10457

ELEMENTS

OF

HEBREW SYNTAX

BY

AN INDUCTIVE METHOD

BY

WILLIAM RAINEY HARPER

PROFESSOR OF SEMITIC LANGUAGES, YALE UNIVERSITY

NEW YORK
CHARLES SCRIBNER'S SONS
1888

Press of J. J. Little & Co.,
Astor Place, New York.

TO

MY PARENTS

IN APPRECIATION OF THE HELP

AND ENCOURAGEMENT SO FREELY GIVEN

DURING MY EARLY STUDIES

THIS BOOK

IS AFFECTIONATELY DEDICATED

The study of Syntax by this plan combines (1) the exegetical study of the illustrations cited, (2) the mastery of the principles taught, (3) the translation and interpretation, in connection with the context, of a number of texts, and (4) in certain portions also the pronunciation of the unpointed text. The student may be required to translate beforehand only the texts cited from prophetical and poetical portions, these being the most difficult; the texts taken from the historical portions may with great advantage be read at sight.

For valuable assistance in reading proof-sheets, and in verifying references, as well as for the typographical neatness and accuracy of the book as a whole, the author is indebted to the Rev. John W. Payne, of New Haven, Conn., who for some years has been closely associated in the work of "The Old Testament Student" and "Hebraica." The Indices, which will be found especially full and helpful, have been prepared by the Rev. A. M. Wilson, now carrying on Semitic studies in Yale University. From Dr. C. R. Brown, of Newton Centre, Mass., and from Mr. Charles H. Wissner, of Fredericksburg, Va., the author has received valuable aid which he desires hereby to acknowledge.

The author would express the hope that this work may meet the approval of the many teachers who are now using his other Hebrew text-books, and that in their hands it may prove efficient in aiding to a better knowledge of the Old Testament.

New Haven, Conn., August 4, 1888.

TABLE OF CONTENTS.

I. THE NOUN.

II. USE OF TENSES AND MOODS.

SYNTAX

I. The Noun.

1. THE NOUN, USED COLLECTIVELY.

1. בָּקָר *oxen;* צֹאן *flock;* עַם *people;* גּוֹי *nation.*

2. עֵץ *a tree,*[1] *trees;*[2] אִישׁ *a man,*[3] *men;*[4] חַיָּה *a beast,*[5] *beasts.*[6]

3. אֹרְחָה *caravan;*[7] אֹרַח *traveler;*[8] גֹּלָה *band of exiles;*[9] גָּלֶה *an exile.*

4. אֳנִי *fleet;*[11] אֳנִיָּה *ship;*[12] שֵׂעָר *hair;*[13] שַׂעֲרָה *a hair.*[14]

Collective nouns, that is, nouns which are singular in form, but plural in sense, may be classified as follows:—[a]

1. Those which *always* express a collective idea, the corresponding individual idea being a different word.

2. Those which are used sometimes in an individual, sometimes in a collective sense.[b][c]

3. Those whose feminine form is collective,[d] while, often, the corresponding masculine form is individual.

4. Those whose masculine form is collective, while the corresponding feminine is, generally, individual.

REMARKS.

(a) The very frequent occurrence of collective expressions in Hebrew is in accord with the extreme simplicity of the language.

(b) Here are included the numerous cases in which words, for the most part or even always used of individuals in *prose*, have a collective sense in *poetry;* there are, indeed, few nouns which may not be thus used.

(c) Adjectives, used as substantives, have frequently a collective sense.

(d) Compare with this use of the feminine, its employment in abstract nouns.

[1] Gen. 2:9; Ps. 1:3.
[2] Gen. 1:11; Ps. 74:5.
[3] Gen. 4:1.
[4] Isa. 21:9.
[5] Gen. 37:20.
[6] Gen. 1:25.
[7] Gen. 37:25.
[8] Judg. 19:17.
[9] Ezr. 1:11.
[10] 2 Sam. 15:19.
[11] 1 Kgs. 9:26, 27.
[12] Jon. 1:3, 5.
[13] Judg. 16:22.
[14] Judg. 20:16; cf. also 1 Sam. 14:45.

REFERENCES FOR STUDY.

2. GENDER OF NOUNS.

1. אִישׁ man; בֵּן son; בָּשָׂר flesh; מָאוֹר luminary.

   a. אֲבָנִים שְׁלֵמוֹת[2] whole stones.;[1]הַמְּאֹרֹת הַגְּדֹלִים cf.

   b. מֵת[3] dead (f.); דֹּב שַׁכּוּל[4] a bear robbed of her young; אַלּוּף[5] cow.

   c. הֵמָּה[6] they (f.); עִמָּכֶם, מִכֶּם, לָכֶם,[7] to, from, with you (f.); שְׁתֵּיהֶם[8] they two (f.); אֲבִיכֶם[9] your (f.) father: אֹתָם[10] them (f.); צֹאנָם[11] their (f.) flock.

2. a. אֵם mother (cf. אָב); רָחֵל ewe (cf. אַיִל); אָתוֹן she-ass (cf. חֲמוֹר); נַעֲרָה maiden (cf. נַעַר); עֶגְלָה calf (cf. עֵגֶל); פָּרָה heifer (cf. פַּר). גָּמָל fem. (Gen. 32:16), masc. (Gen. 24:63); בָּקָר fem. (Job 1:14), masc. (Ex. 21:37).

   b. אִמָּה metropolis (cf. אֵם); פֵּיָה edge (cf. פֶּה); יְרֵכָה hinder part (cf. יָרֵךְ); צְדָקָה righteousness; יְשׁוּעָה deliverance; פֶּחָה governor; קֹהֶלֶת preacher; אֹרְחָה caravan; גֹּלָה exiles; אֳנִיָּה a ship; שַׂעֲרָה a hair.

   c. צֹר[12] Tyre; אֲרָם[13] Syria; מוֹאָב[14] Moab; מִצְרַיִם[15] Egypt.

תֵּימָן, צָפוֹן, שָׁאוּל, מַחֲנֶה, חָצֵר, אֹרַח, דֶּרֶךְ, עִיר, תֵּבֵל, אֶרֶץ, בֶּטֶן, שֵׁן, קֶרֶן, כָּנָף, אַף, עַיִן, כָּתֵף, בֶּרֶךְ, רֶגֶל, כַּף, יָד, שֶׁמֶשׁ, נֹגַהּ, אֵשׁ, נֶפֶשׁ, רוּחַ, נַעַל, כּוֹס, אֶבֶן, חֶרֶב (also m.).

---

[1] Gen. 1:16.　　　[6] Ruth 1:22.　　　[11] Ex. 2:17.
[2] Deut. 27:6.　　[7] Ruth 1:8, 9, 11, 13.　[12] Isa. 23:15.
[3] Gen. 23:4.　　　[8] Ruth 1:19.　　　[13] 2 Sam. 10:11.
[4] Hos. 13:8, cf. 2 Kgs. 2:24.　[9] Gen. 31:9.　[14] Jer. 48:4, 9.
[5] Ps. 144:14.　　[10] Gen. 41:23.　　[15] Joel 4:19.

  * Also used individually, Deut. 4:18; Jon. 2:2.

3. *a.* טוֹב[1] *that which is good;* טוֹבָה,[2] *same;* מַה־זֹּאת[3] בָּה אֲרַע.[4]

　　b. כָּל־הַקֹּרֹת אֹתָם[5] *all that befell them;* קָשׁוֹת *hard things.*[6]

1. Under *masculine* nouns are included the names of male beings, and, with the exception of those referred to below under 2. *a* and *c*, all nouns without a distinctively feminine ending. It is to be noted that

　　a. In masculines which have plurals in וֹת (and likewise, in feminines which have plurals in ־ים), this termination does not affect the gender.[a]

　　b. In some instances, a masculine form occurs where the sense, and rarely also the construction, demands a feminine ; and this, sometimes, when a feminine form is in existence.

　　c. In the case of pronouns and pronominal suffixes the masculine, instead of the feminine, often occurs as being the primary form, or as being superior to the feminine and including it.

REMARKS.

(*a*) There are exceptions to this; cf. נשׁים (Gen. 7:13); משׁכנות (Ps. 84:2).

(*b*) The feminine rarely so occurs for the masculine; both irregularities may be attributed, in many cases, to colloquial inaccuracy, or to carelessness on the part of the writer.

2. Under *feminine* nouns are included three classes :

　　a. Nouns which refer to female beings ; of these

　　　　(1) some are distinguished from corresponding masculines by having an entirely distinct form ;

　　　　(2) some are so distinguished by the addition of a feminine termination ;

　　　　(3) some (called *epicene*) are so distinguished only by the construction, both masculine and feminine forms being the same.[a]

　　b. Nouns which do not refer to female beings, yet have a feminine termination ; here belong

　　　　(1) nouns designating things without life ;[b]

　　　　(2) nouns indicating abstract ideas[c] or official designations ;[d]

　　　　(3) nouns used collectively[e] (§ 1. 3), or individually (§ 1. 4).

　　c. Nouns which neither imply distinction of sex, nor have a feminine termination, but are always construed as feminine ; here belong

　　　　(1) names of countries, cities, towns ;[f g h]

　　　　(2) common nouns designating countries, localities, limited space, points of compass, etc.;

---

1 Gen. 2:17.　　　　3 Gen. 3:13.　　　　5 Gen. 42:29.
2 1 Sam. 24:18.　　　4 Gen. 24:14.　　　6 Gen. 42:7, 30.

(3) names of members of the body, especially those which are double ;[i]

(4) names of instruments, utensils, powers of nature.[j]

3. There being in Hebrew no separate designation of the *neuter*, there is used in place of it,

    a. When the word is *singular*, either a masculine or feminine form.

    b. When the word is *plural*, generally a feminine form (except in poetry).

REMARKS.

(*a*) Certain species of animals are treated as masculine, because regarded as strong; others as feminine, because regarded as weak; cf. כֶּלֶב *dog*, זְאֵב *wolf*; but יוֹנָה *dove*, חֲסִידָה *stork*.

(*b*) These are really *neuter*, the signification passing, in many cases, from something living, to that which is without life.

(*c*) So adjectives, when used as neuter substantives, assume the feminine form.

(*d*) Compare our abstract terms "Lordship," "Majesty," "Excellency," etc.

(*e*) Collectives without a feminine ending are often treated as feminines; cf. Ex. 8:2, 13, 14; 16:13; 2 Sam. 24:9.

(*f*) These are treated as "mothers" or "nurses" of the inhabitants; cf. בְּנֵי צִיּוֹן Ps. 149:2, also the word *metropolis*.

(*g*) When these words refer to the inhabitants, they are construed as masculine.

(*h*) It is common, in poetry, to personify nations, countries and cities, as female beings; cf. Isa. 47:1; 50:1; Lam. 1:1.

(*i*) Some of these also appear, at times, as masculine; always masculine are אַף *nose*, מֵצַח *forehead*, צַוָּאר *neck*, עֹרֶף *neck*, פֶּה *mouth*, עָקֵב *heel*, זָנָב *tail*.

(*j*) The exceptions to the principles here given are very numerous, great variation existing in the usage of the language.

REFERENCES FOR STUDY.

3. NUMBER.

1. *a.* יָמִים¹ *days;* מוֹעֲדִים² *seasons;* פְּנֵי³ *faces of;* אֹתֹת⁴ *signs.*

   b. בָּקָר *oxen;* אָדָם *mankind;* אֹרְחָה *caravan;* אֳנִי *fleet.*   [*heart.*

   c. אִישׁ וָאִישׁ⁵ *every man;* גֻּבִּים גֵּבִים⁶ *many ditches;* לֵב וָלֵב⁷ *double*

2. *a.* שָׁמַיִם *heavens;* פָּנִים *face, surface;* מַיִם *water;* תַּחְתִּיוֹת⁸ *lower parts of the earth.*   [הוֹלֵלוֹת]¹² *foolishness.*

   b. בְּתוּלִים⁹ *virginity;* אֲהָבִים¹⁰ *loveliness;* נְעוּרִים¹¹ *childhood;*

   c. אֱלֹהִים *God;* קְדֹשִׁים¹³ *Holy;* אֲדֹנָי *Lord;* בְּהֵמוֹת¹⁴ *hippopota-*

3. כֶּסֶף *silver,* כְּסָפִים¹⁵ *pieces of silver;* עֵץ *tree,* עֵצִים¹⁶ *wood.*   [*mus.*

   כִּכָּרִים¹⁷ *talents,* כִּכָּרוֹת¹⁸ *loaves;* פְּעָמִים¹⁹ *footsteps,* פְּעָמוֹת²⁰ *feet* (*artif.*).

4. גִּבּוֹרֵי חַיִל²¹ *heroes of valor;* בֵּית אָבוֹת²² *families;* בְּנֵי אֵלִים²³ *sons of God;* בֵּית עֲצַבֵּיהֶם²⁴ *their idol-houses.*

5. *a.* אָזְנַיִם *ears;* אַפַּיִם *nostrils;* מֹאזְנַיִם *pair of scales;* נְעָלַיִם *sandals.*

   b. יוֹמַיִם²⁵ *period of two days;* כִּכְּרַיִם²⁶ *two talents;* נַהֲרַיִם²⁷ *two*

   c. שְׁנַיִם *two;* כִּפְלַיִם²⁸ *double;* אַלְפַּיִם *two thousand.*   [*rivers.*

1. The *plural-idea* is indicated in one of three ways:—

   a. By means of plural affixes (־ים, ־ִי, וֹת).

   b. By means of words which have a collective signification (§ 1.).

   c. By the repetition of a word with or without a connective[a] (§ 6. 3).

2. The *plural-termination* is often employed in Hebrew in the designation of ideas for which in other languages the singular is employed:—

   a. Portions of space or time, "their unity being regarded as a compound of an immense number of single particles or dates."

   b. Abstract ideas, the particular quality or condition contained in the stem being thus heightened or intensified;[b][c] closely connected with these are

---

[1] Gen. 1:14.
[2] Gen. 1:14.
[3] Gen. 1:2.
[4] Gen. 1:14.
[5] Ps. 87:5.
[6] 2 Kgs. 3:16.
[7] Ps. 12:3.
[8] Isa. 44:23.
[9] Lev. 21:13.
[10] Prov. 5:19.
[11] Gen. 46:34.
[12] Eccl. 1:17, 2:12.
[13] Hos. 12:1.
[14] Job 40:15.
[15] Gen. 42:25.
[16] Gen. 22:3.
[17] 2 Kgs. 5:23.
[18] Judg. 8:5.
[19] Ps. 119:133.
[20] Ex. 25:12.
[21] 1 Chron. 7:2, 9.
[22] Num. 1:2.
[23] Ps. 29:1.
[24] 1 Sam. 31:9.
[25] Ex. 16:29.
[26] 2 Kgs. 5:23.
[27] Gen. 24:10.
[28] Job 11:6.

c. Ideas of power and greatness, in which the plural magnifies or increases the original idea.[d][e]

3. The *plural form* of certain nouns often conveys a different shade of meaning from the singular ; and, further, the *feminine* plural of a noun is sometimes used in a different sense from the *masculine* plural.[f]

4. The *pluralizing* of compound ideas is accomplished either by pluralizing the first of two nouns, or the second, or both.

5. The *dual* was, in use, limited to

a. Things which in nature exist in pairs,[g] or are made double by art.

b. Objects which are regarded as going together, especially measures of time or quantity.

c. A few numerals, and anomalous forms.[h]

REMARKS.

(a) This repetition indicates in some cases *entirety;* in others, *distribution;* in still others, *multitude,* or *diversity.*

(b) It is important to note the close connection, (1) between the abstract and the collective, both being frequently expressed by the feminine; and (2) between the abstract and the plural, the latter expressing in its totality that quality which is common to all the units of which it is composed.

(c) The plural form of abstracts often expresses " a high degree of a given quality or repeated exhibitions and embodiments of it."

(d) The use of this plural (called *the plural of majesty*) is limited to a few words and in construction these words are generally treated as singular.

(e) Compare the plurals in the mouth of God, e. g. Gen. 1:26; 11:7; Isa. 6:8.

(f) In poetry feminine plurals are found instead of masculine, without any difference of meaning.

(g) The names of double members of the body often have a *feminine plural* termination instead of a dual, but only when they have been transferred to inanimate objects.

(h) Irregular are (1) שְׂפָתוֹת instead of שְׂפָתַיִם (Ps. 45:3; Is. 59:3); (2) חֹמֹתַיִם *two walls* (2 Kgs. 25:4), and (3) לֻחֹתַיִם *deck* [double] (Ezek. 27:5).

REFERENCES FOR STUDY.

4. DETERMINATION OF NOUNS.

1. *a.* מִצְרַיִם *Egypt;* חֶבְרוֹן *Hebron;* שָׂרָה *Sarah;* תְּהוֹם *abyss.*

　b. אָנֹכִי *I;* זֶה *this;* מִי *who?* בְּנִי *my son;* but הַיּוֹם הַזֶּה.

2. *a.* בֵּית אֵל *the house of God;* אֵשֶׁת אַבְרָם *the wife of Abram;* בְּנֵי
יִשְׂרָאֵל *the sons of Israel.*

　b. עֳנִי עַמִּי[1] *the affliction of my people;* רָאשֵׁי שִׁבְטֵיכֶם[2] *the heads
of your tribes.* [war.

　c. שֵׁם הַמָּקוֹם[3] *the name of the place;* אַנְשֵׁי הַמִּלְחָמָה[4] *the men of*

1. Certain nouns are in their very nature definite, and require no sign
to indicate their definiteness; these are

　a. Proper names which were not originally appellatives, and words
in which the appellative force, originally existing, has almost or entirely
been lost.[a]

　b. All pronouns (except the Demonstrative when attributive), and
pronominal suffixes.[b c d]

2. Nouns may become definite (or determinate) by position or construction,[e] as in the case of

　a. Nouns in the construct state before a proper noun.

　b. Nouns in the construct state before a noun with a suffix.

　c. Nouns in the construct state before a noun with the article.

---

1 Ex. 3:7.　　　2 Deut. 1:15.　　　3 Gen. 28:19.　　　4 Deut. 2:14.

REMARKS.

(a) In many cases the usage varies; e. g. גִלְעָד (Num. 32:1), הַגִּלְעָד (Gen. 31:21 ff.).

(b) A noun with a suffix is definite and does not receive the article; exceptions are seen in Lev. 27:23; Josh. 7:21; 8:33; 2 Kgs. 15:16; Mic. 2:12.

(c) The Infinitive, being essentially a verbal form, never receives the article; דַעַת knowledge, really a substantive is an exception (as in Gen. 2:9, 17).

(d) The following words, archaic and poetic, never receive the article: (1) אֱלֹהַּ God, (2) רֹזֵן prince, (3) שָׂדַי field, (4) שַׁדַי the Almighty, (5) שְׁאוֹל underworld, (6) תֵּבֵל world, (7) תְּהוֹם abyss, (8) תּוּשִׁיָה help.

(e) Every noun in a chain of several constructs is definite, provided the last noun in the chain is for any reason (§ 4. 1. a. b) definite.

3. a. הַיּוֹם¹ to-day; הַלַּיְלָה² this night; הַפַּעַם³ this time.

b. הָרָקִיעַ⁴ the expanse; הַתֵּבָה⁵ the ark; הָאִשָּׁה⁶ the woman;

"הָאִישׁ אֲשֶׁר לֹא הָלַךְ וגו'⁷ the man who hath not walked, etc.

אֶת־הָאֵשׁ וְאֶת־הַמַּאֲכֶלֶת⁸ the fire and the knife (required for the sacrifice).

c. אֶת־הַסּוּס וְאֶת־הָרֶכֶב⁹ the horses and the chariots (of the enemy).

וַתִּקַּח הַצָּעִיף¹⁰ and she took the veil (usually worn by women).

d. הַכְּנַעֲנִי¹¹ the Canaanite; תֹּאכַל הַחֶרֶב¹² the sword devours;

כַּבָּקָר¹³ like oxen; כַּאֲשֶׁר תַּעֲשֶׂינָה הַדְּבֹרִים¹⁴ as bees do;

הַחֵמָר....לַחֹמֶר¹⁵ slime....for mortar; הַזָּהָב¹⁶ gold;

בַּסַּנְוֵרִים¹⁷ with blindness; הָאֱמֶת וְהַשָּׁלוֹם¹⁸ truth and peace.

e. הַבַּיִת¹⁹ the house; הָאָרוֹן²⁰ the ark; הָאֱלֹהִים²¹ the God.

הַשָּׁמַיִם²² O heaven! הַבַּעַל²³ O Baal! הָרוּחַ²⁴ O Spirit!

הַשָּׁמַיִם²⁵ the heaven; הַשֶּׁמֶשׁ²⁶ the sun; הָאָרֶץ²⁷ the earth;

הַלְּבָנוֹן²⁸ Lebanon (= the white); הַיַּרְדֵּן²⁹ Jordan (= the descender).

f. הַסֹּבֵב³⁰ that which encompasses; הַבֹּטְחִים³¹ they who trust.

הַבָּאָה³² (she) that hath come; הַהֹלְכוּ(א)³³ they who wait.

---

1 Gen. 4:14.	12 2 Sam. 11:25.	23 1 Kgs. 18:26.
2 Gen. 19:5.	13 Isa. 11:7.	24 Ezek. 37:9.
3 Gen. 29:35.	14 Deut. 1:44.	25 Gen. 1:1.
4 Gen. 1:7.	15 Gen. 11:3.	26 Gen. 15:12.
5 Gen. 6:14.	16 Gen. 2:11.	27 Gen. 1:1.
6 Ex. 2:9.	17 Gen. 19:11.	28 1 Kgs. 5:20,23.
7 Ps. 1:1.	18 Zech. 8:19.	29 Gen. 13:10.
8 Gen. 22:6.	19 Mic. 3:12.	30 Gen. 2:11.
9 1 Kgs. 20:21.	20 Ex. 25:14.	31 Ps. 125:1.
10 Gen. 24:65.	21 Gen. 5:22.	32 Gen. 18:21.
11 Gen. 13:7.	22 Deut. 32:1.	33 Josh. 10:24.

3. Nouns, not determinate *in themselves* or *by position*, may be made determinate by prefixing the article. The article, as thus employed, may be classified and named as follows :—

a. The *demonstrative*, which was the original use, but is now found only in a few stock expressions.

b. The *objective*, including those cases in which the article occurs with an object or person,

(1) which has just been described in the narrative ; or
(2) which is described by words (particularly, a relative clause) which immediately follow ; or
(3) which is defined more or less closely by the circumstances involved in the particular case.

c. The *subjective*, used with nouns which, though in no way described, are definite in the writer's mind and, consequently, supposed to be so in the mind of the reader.[a]

d. The *generic*, used with words which describe a class of objects, or several objects of a class ; here may be noted,

(1) the more general use of the generic article "with a common appellative, which is used collectively to denote all, or an indefinite number of, the individuals belonging to it ;"
(2) its special use in *comparisons*, when the object compared is taken as a class and not as an individual ;
(3) its special use, also with nouns of material and class-nouns, which are generally known and employed in a general sense ;[b]
(4) its special use with *abstract nouns*, employed in their widest significance.

e. The *distinctive*, used to convey the idea of pre-eminence, as when

(1) a particular object, of a certain class, is made to have a pre-eminence over all other objects in that class ; or
(2) a noun in the vocative is, by its use, made more pointed ; or
(3) a particular object or individual is emphasized as being the only one in a class ; or
(4) a proper name, originally an appellative, continues to retain the article which it first received because it was regarded (see (1) above) as the chief member of its class (cf. § 4. 1. *a*).[c]

f. The *relative*, which, when prefixed to the participle (and, rarely, to a finite form), has the general force of a relative pronoun.

REMARKS.

(*a*) In these cases the idea may often be well expressed by the employment of an unemphatic possessive pronoun.

(b) With this may be compared cases like הַפָּלִיט (Gen. 14:13), הָאֲרִי (1 Sam. 17:34), בְּמִקְנֶה בְכֶסֶף וּבַזָּהָב (Gen. 13:2), in which the individual, though really indeterminate, is to be represented as being made definite by the context.

(c) In the case of many such nouns the usage varies.

REFERENCES FOR STUDY.

5. DETERMINATION OF NOUNS (CONT.).

1. אַנְשֵׁי הַמִּלְחָמָה[1] the men of war; דְּבַר הַנָּבִיא[2] the prophet's word.

   a. כָּל הַדּוֹר[3] the whole generation; כָּל הָעָם[4] all the people;
   כָּל־בְּכוֹר[5] every first-born; כָּל־עֵץ[6] every tree.

   b. בֶּן־הַיְמִינִי[7] the Benjamite; בֵּית הַלַּחְמִי[8] the Bethlehemite.

2. הַמָּאוֹר הַגָּדֹל[9] the great luminary; הַדְּבָרִים הָאֵלֶּה[10] these things;
   יוֹם הַשְּׁבִיעִי[11] the seventh day; בַּלַּיְלָה הוּא[12] in that night.

3. סַל אֶחָד[13] a basket; אִישׁ אֶחָד[14] a man; נָבִיא אֶחָד[15] a prophet.

---

[1] Num. 31:49.
[2] Jer. 28:9.
[3] Ex. 1:6.
[4] Ezek. 45:16.
[5] Ex. 13:2.
[6] Lev. 19:23.
[7] Judg. 3:15.
[8] 1 Sam. 17:58.
[9] Gen. 1:16.
[10] Gen. 15:1.
[11] Gen. 2:2.
[12] Gen. 19:33.
[13] Ex. 29:3.
[14] Judg. 13:2.
[15] 1 Kgs. 20:13.

4. מַלְכֵי־אֶרֶץ [1] *kings of the earth;* אַתָּה בֹקֶר [2] *the morning comes.*

1. An idea, expressed by means of two nouns in the construct relation, is made definite by prefixing the article to the second noun.[a][b] Worthy of notice, however, is

   a. (1) The use of the article after כֹּל, when this word means *all* or *whole.*

      (2) The absence of the article after כֹּל, when it means *any* or *every.*[c]

   b. The use of the article with the second part of a compound word.

2. An adjective or demonstrative pronoun, connected attributively with a definite noun, must be marked as definite by having the article prefixed.[d]

3. Indefiniteness is expressed by the numeral אֶחָד, rarely, however, and chiefly in later writers.[e]

4. The article may be omitted in poetry, when in prose it would be required; this omission is explained by the brevity, vividness and emphasis characteristic of poetic style.

REMARKS.

(*a*) When the first of two nouns expressing one idea is to be marked as indefinite, a construction with the preposition לְ is employed (§ 9. 5).

(*b*) On the occurrence of the article with the *first* of two nouns in the construct relation, see § 9. 2.

(*c*) Compare the similar usage of πᾶς *all* or *every.*

(*d*) There are not a few exceptions to this, the article being sometimes omitted from the noun, sometimes from the attributive.

(*e*) This numeral is sometimes found in the construct relation with the noun which it limits (cf. Job 2:10); its use with things is more rare than with persons

REFERENCES FOR STUDY.

Gen. 1:31; 10:12; 19:25; 28:19; 30:16;	1 Sam. 2:23; 14:29; 17:12..... 2
32:23................................ 2	1 Sam. 16:18..... ....1*b*.
Gen. 7:21; 26:4....................1*a*.	2 Sam. 6:3; 12:4............................2
Gen. 23:19.............................1	1 Kgs. 19:4................................3
Ex. 20:4.............................1*a*.	Isa. 1:5; 13:7; 28:24..................... 1*a*.
Lev. 7:27; 14:45.....................1*a*.	Isa. 10:1; 24:12............................4
Num. 9:7.............................2	Neh. 1:5...................................4
Num. 35:23.... ....1*a*.	Hab. 1:4...................................4
Deut. 1:35; 9:6; 11:7.....................2	Zech. 14:15................................1*a*.
Deut. 11:12..........................4	Ps. 12:8...................................2
Josh. 3:13..............................1*a*.	Ps. 72:17; 148:10.. 4
Judg. 6:11.............................1*b*.	Job 9:24...................................4
1 Sam. 1:1.............................3	Dan. 8:3, 13................................3

---

[1] Ps. 2:2.　　　　　[2] Isa. 21:12.

6. APPOSITION OF NOUNS.

1. *a.* הַבָּקָר הַנְּחֹשֶׁת[1] *the oxen the brass = the brazen oxen;* הַמַּבּוּל
    מַיִם[2] *= the deluge* (of) *water.*   *[offerings.*

  b. אֲמָרִים אֱמֶת[3] *words, truth = true words;* זְבָחִים שְׁלָמִים[4] *peace-*

  c. הָאָרֶץ כְּנַעַן[5] *the land* (of) *Canaan;* הַנָּהָר פְּרָת[6] *the river Euphrates*

  d. אִשָּׁה אַלְמָנָה[7] *a woman, a widow;* דֶּשֶׁא עֵשֶׂב[8] *greenness, herb.*

  e. יָמִים מִסְפָּר[9] *days, a number;* שְׁנָתַיִם יָמִים[10] *two years, time.*

2. שְׁלֹשׁ סְאִים קֶמַח[11] *three seahs, meal;* שְׁלֹשָׁה יָמִים[12] *a triad, days.*
    שֶׁבַע שָׁנִים[13] *seven years;* אֵיפָה שְׂעֹרִים[14] *an ephah, barley.*

3. *a.* בִּמְאֹד מְאֹד[15] *in high degree, high degree;* גָּבְהָה גִּבְהָהּ[16] *proudly,*
    proudly.   *[generation.*

  b. שִׁבְעָה שִׁבְעָה[17] *seven by seven;* מִדֹּר דֹּר[18] *from generation to*

  c. בְּאֵרֹת בְּאֵרֹת[19] *many wells;* גֵּבִים גֵּבִים[20] *many ditches.*

  d. הַנָּהָר הַגָּדוֹל נְהַר פְּרָת[21] *the great river, the river Euphrates.*

Apposition, because of a scarcity of adjectives, and a desire for brev-ity, is of much more frequent occurrence, and of far wider range in He-brew, than in languages generally. The various kinds of apposition may be grouped as follows:—

1. Cases in which the *first* of two nouns contains the principal idea, the second being added for fuller explanation.*ab* Here belong the instan-ces in which

    a. The first noun denotes a *thing*, the second, the *material* of which that thing is composed.

    b. The first noun denotes a *thing*, the second, a *quality* of it.

    c. The first noun denotes a *person* or *thing*, the second, its *name.c*

    d. The first noun denotes a *genus*, the second, a *species;* or the sec-ond gives a more precise idea than the first.

    e. The first noun denotes a *thing*, the second, the *number, weight,* or *measure* of it.*de*

1 2 Kgs. 16:17.	8 Gen. 1:12.	15 Gen. 17:2.
2 Gen. 6:17.	9 Deut. 4:27.	16 1 Sam. 2:3.
3 Prov. 22:21.	10 Gen. 41:1.	17 Gen. 7:2.
4 Ex. 24:5.	11 Gen. 18:6.	18 Ex. 17:16.
5 Num. 34:2.	12 1 Sam. 30:12.	19 Gen. 14:10.
6 1 Chron. 5:9.	13 Gen. 5:7.	20 2 Kgs. 3:16.
7 2 Sam. 14:5.	14 Ruth 2:17.	21 Gen. 15:18.

REMARKS.

(a) Where the first noun is definite, and the second indefinite, the latter may be regarded as an accusative of limitation (cf. § 40. 2); cf. 1 Chron. 28:18; Ps. 71:7; Hab. 3:8; Lev. 26:42; Jer. 33:2.

(b) The appositional relation is, at times, so loose that one or more words may stand between the nouns thus connected.

(c) Sometimes the "name" is the first noun (Isa. 37:2); if the "name" is the second noun and a preposition stands before the first, the preposition must be repeated before the second (Gen. 24:4; cf. Gen. 22:20).

(d) For all these cases, there are parallel cases in which, by the introduction of a copula, a complete sentence is formed; cf. Gen. 1:2; 11:1; 14:10; 47:9; Ex. 9:31; Deut. 33:6; 2 Sam. 17:3; Isa. 5:12; 19:11; Jer. 24:2: Ezek. 45:11; Ps. 23:5; 45:9; 110:3.

(e) While nouns like כֹּל all, יֵשׁ there is, and אַיִן there is not generally stand in the *construct* relation with what follows, they sometimes stand in apposition with a following, and rarely with a preceding, noun.

2. Cases in which the *second* word conveys the principal idea, the first marking the *measure, weight,* or *number* of it.[a][b]

3. Cases in which the first word is simply repeated. [Here belong those instances in which the second word is a *pronoun* repeating a preceding *noun*, or a *noun* repeating a preceding *pronoun* (whether expressed, or implied in a verbal form) (see § 11. 1. *a*).] The appositional repetition serves

   a. To express *emphasis, intensity*.

   b. To express *distribution, entirety*.

   c. To express *multitude*.

   d. To afford an opportunity for the addition of a new idea without rendering the construction faulty.[c]

REMARKS.

(a) In the great majority of cases under this head, the construct relation may be employed (§ 8. 2).

(b) It is probable that the second noun, in these cases, is an accusative of limitation (§ 40. 5), rather than in apposition.

(c) The two constructions, apposition and annexion (i. e., the construct relation), are closely related. In the expression of many ideas the one or the other may be used according to choice. Apposition was the earlier construction, and out of it grew annexion.

REFERENCES FOR STUDY.

7. THE NOMINATIVE ABSOLUTE.

1. הָאָרֶץ אֲשֶׁר אַתָּה שֹׁכֵב עָלֶיהָ לְךָ אֶתְּנֶנָּה[1] *the land upon which thou art lying,—to thee will I give it.*

2. שְׁכֶם בְּנִי חָשְׁקָה נַפְשׁוֹ בְּבִתְּכֶם[2] *Shechem my son,—his soul hath longed for your daughter.*

3. הָאִישׁ מִיכָה לוֹ בֵית אֱלֹהִים[3] *the man Micah,—to him was a house of God.*

4. אֲנִי הִנֵּה בְרִיתִי אִתָּךְ[4] *I—behold my covenant is with thee.*

5. אֶת־כָּל־הָאָרֶץ אֲשֶׁר־אַתָּה רֹאֶה לְךָ אֶתְּנֶנָּה[5] *all the land which thou seest—to thee I will give it.*

6. יְהוָֹה הוּא נַחֲלָתוֹ[7]; יְהוָֹה הוּא הָאֱלֹהִים[6] *Yahweh,* HE *is the God; Yahweh,* HE *is his inheritance;* הַדָּם הוּא הַנֶּפֶשׁ[8] *the blood,* THAT *is the life.*

7. הָאֲנָשִׁים הָאֵלֶּה שְׁלֵמִים הֵם[9] *these men—they are at peace;* חֲלוֹם פַּרְעֹה אֶחָד הוּא[10] *the dream of Pharaoh—it is one;* [holy. הַמָּקוֹם ....קֹדֶשׁ הוּא[11] *the place (upon which thou standest)—it is*

---

1 Gen. 28:13.	4 Gen. I7:4.	7 Deut. 10:9.	10 Gen. 41:25.
2 Gen. 34:8.	5 Gen. 13:15.	8 Deut. 12:23.	11 Josh. 5:15.
3 Judg. 17:5.	6 1 Kgs. 18:39.	9 Gen. 34:21.	

For the sake of emphasis, and for the avoidance of unwieldy sentences, a noun or pronoun is frequently placed at the beginning of the sentence with no grammatical relation to the other words of the sentence, but represented in the body of the sentence by a pronominal suffix. This noun or pronoun is said to be a Nominative Absolute. The various cases may be classified as follows :—

.1. Where this nominative absolute is, logically, the object of the sentence.

2. Where it is, logically, the subject of the sentence.

3. Where it is, logically, the object of a preposition occurring farther along in the sentence.

4. Where it is a pronoun, and is, logically, the subject or object of the sentence, or a genitive after a noun.

5. Where it is preceded by אֵת, the sign of the object.

6. Where, standing as the logical subject, it is resumed by the pronoun הוּא, which then, though really the grammatical subject of the following predicate, is practically equivalent to a copula.

7. A similar usage to that just given, except that the pronoun *follows*, instead of *preceding*, the predicate.

REFERENCES FOR STUDY.

8. ANNEXION, OR THE CONSTRUCT RELATION.

1. *a.* חֲמַס יְדֵיכֶם[1] *cruelty of* (= *done by*) *your hands;* יֵצֶר לֵב הָאָדָם[2] *the imagination of man's heart;* פַּחְדְּכֶם[3] *your fear* (= *which you have*); כַּעֲשׂוֹ[4] *his vexation.*

    b. חֲמַס לְבָנוֹן[5] *cruelty of* (= *done to*) *Lebanon;* שְׁמֻעַת שָׁאוּל[6] *report about Saul;* חִתְכֶם[7] *fear of* (= *concerning*) *you;* זַעֲקַת סְדֹם[8] *cry concerning Sodom.*

2. *a.* שְׁנֵיהֶם[9] *they two* (not, *two of them*); שְׁנֵי הַמְּאֹרֹת[10] *the two luminaries;* שְׁנֵי לְאֻמִּים[11] *two peoples;* שְׁלֹשׁ הֶעָרִים[12] *the three cities.*

    b. כָּל־הָעֵץ[13] *all* (*of*) *the tree(s);* רֹב שָׁלוֹם[14] *much* (*of*) *peace;* דֵּי חָלָב[15] *enough* (*of*) *milk;* cf. also יִשְׂרָאֵל כֻּלֹּה[16] *all of Israel.*

    c. לַחְמָם לְנַפְשָׁם[17] *their food is for themselves;* פָּנַי יֵלֵכוּ[18] *my presence* (= *I myself*) *shall go;* עֶצֶם הַיּוֹם הַזֶּה[19] *that very day;* עֶצֶם הַשָּׁמַיִם[20] *heaven itself.*

    d. בְּלִי מִסְפָּר[21] *without number;* אֵין מִלְחָמָה[22] *without war;* בְּלִי נִשְׁמָע[23] *without clothing;* בְּלִי מָשִׁיחַ[24] *unanointed;* בְּלִי נִשְׁמָע[25] *unheard;* לֹא־אֵל[26] *a non-God;* אַל־מָוֶת[27] *immortality;* בְּלֹא אֵיבָה[28] *without enmity.*

    e. בְּיוֹם דִּבֶּר יְהֹוָה[29] *on the day* (that) *Jehovah spake.* יְמֵי הִתְהַלַּכְנוּ אִתָּם[30] *the days we walked with them.* יוֹם אִירָא[31] *the day I fear;* עֵת נִשְׁבֶּרֶת[32] *the time thou wast broken.*

3. *a.* דַּם הַנָּקִי[33] *the innocent blood;* גַּיְא גְדֹלָה[34] *a large ravine;* בַּיִת גָּדֹל[35] *a large house;* חַיִל כָּבֵד[36] *a strong force;* מְקוֹם קָדוֹשׁ[37] *the holy place;* אֵשֶׁת רָע[38] *a bad woman;* כְּלֵי הַקָּטֹן[39] *the smallest vessels.*

---

1 Ps. 58:3.
2 Gen. 8:21.
3 Prov. 1:26.
4 Prov. 12:16.
5 Hab. 2:17.
6 2 Sam. 4:4.
7 Gen. 9:2.
8 Gen. 18:20.
9 Gen. 2:25.
10 Gen. 1:16.
11 Gen. 25:23.
12 Num. 35:14.
13 Gen. 1:29.
14 Ps. 37:11.
15 Prov. 27:27.
16 2 Sam. 2:9.
17 Hos. 9:4.
18 Ex. 33:14.
19 Gen. 7:13.
20 Ex. 24:10.
21 Gen. 41:49.
22 1 Kgs. 22:1.
23 Job 24:10.
24 2 Sam. 1:21.
25 Ps. 19:4.
26 Deut. 32:5, 17, 21.
27 Prov. 12:38.
28 Num. 35:22b.
29 Ex. 6:28.
30 1 Sam. 25:15.
31 Ps. 56:4.
32 Ezek. 27:34.
33 Deut. 19:13.
34 Zech. 14:4.
35 2 Kgs. 25:9.
36 2 Kgs. 18:17.
37 Eccles. 8:10.
38 Prov. 6:24.
39 Isa. 22:24.

b. מְתֵי מְעַט[1] *few people;* דְּמֵי חִנָּם[2] *blood shed causelessly;*

אֱלֹהֵי מִקָּרֹב[3] *a God from near;* עוֹלַת תָּמִיד[4] *continual offering.*

c. נְהַר פְּרָת[5] *the river Euphrates;* שֵׁבֶט הַלֵּוִי[6] *the tribe of Levi.*

d. גִּבּוֹר חַיִל[7] *a strong hero;* אֲרוֹן עֵץ[8] *a wooden chest;*

בִּגְדֵי קֹדֶשׁ[9] *holy garments;* אֱלִילֵי כֶסֶף[10] *silver idols.*

e. אִישׁ דְּבָרִים[11] *an eloquent man;* בַּעַל הַחֲלֹמוֹת[12] *having dreams;*

בְּנֵי חַיִל[13] *sons of strength;* בֶּן־לַיְלָה[14] *son of a night;*

בֶּן־חֲמֵשׁ מֵאוֹת שָׁנָה[15] *(Noah was) a son of five hundred years =*
five hundred years old.

f. נְסִיכֵי אָדָם[16] *the anointed of men;* אֶבְיוֹנֵי אָדָם[17] *the poor of men;*

פֶּרֶא אָדָם[18] *a wild ass of a man;* פֶּלֶא יוֹעֵץ[19] *a wonder of a coun-*
sellor.

4. a. חָכְמַת וָדַעַת[20] *wisdom and knowledge;* שְׁכֻרַת וְלֹא מִיָּיִן[21].

b. בְּתוּלַת בַּת צִיּוֹן[22] אֵשֶׁת בַּעֲלַת אוֹב[23] *a woman possessed of a spirit;*

c. אֶת־שׁוֹר מִי לָקָחְתִּי[24] *whose ox have I taken?* חָכְמַת־מַה לָהֶם[25]

That relation between two nouns which is indicated in Latin or Greek by placing the second noun in the *genitive*, is expressed in Hebrew by pronouncing the two words as one.[a] As a result of this, the tone passes to the second word, and the first word is, if possible, shortened. This construction may for convenience be called *annexion*.[b] The varieties of *annexion* may be classified as follows :—

1. Cases in which the two nouns, thus joined, contain distinct ideas of equal value ; this is seen

a. When the second noun designates a person or thing which is the *subject* or possessor of that which is indicated by the preceding noun.[c]

b. When the second noun designates the *object* of an action or feeling expressed by the preceding noun.

REMARKS.

(a) The remnants of original case-endings are quite numerous (El. § 121. 1-3), but these remnants (except in the case of the accusative הָ֯) no longer have any signification.

1 Deut. 26:5.	8 Deut. 10:1.	14 Jon. 4:10.	20 Isa. 33:6.
2 1 Kgs. 2:31.	9 Ex. 28:2.	15 Gen. 5:32.	21 Isa. 51:21.
3 Jer. 23:23.	10 Isa. 2:20.	16 Mic. 5:4.	22 1 Sam. 28:7.
4 Num. 28:6.	11 Ex. 4:10.	17 Isa. 29:19.	23 Isa. 37:22.
5 Gen. 15:18.	12 Gen. 37:19.	18 Gen 16:12.	24 1 Sam. 12:3.
6 Josh. 13:33.	13 Deut. 3:18.	19 Isa. 9:55.	25 Jer. 8:9.
7 Judg. 11:1.			

(b) A noun with a pronominal suffix is to be regarded, syntactically, as in *annexion* with that suffix.

(c) Because of their inflexibility, proper names are seldom found in annexion with a following noun. In cases like אוּר כַּשְׂדִּים *Ur (city) of the Chaldees* (Gen. 11:28), יְהוָה צְבָאוֹת *Jehovah (God) of hosts*, there is an ellipsis to be supplied (cf. 2 Sam. 5:10).

2. Cases in which the second of two nouns, thus joined, is the more important, the first merely indicating its number, size, nature, etc.; this is seen,

a. In the usage of numerals 2–10, which may stand in the construct state before the substantive which they number.*a*

b. In the usage of certain nouns, e. g., כֹּל *totality*, רֹב *abundance*, דַּי *sufficiency*, which have almost come to have the force of adjectives.*b*

c. In the usage of certain commonly occurring nouns as "purely mental concepts," e. g., נֶפֶשׁ, פָּנִים and עֶצֶם = *self* (the first used of animate objects, the second of persons, the third of inanimate objects); cf. also קוֹל = *voice of* = *Hark!* *c d e*

d. In the usage of words designating the existence or non-existence of a nominal idea; e. g., יֵשׁ *there exists*, אַיִן and בִּלְתִּי *non-existence* (and in poetry, לֹא, אַל and בְּלִי) = *without, in-, un-, -less;* *f* בַּד *solitariness.*

e. In that usage which permits a noun expressing in a general way *place, time, manner* to stand in *annexion* with a following relative clause (in which, however, the relative may be omitted).*g*

REMARKS.

(a) For other constructions which the numeral may have, see § 15. 1. *b.*

(b) In reference to כֹּל the following points may be noted: (1) It regularly precedes in the construct the noun it modifies (Isa. 2:2), but (2) sometimes follows with the idea of the modified noun repeated in the form of a pronominal suffix (2 Sam. 2:9); and (3) rarely occurs with the article after a preceding noun in the construct state (Isa. 29:11).

(c) For examples of this use of קוֹל, see Cant. 2:8; 5:2; Ps. 29:3-9 (?).

(d) The common use of נֶפֶשׁ with suffixes to express a reflexive idea is to be noted; e. g., נַפְשִׁי *I myself*, נַפְשָׁם *they themselves.*

(e) Compare also some of the indefinite uses of דָּבָר *thing*, for which, however, see the lexicon.

(f) The use of לֹא and אַל in poetry to form a noun with an exactly opposite meaning to that conveyed by the noun itself, is not uncommon (cf. Deut. 32:5, 17, 21; Amos 6:13).

(g) See, more in detail, § 13. 2.

3. Cases in which the *first* of two words, thus joined, is the more important, the second merely indicating its character, number, size, or contents; this is seen,

a. When the second word is an *adjective*. This use is late, and occurs chiefly in the case of a few common adjectives like רַע, טוֹב, קָטֹן, גָּדֹל.*a b.* When the second word is an attributive word, whether noun, adverb or prepositional phrase.

c. When the second word, a proper noun, is the name of the first

d. When the second word is used "by circumlocution to describe a property of the first." This usage is very common on account of the scarcity of adjectives.

e. When the second word, a neuter or abstract noun, is joined to a preceding general noun like אִישׁ, בַּעַל, בֶּן, בַּת, denoting *possessor, origin, derivation.*[c]

f. When the second word designates the *whole* of which the first noun is a *part;*[f] or when the second word is a literal term. the first being *figurative.*[d]

4. Peculiar and rare is the occurrence of a construct,

    a. Before the conjunction וְ *and.*

    b. With a noun which, in sense, is in apposition with it.

    c. Before the interrogative pronoun.[e]

REMARKS.

(a) The adjective in this case is really treated like a neuter noun. Compare יַד הַיָּמִין *the right hand,* in which the word יָמִין, originally an adjective, has become a substantive.

(b) Here, of course, the appositional construction is much more common.

(c) Compare the peculiar cases of this construction seen in Isa. 5:11; Eccles. 12:11.

(d) For cases in which three or more nouns are joined together by annexion, see Gen. 40:3; 47:9; Josh. 3:15; Judg. 9:1; Isa. 10:12.

(e) The form אַחַד (e. g., in 2 Sam. 17:22) is sometimes used as an absolute and not as a construct.

(f) On the use of the preposition מִן *from* to express the partitive idea, see the lexicon.

REFERENCES FOR STUDY.

9. ANNEXION (CONTINUED).

1. *a.* רֹעֵה צֹאן[1] *keeper of sheep;* מְאִירַת עֵינַיִם[2] *enlightening the eyes;* אֹכְלֵי עַמִּי[3] *consumers of my people;* יֹרְדֵי עָפָר[4] *who go down to the dust.*

   b. מֻכֵּה אֱלֹהִים[5] *stricken of God;* בְּזוּי עָם[6] *despised by the people;* מִקְנַת־כֶּסֶף[7] *bought with money;* מֻכֵּי חָרֶב[8] *slain by the sword.*

   c. כְּבַד־פֶּה[9] *slow of speech;* קְשֵׁה עֹרֶף[10] *stiff of neck;* חֲכַם לֵב[11]; נוֹרָא תְהִלֹּת[12] *fearful in praises;* מֵתֵי מִלְחָמָה[13] *dead in battle.*

2. *a.* פְּנֵי הַמַּיִם[14] *face of the waters;* בֵּיתָה יוֹסֵף[15] *to the house of Joseph.*

   b. נְבִיאֵי מִלִּבָּם[16] *prophets out of their own heart;* הָרֵי בַגִּלְבֹּעַ[17] *mountains in Gilboa;* חוֹסֵי בוֹ[18] *those trusting in him;* מִיָּמִין לַבָּיִת[19] *on the right of the house.*

   c. בְּנֵי דָוִד וּבְנֹתָיו *the sons and daughters of David;* אֱלֹהֵי הַשָּׁמַיִם וֵאלֹהֵי הָאָרֶץ[20] *the God of heaven and earth.*

   d. הַר־קָדְשִׁי[21] *my holy hill;* יַד־אֱלֹהָיו הַטּוֹבָה[22] *the good hand of his God;* גַּל־אֲבָנִים גָּדוֹל[23] *a great heap of stones.*

---

1 Gen. 4:2.	7 Gen. 17:12.	13 Isa. 22:2.	19 Ezek. 10:3.
2 Ps. 19:9.	8 Jer. 18:21.	14 Gen. 1:3.	20 Gen. 24:3.
3 Ps. 53:5.	9 Ex. 4:10.	15 Gen. 43:17.	21 Ps. 2:6.
4 Ps. 22:30.	10 Deut. 9:6.	16 Ezek. 13:2.	22 Ez. 7:9.
5 Isa. 53:4.	11 Job 9:4.	17 2 Sam. 1:21.	23 Josh. 7:2
6 Ps. 22:7.	12 Ex. 15:11.	18 Ps. 2:12.	

1. Participles and adjectives are frequently joined by annexion with a following substantive. This is a closer construction than a following object-accusative or accusative of specification would be. Here may be noted,

a. The usage in the case of *active* participles, in which the noun expresses the object of the action, or, as sometimes in poetry, the sphere *in* which the action is exerted.[a][b]

b. The usage in case of *passive* participles, in which the noun expresses, sometimes the author of the action, sometimes the secondary agent or instrument.

c. The usage in the case of *adjectives* (denoting a property or quality) in which the noun has the force of an accusative of limitation or specification.

REMARKS.

(a) Cases of the construct before אֵת occur, e. g., Jer. 33:22.

(b) The accusative rather than a genitive is used (1) after a participle or adjective when it (the participle) has the article, and (2) when a word is for any reason inserted between the participle and the word which would, otherwise, be in the genitive; cf. Isa. 40:20; Job 15:10; 32:6.

2. Words in *annexion* form one complex idea, and therefore *cannot be separated by intervening words*. Here are to be noted certain points:—

a. The *article* and *He locative* everywhere form exceptions to the general law just given ; but aside from these only a few anomalous cases occur of the interposition of words.[a]

b. Prepositions, particularly the shorter ones and especially in poetry, quite frequently occur prefixed to the second of two nouns in annexion, thus defining more exactly the relationship existing between the two nouns.[b]

c. As *one* result of this inseparability, two or more nouns joined by "and" cannot stand in annexion with a single genitive ; but the genitive is employed with the first, and in the form of a suffix with the second;[c][d][e] while further, a single construct does not usually stand in annexion with two or more genitives, but is repeated with each.[f]

d. As a *second* result of this inseparability, a word or suffix limiting the construct must be placed after the following genitive and not between the construct and the genitive.[g]

REMARKS.

(a) כֹּל *all*, having almost come to be an adjective, occasionally allows the interposition of a word before its genitive, e. g., 2 Sam. 1:9; other cases in which this is claimed to occur are capable of a different explanation; e. g., Job 27:3; Ps. 45:7; Isa. 28:1; 36:9. Cf. also the bold poetic constructions in Gen. 49:11; Isa. 19:8; 22:16.

(b) This is most frequent with participles of verbs which are regularly followed by a preposition, e. g., חָסָה בְ trust in; שָׁכַן בְּ dwell in, etc.

(c) Hence one may not say, "*the sons and daughters of David*," but "*the sons of David and his daughters*;" and it is better to say "*the God of heaven and the God of earth*," than "*the God of heaven and earth*;" but see Gen. 14:19.

(d) The same holds true of pronominal suffixes; instead of "*his sons and daughters*" one must say "*his sons and his daughters*."

(e) Sometimes the suffix is omitted, or there is substituted for it the article, in which case the absolute state is employed, e. g., Gen. 40:1.

(f) Exceptions occur: (1) when the second of the two nouns joined by "and" is a repetition or a synonym of the first; and (2) in poetry where greater liberty is allowed, e. g., Job 20:17; Ezek. 39:4; 2 Sam. 20:19.

(g) Whether the modifying word which follows two nouns in annexion limits the construct, or the genitive, or the complex idea expressed by both together must be determined from the agreement and from the context. When there would be manifest ambiguity, resort is had to a periphrastic construction (§ 9. 5.).

3. a. אַנְשֵׁי הַמִּלְחָמָה[1] not *men of the war*, but *the men of war*.

   b. פְּנֵי רְקִיעַ הַשָּׁמַיִם[2] *the face of the expanse of the heavens*.

   בְּצֶלֶם אֱלֹהִים בָּרָא אֹתוֹ[3] *in the image of God he created him*.

   רָאשֵׁי שִׁבְטֵיכֶם[4] *the heads of your tribes*.

4. a. עֶבֶד עֲבָדִים[5] *a servant of servants*, i. e. *the lowest servant*.

   נְשִׂיא נְשִׂיאֵי הַלֵּוִי[6] *the prince of the princes of Levi*. [dwell.

   b. בַּעֲרוּץ נְחָלִים לִשְׁכֹּן[7] *in the most frightful of valleys they must*

   מִגְּדֹלָם וְעַד־קְטַנָּם[8] *from the greatest of them even to the least of them*.

5. a. בִּשְׁנַת שְׁתַּיִם לַמֶּלֶךְ[9] *in the year two of the king*.

   עִיר־גְּדֹלָה לֵאלֹהִים[10] *a great city of God*.

   בֵּן אֶחָד לַאֲחִימֶלֶךְ[11] *one son of Ahimelech*.

   b. בֶּן לְיִשַׁי[12] *a son of Jesse*.

   עֶבֶד לְשַׂר הַטַּבָּחִים[13] *a servant of the captain of the guard*.

   רָאשִׁים לְאָבוֹת[14] *heads of fathers*.

   מִזְמֹר לְדָוִד[15] *a psalm of David*.

   כֹּהֵן לְאֵל עֶלְיוֹן[16] *a priest of the most high God*.

---

1 Num. 31:49.   5 Gen. 9:25.   9 Hag. 1:1.   13 Gen. 41:12.
2 Gen. 1:20.   6 Num. 3:32.   10 Jon. 3:3.   14 Neh. 11:13.
3 Gen. 1:27.   7 Job 30:6.   11 1 Sam. 22:20.   15 Ps. 3:1.
4 Deut. 1:15.   8 Jon. 3:5.   12 1 Sam. 16:18.   16 Gen. 14:18.

c. לְדָוִד[1] (a psalm) of David.

אַמְנֹן לַאֲחִינֹעַם[2] Amnon (son) of Ahinoam.   [the month.

d. בְּשִׁבְעָה וְעֶשְׂרִים יוֹם לַחֹדֶשׁ[3] on the seven and twentieth day of

רִאשׁוֹן לְכֹל[4] the first of all.

e. חֶלְקַת הַשָּׂדֶה לְבֹעַז[5] the portion of the field of Boaz.

סֵפֶר דִּבְרֵי הַיָּמִים לְמַלְכֵי יִשְׂרָאֵל[6] the book of the chronicles of
the kings of Israel.

אֲבִיר הָרֹעִים אֲשֶׁר לְשָׁאוּל[7] the chief of the herdmen of Saul.

3. The construct, containing only a portion of the idea intended to be
conveyed, is incomplete and, in itself, *indefinite;* hence

  a. The construct cannot receive the article ;[a] or be definite in itself
(§ 4. 1.).[b]

  b. The construct, however, becomes definite *by position* (§ 4. 2),
whenever its following genitive is, for any reason, definite.[c] [d]

4. The use of *annexion* to express the superlative idea is worthy of
special notice. This is seen,

  a. When the *two* nouns in *annexion* are the same, the former being
singular, the latter plural.

  b. When the relation between the nouns is a partitive one (§ 8. 3. *f*).

5. Instead of *annexion*, there is often employed a periphrasis, made
by means of the preposition לְ.[e] [f] This is substituted when there is a
desire on the part of the writer,

  a. To interpose a word between the construct and genitive.

  b. To mark the first noun as indefinite, when the second is definite.

  c. To omit entirely the noun which would be in the construct, as in
inscriptions, and in the case of common words like *son, day*, etc.

  d. To designate explicitly relations of place and time.

  e. To avoid a long series of constructs.

REMARKS.

(a) Exceptions to this may be classified as follows: (1) Cases where the article
seems to have a demonstrative force, Josh. 8:33; cf. also Ps. 123:4; Ezek. 17:15; 1 Kgs.
14:24. (2) Cases where the genitive is a proper name, e. g., 2 Kgs. 23:17; Gen. 31:13;
Isa. 36:8. (3) Cases where what seems to be a construct is a participle with an accusative suffix, e. g., Ps. 18:33; Isa. 9:12. (4) Cases where the connection is loose, the second
noun denoting the material (and to be regarded in many instances as an adverbial

---

1 Ps. 69:1.   3 Gen. 8:14.   5 Ruth 2:3.   7 1 Sam. 21:8.
2 2 Sam. 3:2.   4 2 Sam. 19:21.   6 1 Kgs. 15:31.

accusative), e. g., 2 Kgs. 16:14; Zech. 4:10. (5) Cases where, the connection being loose, a preposition is inserted, e. g., Ps. 113:5; Judg. 8:11.

(b) Proper names, therefore, except when applied to more than one object, cannot stand in the construct.

(c) The construct cannot be indefinite and the genitive definite; nor can the genitive be indefinite and the construct definite; either both are definite or both indefinite. To both of these cases, however, exceptions are found, where there would be no room for ambiguity; e. g., Gen. 16:7; 42:19; 9:20; Lev. 14:34; 1 Sam. 17:17; Deut. 22:19.

(d) On the determination of words in annexion, see § 5. 1.

(e) The pronoun אֲשֶׁר is frequently inserted before the preposition to secure greater clearness.

(f) The preposition מִן from is sometimes employed as a substitute for annexion; e. g., 2 Sam. 19:18; Isa. 6:6; 1 Kgs. 20:35; Ps. 16:4. The sense, in this usage, is generally partitive.

REFERENCES FOR STUDY.

10. THE ADJECTIVE.

1. *a.* חֵיל כָּבֵד[1] *a host of mighty = a mighty host;* דָּם־הַנָּקִי[2] *the inno-*
   b. קֹרֶשׁ הֵיכָלֶךָ[3] *the holy of thy temple = thy holy temple.* [*cent blood.*

2. הַמָּאוֹר הַגָּדֹל[4] *the great luminary;* הַדְּבָרִים הַטּוֹבִים[5] *the good things;*
   בְּנוֹ הַגָּדֹל[6] *his eldest son;* הַמָּקוֹם הַזֶּה[7] *this place;*
   הַשָּׁנִים הַטֹּבוֹת הַבָּאֹת הָאֵלֶּה[8] *these good years that are to come.*

3. טוֹב יְהוָה[9] *Yahweh (is) good;* גָּדוֹל כְּבוֹדוֹ[10] *his glory (is) great;*
   טוֹבָה הָאָרֶץ[11] *the land (is) good;* כֹּחוֹ גָּדוֹל[12] *his strength (is) great;*
   אַתָּה צַדִּיק[13] *thou (art) righteous.*

4. *a.* מָתוֹק מִדְּבַשׁ[14] *sweeter than honey;* טוֹב מֵחַיִּים[15] *better than life;*
   וַיֶּאֱהַב אֶת־רָחֵל מִלֵּאָה[16] *and he loved Rachel more than Leah.*
   b. וְדָוִד הוּא הַקָּטָן וּשְׁלֹשָׁה הַגְּדֹלִים הָלְכוּ אַחֲרֵי שָׁאוּל[17] *and Da-*
   vid was the smallest, and the three oldest had followed Saul.

   מִגְּדוֹלָם וְעַד־קְטַנָּם[18] *from the greatest among them even unto the*
   least among them.

   גָּדוֹל מִכָּל־בְּנֵי־קֶדֶם[19] *greatest of all the men of the East.*

   הַיָּפָה בַּנָּשִׁים[20] *the fairest among women.*   [*priests.*

   גְּדֹלֵי הָעִיר[21] *the greatest of the city;* זִקְנֵי הַכֹּהֲנִים[22] *the oldest of the*

5. אִישׁ דְּבָרִים[23] *an eloquent man;* בַּעַל הַחֲלֹמוֹת[24] *having dreams;*
   בְּנֵי חַיִל[25] *sons of strength, valiant;* בֶּן־לַיְלָה[26] *son of a night.*

1. The adjective is frequently treated as if it were a *substantive:*
   a. When it stands in the genitive after a noun in the construct state
(§ **8. 3.** *a.*).
   b. When it stands in the construct state with a following genitive.[a]
2. The adjective (here including participles and demonstratives) when
used in an attributive sense,
   a. Follows[b] the noun which it modifies.
   b. Agrees[c] with it in number and gender.

---

1 Isa. 36:2.	8 Gen. 41:35.
2 Deut. 19:13.	9 Ps. 34:9.
3 Ps. 65:5.	10 Ps. 21:6.
4 Gen. 1:16.	11 Num. 14:7.
5 Josh. 23:14.	12 Judg. 16:5.
6 Gen. 27:1.	13 Neh. 9:33.
7 Gen. 28:17.	14 Judg. 14:18.

15 Ps. 63:4.	21 2 Kgs. 10:6.
16 Gen. 29:30.	22 Isa. 37;2.
17 1 Sam. 17:14.	23 Ex. 4:10.
18 Jon. 3:5.	24 Gen. 37:19.
19 Job 1:3.	25 Deut. 3:18.
20 Cant. 1:8.	26 Jon. 4:10.

c. Receives[d] the article, if the noun which it modifies is for any reason a definite noun.

3. The adjective (here including participles and demonstratives) when used as a predicate, regularly precedes the subject, yet frequently follows it, when the sense is clear.[e]

4. The comparison of adjectives is expressed as follows :—

a. The *comparative* degree, by the use of the preposition מִן *from* prefixed to the word with which comparison is made.[f] [g]

b. The *superlative* degree,

(1) By the emphatic use of the *positive* with the article, a pronominal suffix or a following genitive.[h]

(2) By employing the phrase מִכֹּל, or בְּ.

(3) By the constructions referred to in § 9. 4.

5. The adjectival idea, because of the scarcity of adjectives, is frequently expressed by certain nominal constructions (see § 8. 3. *e.*).

REMARKS.

(*a*) This does not include the cases cited under § 9. 1. *c.*

(*b*) Very rarely does the adjective precede; and in most of these cases the adjective or demonstrative is treated as a substantive; e. g., Ex. 32:1; Ps. 104:25; Ps. 32:10.

(*c*) It is to be noted that the adjective is plural when the noun is dual, and that with collectives the construction is often one according to sense; e. g., Isa. 42:7; 1 Sam.

(*d*) The article is quite frequently omitted (see § 5. 2. Rem. *d*).   [13:15; 17:28.

(*e*) Note also the use of a substantive (or a substantive and preposition) as predicate instead of an adjective, thus emphasizing the idea; Gen. 1:2; Job 3:4; Ps. 25:10; Isa. 5:12.

(*f*) This use of מִן is frequent also after verbs; e. g., 1 Sam. 10:23; Gen. 37:3.

(*g*) The adjective is often omitted and is to be supplied from the context; Mic. 7:4; Job 11:17.

(*h*) The individual is thus designated as possessing in a pre-eminent degree the quality referred to.

REFERENCES FOR STUDY.

11. PERSONAL PRONOUN AND SUFFIXES.

1. *a.* מוֹתִי¹ אָנִי *my death, mine;* לְשֵׁת גַּם־הוּא² *to Seth also to him.*

 b. מַמְרֵא הוּא חֶבְרוֹן⁴ *Bela, that is Zoar;* בֶּלַע הִיא צֹעַר³ *Bela, that is Zoar.*

 c. הָאָרֶץ הַהוּא⁵ *that land;* הָאִישׁ הַהוּא⁶ *that man.*

 d. אֱלֹהִים שֹׁפֵט⁷ *God is Judge;* הוּא⁸ שְׁמוֹ *is its name.*

2. *a.* בְּרָאָם⁹ *he created them;* בָּרָא אֹתָם¹⁰ *he created them;*

 הַצַמְתֶּנִי¹¹ *did ye fast for me?* נְתַתָּנִי¹² *thou hast given me.*

 b. אֹתְךָ הֲרַגְתִּי¹³ *thee I had killed;* וְהִרְאַנִי אֹתוֹ¹⁴ *and he will make
 me see it;* וּבָחֹר אֹתוֹ¹⁵ *and the choosing him;* בְּלִדְתָּהּ אֹתוֹ¹⁶ *when
 she bare him;* הֵם מַכְעִיסִים....אֹתָם¹⁷ *they provoke themselves;*
 הַכּוֹת־אֹתוֹ¹⁸ *to smite him.*

 c. לוֹ¹⁹ *to him;* מִמֶּנּוּ²⁰ *from it;* עָלַי²¹ *upon me;* לֶךְ־לְךָ²² *go for thee*
 = *take thyself;* נָם לוֹ²³ *he fled for himself.*

 d. חֲמָסִי²⁴ *my wrong;* יִרְאָתוֹ²⁵ *his fear* (caused by him).

1. The Personal Pronoun, in its separate form,ᵃ aside from its ordinary use,ᵇ ᶜ ᵈ ᵉ is employed,

 a. In apposition with a noun or pronoun in an oblique case, for emphasis (§ 6. 3); and in the case of the *third* person,

 b. As a brief explanatory particle equivalent to *that is.*

 c. As a remote demonstrative (see § 12. 1. *b.*).

 d. As a sort of copula (see § 7. 6, 7).

2. The Pronominal Suffixes are substituted for the personal pronouns in all oblique cases. Here may be noted their use,

 a. With verbs ;ᶠ ᵍ in which case the suffix is

 (1) generally the direct object of the verb as an accusative, either directly appended to the verb, or joined to אֵת (see *b.* below);

 (2) sometimes, for brevity, the indirect object, as a dative.

 b. With the sign of the definite object אֵת ;ʰ ⁱ this occurs

 (1) when for emphasis the pronominal idea must be expressed first ;

---

¹ 2 Sam. 19:1.	⁸ Gen. 2:19.	¹⁴ 2 Sam. 15:25.	²⁰ Gen. 3:3.
² Gen. 4:26.	⁹ Gen. 5:2.	¹⁵ 1 Sam. 2:28.	²¹ 2 Sam. 15:33.
³ Gen. 14:8.	¹⁰ Gen. 1:27.	¹⁶ Gen. 38:5.	²² Gen. 12:1.
⁴ Gen. 23:19.	¹¹ Zech. 7:5.	¹⁷ Jer. 7:19.	²³ Isa. 31:8.
⁵ Gen. 2:12.	¹² Josh. 15:19.	¹⁸ Gen. 4:15.	²⁴ Jer. 51:35.
⁶ Job 1:1.	¹³ Num. 22:33.	¹⁹ 1 Sam. 1:2.	²⁵ Ex. 20:20.
⁷ Ps. 50:6.			

(2) when a verb has two pronominal objects, only one of which can be joined directly to the verb ;

(3) when it is the object of an Infinitive Absolute which cannot receive a suffix ;

(4) when it is the object of an Infinitive Construct whose subject is a pronominal suffix, or a noun which must stand near it ;

(5) when the pronominal idea is a reflexive one ;

(6) when, by the use of אֵת, ambiguity is avoided, or greater distinctness secured.

  c. With prepositions :—

(1) In all the various uses which occur in the case of nouns; and besides

(2) In the so-called "ethical dative," which marks "an intimate relation sustained by the subject to the act."ⱼ

  d. With nouns ; here the noun is properly a construct (§ 8. Rem. b), and the suffix a genitive, subjective or objective (§ 8. 1. a. b).ᵏ ˡ

REMARKS.

(a) The personal pronoun, in its separate form, may be used only as a nominative, except in the case cited in 1. a. above.

(b) While the personal pronoun is included in the finite verb, it is also written separately (1) for emphasis or contrast; e. g., Ps. 71:22; Gen. 48:19; (2) if a second subject besides the pronoun follows the verb; e. g., Gen. 6:18; 13:1; (3) superfluously, chiefly by later writers; e. g., Lev. 18:26; Eccles. 2:12.   [24:36; 19:24.

(c) It is not uncommon to repeat a noun rather than employ a pronoun; e. g., Gen.

(d) The *third* person rather than the *first* is generally used by authors in speaking of themselves; e. g., Jer. 7:1; but cf. Isa. 6:1; Jer. 1:4.

(e) The terms *thy servant, thy handmaid* for the first person, and of *my Lord, the king* for the second person are common; e. g., Gen. 18:3; 19:19; 44:18; 2 Sam. 14:12.

(f) The suffix, when the object of a verb, is often omitted when it can be easily supplied from the context; e. g., Gen. 2:19; 9:22; 38:17; Ex. 2:3.

(g) It is, on the other hand, sometimes expressed redundantly; e. g., Ex. 2:6; 1 Sam. 21:14; Ezek. 10:3; Isa. 17:6; Josh. 1:2.

(h) As the language grows older there is an increasing tendency to separate the pronoun from the verb which it modifies.

(i) For the usage of the sign of the definite object אֵת with nouns, see § 12. 2. b.

(j) "In most cases this mode of expression indicates a special participation in the action by the agent or speaker, a certain earnestness or zeal with which he acts; but it occurs, as an expression of heartiness, more in the diffuse and easy-going popular style, both in poetry and in unimpassioned prose, and especially in sentences in which advice is tendered, or a question asked."—EWALD.

(k) The suffix, in a few cases, seems almost entirely to have lost its original force; e. g., (1) אֲדֹנָי = *my lords* (§ 3. 2. c) = *the Lord*, used only of *God* (Gen. 15:2; 18:3); (2) יַחְדָּו = *his joinings* = *he together* = *together* (Ex. 19:8; 1 Kgs. 3:18).

(l) On the inaccurate, and largely colloquial, interchange of masculine and feminine pronouns and suffixes. see § 2. 1. c.

REFERENCES FOR STUDY.

12. DEMONSTRATIVE AND INTERROGATIVE PRONOUN.

1. a. הַמָּקוֹם הַזֶּה[1] this place; הַדְּבָרִים הָאֵלֶּה[2] these things.

   b. הָאִישׁ הַהוּא[3] that man; בַּיָּמִים הָהֵם[4] in those days.

   c. הַפַּעַם[5] this stroke = now; הַלַּיְלָה[6] this night = to-night.

   d. זֶה יְלָדְךָ[7] who begat thee; זֶה שָׁכַנְתָּ בּוֹ[8] in which thou dwellest.

   e. זֶה הַיָּם[9] the sea there; עֲלוּ זֶה[10] come up here;

   זֶה יָמִים רַבִּים[11] now many days; זֶה פַעֲמַיִם[12] now twice;

   מִי זֶה[13] who then? לָמָּה זֶּה[14] why then? מַה־זֶּה[15] how is it that?

   f. וַאֲשֶׁר אִתּוֹ רַגְלַי כְּאַיָּלוֹת[16] my feet are like those of hinds;

   בַתֵּבָה[17] and those who were with him in the ark.

   g. וַיֹּאמֶר זֶה בְּכֹה וְזֶה אֹמֵר בְּכֹה[18] and this one said so, and that one said so; אֵלֶּה מִזֶּה וְאֵלֶּה מִזֶּה[19] these hither and those thither.

2. a. מִי הָאִישׁ[20] who is the man? מִי אֵלֶּה[21] who are these?

   מִי לְךָ כָּל־הַמַּחֲנֶה הַזֶּה[22] מִי כָל־בָּשָׂר[23] who is all flesh?

   b. בַּת־מִי אַתְּ[24] whose daughter art thou? אֶת־מִי אֶשְׁלַח[25] whom shall I send?

---

1 Gen. 28:17.   8 Ps. 74:2.   14 Gen. 18:13.   20 Gen. 24:65.
2 Gen. 15:1.   9 Ps. 104:25.   15 Judg. 18:24.   21 Gen. 33:5.
3 Job 1:1.   10 Num. 13:17.   16 2 Sam. 22:34.   22 Deut. 5:23.
4 Gen. 6:4.   11 Josh. 22:3.   17 Gen. 7:23.   23 Gen. 33:8.
5 Gen. 2:23.   12 Gen. 27:36.   18 1 Kgs. 22:20.   24 Gen. 24:23.
6 Gen. 19:5.   13 Job 38:2.   19 2 Sam. 2:13.   25 Isa. 6:8.
7 Prov. 23:22.

c. מָה־אָמְרוּ[1] *what did they say?* חָכְמַת־מֶה[2] *what wisdom?*

לָמָה[3] *for what?* יַעַן מֶה[4] *on account of what?* עַל־מָה[5] *upon what?*

d. לֹא־יֵדַע מִי־אֹסְפָם[6] *he knows not who shall gather them.*

לֹא יָדְעוּ מַה־הוּא[7] *they knew not what it was.*

e. מִי־יָרֵא וְחָרֵד יָשֹׁב[8] *let whoever is fearful and timid return.*

מַה־תֹּאמַר נַפְשְׁךָ וְאֶעֱשֶׂה־לָּךְ[9] *whatever thy soul desires I will do
for thee.*   [*thou?*

f. אֵי־זֶה בַיִת[10] *which house?* אֵי־מִזֶּה עִיר אָתָּה[11] *from what city art*

1. In reference to the *demonstrative* pronoun, it may be noted that

a. The demonstrative, when attributive, is treated as an adjective
(§ **10.** 2.).

b. The personal pronoun of the third person is used as a remote
demonstrative*a* (§ **11.** 1. *c.*).

c. The article sometimes still retains its original demonstrative
force (§ **4.** 3. *a*).

d. The pronoun זֶה, especially in poetry, is often used as a relative
pronoun.*b*

e. The pronoun זֶה (sometimes having a preposition) is also used as
a demonstrative adverb, sometimes referring to *place* and sometimes to
time; and frequently serves as an enclitic to emphasize words of interrogation (cf. English *then*).*c*

f. The demonstrative is omitted whenever, if expressed, it would
stand as a construct before a genitive, or before a relative pronoun.

g. The demonstratives are often used antithetically = *this—that,
these—those.*

2. In reference to the *interrogative* pronouns it may be noted that

a. מִי, either singular or plural, refers generally to *persons*, though
very seldom to *things.d*

b. מִי may be used as a genitive after a construct, an accusative with
אֵת, or with prepositions.

c. מָה, referring always to things, may stand as a nominative, accusative, or genitive, or with prepositions.

d. Either מִי or מָה may introduce indirect as well as direct questions.*e*

---

1 Isa. 39:3, 4.	4 Hag. 1:9.	7 Ex. 16:15.	10 Isa. 66:1.
2 Jer. 8:9.	5 Job 38:6.	8 Judg. 7:3.	11 2 Sam. 15:2.
3 Ps. 2:1.	6 Ps. 39:7.	9 1 Sam. 20:4	

e. Either מִי or מָה may be used as indefinite pronouns, *whoever, whatever.ᶠ ᵍ ʰ*

f. By prefixing אֵי (construct of אַי *where*) to the demonstrative זֶה a quite common interrogation is formed.

REMARKS.

(*a*) It is important to distinguish closely between זֶה and הוּא; e.g., Judg. 7:4.

(*b*) In the same manner our English *that* may be used as a relative.

(*c*) הוּא also is sometimes an enclitic emphasizing the preceding interrogative; e. g., Ps. 24:10.

(*d*) In most cases the objects to which מִי refers involve individual beings.

(*e*) In the Semitic languages the difference between direct and indirect sentences is scarcely felt.

(*f*) Compare דְּבַר מַה *whatever*, Num. 23:3; and also מְאוּמָה *anything whatever.*

(*g*) In a few cases מִי and מַה qualify a following word; e. g., מִי־אֵל (Deut. 3:24) *what God?* מַה־דְּמוּת (Isa. 40:18) *what likeness?* also Ps. 77:14; Jer. 2:5.

(*h*) Notice should be taken of those cases in which מַה, asking the *mode* of an action, is equivalent to *how?* e. g., Num. 23:8; 1 Sam. 10:27; Gen. 28:17; Ps. 8:2; 84:2.

REFERENCES FOR STUDY.

Gen. 4:10; 47:8	2c.	1 Kgs. 13:12	2f.
Gen. 15:18	1b.	1 Kgs. 17:24; 19:5	1e.
Gen. 16:8	2f.	2 Kgs. 19:22	2b.
Gen. 24:23, 32:18	2b.	Isa. 2:17	1b.
Gen. 27:21	1e.	Isa. 3:9	1f.
Gen. 28:15; 31:1	1f.	Isa. 54:15	2e.
Ex. 2:11	1b.	Joel 3:2	1b.
Ex. 5:22	1e.	Jon. 1:8	2f.
Ex. 24:14	1e, 2e.	Mic. 3:4	1b.
Num. 14:22	1e.	Mic. 5:4	1e.
Deut. 8:2, 4; 9:12	1e.	Zech. 5:5	2d.
Deut. 17:9	1b.	Zech. 7:3	1e.
Judg. 9:28	2a.	Mal. 1:7	2c.
1 Sam. 12:3; 17:55-58	2b.	Ps. 12:5; 77:14	2a.
1 Sam. 14:17	2d.	Ps. 20:8; 75:8	1g.
1 Sam. 30:13	2f.	Ps. 104:8	1d.
2 Sam. 19:43	1e.	Prov. 19:12	1f.
1 Kgs. 1:27; 14:3	2d.	Job 13:13	2e.
1 Kgs. 3:23	1g.	Job 19:19	1d.
1 Kgs. 12:16	2c.	Eccles. 7:14	1g.

13. THE RELATIVE PRONOUN.

1. הַשָּׂר אֲשֶׁר שְׁלָחוֹ הַמֶּלֶךְ[1] *the general whom the king has sent.*

גּוֹי אֲשֶׁר לֹא־תִשְׁמַע לְשֹׁנוֹ[2] *a nation whose tongue thou wilt not hear.*

הַחֲוִילָה אֲשֶׁר־שָׁם הַזָּהָב[3] *Havilah where is gold.*

---

[1] Isa. 37:4.   [2] Deut. 28:49.   [3] Gen. 2:11.

¹בָּרָד אֲשֶׁר לֹא־הָיָה כָמֹהוּ בְּמִצְרָיִם *hail such as has not been in* Egypt.

²עַבְדִּי אַתָּה אֲשֶׁר בְּךָ אֶתְפָּאָר *thou art my servant in whom I will*

2. ³לַאֲשֶׁר קָנָהוּ מֵאִתּוֹ *to him from whom he bought it.* [*be glorified.*

⁴עַל אֲשֶׁר־עָשָׂה *on account of that which he did.*

⁵בְּיַד אֲשֶׁר שָׂנֵאת *in the hand of him whom thou hatest.*

⁶בַּאֲשֶׁר תָּמוּתִי אָמוּת *in the place in which thou diest, I will die.*

⁷מֵאֲשֶׁר יָקַרְתָּ בְעֵינַי *from the time in which thou wast precious in mine*

⁸אֵת אֲשֶׁר־תְּבָרֵךְ מְבֹרָךְ *he whom thou blessest is blessed.* [*eyes.*

3. *a.* ⁹בְּאֶרֶץ לֹא לָהֶם *in a land which is not theirs.*

¹⁰הֵבֵאתָ יוֹם־קָרָאתָ *thou hast brought the day thou hast called.*

¹¹יוֹם אוּלַד בּוֹ *the day on which I was born.*

b. ¹²מְקוֹם לֹא־יָדַע אֵל *the place of him who knows not God.*

¹³בְּיַד־תִּשְׁלָח *by the hand of any one whom thou wilt send.*

¹⁴יְהוָה אֲהֵבוֹ יַעֲשֶׂה חֶפְצוֹ *he whom Yahweh loves will accomplish*

4. *a.* ¹⁵שְׁמַע לְאָבִיךָ זֶה יְלָדֶךָ *listen to thy father who begat thee.* [*his desire.*

¹⁶זֶה־אָהַבְתִּי נֶהְפְּכוּ־בִי *those I loved are turned against me.*

b. ¹⁷בְּנוֹ הַנּוֹלַד־לוֹ *his son who was born to him.* [*turned.*

¹⁸הַהֹלְכוּא *who went;* ¹⁹הַבָּאָה *which has come;* ²⁰הַשָּׁבָה *who re-*

The word אֲשֶׁר is, strictly speaking, an unchangeable relative particle, and not a *pronoun.* It is used to give a *relative* force to something which follows. Hence,

1. A pronominal suffix or an adverb following this particle, receives from it a *relative* meaning, אֲשֶׁר ....לוֹ = *to whom,* אֲשֶׁר ....אֹתָם = *whom,* אֲשֶׁר ....שָׁם = *where,* etc.[a][b]

2. When the particle אֲשֶׁר is immediately preceded by a preposition, or by אֵת, the sign of the definite object, or by a noun in the construct state, there is always to be supplied as its antecedent, according to the demands of the context, either a demonstrative pronoun, or a word indicating *place* or *time.*[c]

---

1 Ex. 9:18.	6 Ruth 1:17.	11 Job 3:3.	16 Job 19:19.
2 Isa. 49:3.	7 Isa. 43:4.	12 Job 18:21.	17 Gen. 21:3.
3 Lev. 27:24.	8 Num. 22:6.	13 Ex. 4:13.	18 Josh. 10:24.
4 Jer. 15:4.	9 Gen. 15:13.	14 Isa. 48:14.	19 Gen. 18:21.
5 Ezek. 23:28.	10 Lam. 1:21.	15 Prov. 23:22	20 Ruth 4:3.

3. The relative particle may be omitted from any construction in which it is accustomed to be used, as,

a. When it would be the subject or object of the sentence, or used as a genitive or dative ; and even

b. When, by its omission, there is also omitted its antecedent (see 2 above) which is included in it.

4. The relative idea is otherwise expressed,

a. By the demonstrative pronoun זֶה (§ 12. 1. *d*).

b. By the article with a participle and rarely with a finite verb (§ 4. 3. *f*).ᵈ ᵉ

REMARKS.

(*a*) When the pronominal suffix is the *object of a verb*, it may be omitted as easily understood from the context, and in this case the particle serves alone to express the idea, e. g., Gen. 2:8; 21:3; 26:32; Ex. 4:21.

(*b*) Generally one or more words stand between the particle, and the pronoun or adverb which receives from it the relative force.

c) In Gen. 31:32 and Isa. 47:12 the relative particle is said by some to be directly connected with the preposition.

(*d*) The relative particle is used with לְ as a periphrasis of annexion (§ 9. 5. Rem. *e*).

(*e*) The relative particle is largely used in the formation of conjunctions from prepositions and adverbs, but even here it may be omitted, e. g., Josh. 2:22; Gen. 31:20; 1 Sam. 5:9; 2 Sam. 12:22.

REFERENCES FOR STUDY.

Gen. 2:11	4*b*.	Isa. 7:16	1
Gen. 9:24; 39:9	2	Isa. 25:9; 42:24; 43:21	4*a*.
Gen. 13:3; 45:4	1	Isa. 30:6; 54:1	3*a*.
Ex. 4:15; 32:34	2	Isa. 40:29; 41:24; 65:1	3*b*.
Ex. 9:4	3*a*.	Jer. 2:8	3*b*.
Ex. 15:13	4*a*.	Jer. 32:19	1
Lev. 5:8	2	Ezek. 11:12	1
Lev. 16:32	1	Hos. 1:2	3*b*.
Deut. 3:4	1	Hos. 14:4	1
Deut. 4:3	2	Hab. 2:6	3*b*.
Deut. 32:15, 20	3*a*.	Ps. 4:8; 7:7; 49:20	3*a*.
Josh. 10:24	4*b*.	Ps. 9:16; 74:2	4*a*.
Judg. 5:18	3*a*.	Job 10:2; 15:17	4*a*.
Judg. 17:8	2	Ruth 1:16	2
1 Sam. 15:2; 16:3	2	Est. 6:6	1
1 Kgs. 18:12	2	1 Chron. 26:28	4*b*.
2 Kgs. 8:1	2		

14. OTHER PRONOMINAL EXPRESSIONS.

1. *a.* וָאֵחָבֵא[1] *and I hid myself;* וַיִּתְחַבֵּא[2] *and he hid himself.*

   b. אֲדֹנִי הוּא[3] *the Lord himself;* הַיְּהוּדִים הֵמָּה[4] *the Jews themselves.*

     וַיַּעַשׂ לוֹ אֵהוּד חֶרֶב[5] *and Ehud made for himself a sword.*

     וַתַּעֲלֵהוּ עִמָּהּ[6] *and she took him up with herself.*

   c. לֹא־אֵדַע נַפְשִׁי[7] *I know not myself* (lit., *my soul*).

     וַתִּצְחַק שָׂרָה בְּקִרְבָּהּ[8] *and Sarah laughed within herself.*

2. *a.* וַיַּחַלְמוּ....אִישׁ חֲלֹמוֹ[9] *and they dreamed....each his dream.*

     בַּבֹּקֶר בַּבֹּקֶר[10] *every morning;* שְׁנֵי הָעֹמֶר לָאֶחָד[11] *two omers for each;* בְּכָל־יוֹם[12] *in every day;* כָּל־חַי[13] *every one living.*

   b. אַל־יֵצֵא אִישׁ מִמְּקֹמוֹ[14] *let not any one go forth from his place.*

     הֲיִפָּלֵא מֵיהוָה דָּבָר[15] *Is anything too difficult for Yahweh?*

     כֹּל מִצְוֹת י[16] *any of Y's commandments;* כָּל־רָע[17] *anything evil.*

     כֹּל אֲשֶׁר־לְךָ בָּעִיר[18] *whoever belongs to thee in the city.*

     כֹּל אֲשֶׁר־חָפֵץ י עָשָׂה[19] *whatever Y. pleases, he does.*

   c. קַח....מִזִּקְנֵי י[20] *take....some of the elders of Israel.*

     וַיֵּצְאוּ מִן־הָעָם[21] *some of the people went out.*

   d. אֵין אִישׁ שָׂם עַל־לֵב[23] *no-body takes it to heart;* לֹא יִצְלַח לַכֹּל[22] *it is good for nothing;* אַל־תַּעֲשׂוּ דָבָר[24] *do nothing;* כָּל־אָדָם לֹא־יִהְיֶה בָאֹהֶל[25] *nobody shall be in the tent.*

   e. גּוֹי אֲשֶׁר־כָּזֶה[26] *such a people;* כָּזֶה אִישׁ[27] *such a man;* לֹא־הָיָה כֵן אַרְבֶּה כָּמֹהוּ[28] *there were no such locusts as they.*

   f. מִזֶּה אֶחָד וּמִזֶּה אֶחָד[29] *the one on the one side, the other on the other.* וַיִּפָּרְדוּ אִישׁ מֵעַל אָחִיו[30] *and they separated the one from the other.* וְלֹא־קָרַב זֶה אֶל־זֶה[31] *and the one did not draw near the other.* עִיר בְּעִיר מַמְלָכָה בְּמַמְ'[32] *one city against another, one kingdom against another.*

---

1 Gen. 3:10.	9 Gen. 40:5.	17 Isa. 56:2.	25 Lev. 16:17.
2 Gen. 3:8.	10 Ex. 16:21.	18 Gen. 19:12.	26 Jer. 5:9.
3 Isa. 7:14.	11 Ex. 16:22.	19 Ps. 135:6.	27 Gen. 41:38.
4 Est. 9:1.	12 Ps. 7:12.	20 Ex. 17:5.	28 Ex. 10:14.
5 Judg. 3:16.	13 Gen. 3:20.	21 Ex. 16:27.	29 Ex. 17:12.
6 1 Sam. 1:24.	14 Ex. 16:29.	22 Jer. 13:7.	30 Gen. 13:11.
7 Job 9:21.	15 Gen. 18:14.	23 Isa. 57:1.	31 Ex. 14:20.
8 Gen. 18:12.	16 Lev. 4:2.	24 Gen. 19:8.	32 Isa. 19:2.

Certain ideas, expressed in English by means of pronouns, are otherwise expressed in Hebrew. The more important of these are the following:—

1. The *reflexive* pronoun is expressed,

    a. By the Nĭph'äl and Hĭthpä'ēl stems.

    b. By the personal pronoun of the third person and by pronominal suffixes.

    c. By the use of certain nouns like פָּנִים, עֶצֶם, נֶפֶשׁ (§ 8. 2. *c*), קֶרֶב, and לֵב.

2. The indefinite pronouns are expressed variously:—

    a. Each, every, by אִישׁ, or the repetition of a word (§ 3. 1. *c*), or כֹּל, or אֶחָד.

    b. Any, anyone, anything, whoever, whatever, by כֹּל, דָּבָר, אִישׁ.

    c. Some of, by the preposition מִן *from.*

    d. Nothing, nobody, by לֹא ... דָּבָר, אֵין אִישׁ, לֹא ... כֹּל (or אַל), כָּל-אָדָם לֹא.

    e. Such, by כֵּן, כָּזֶה.

    f. The one—the other, by אָח—אִישׁ, אִישׁ—אִישׁ, אֶחָד—אֶחָד—אָחָד or זֶה—זֶה, רֵעַ—אִישׁ, אָחוֹת—אִשָּׁה, or the repetition of a noun.

REFERENCES FOR STUDY.

15. NUMERALS.

1. יוֹם אֶחָד[1] *one day;* תּוֹרָה אַחַת[2] *one law;* יָמִים אֲחָדִים[3] *single days.*

2. *a.* שְׁלֹשֶׁת יָמִים[4] *triad of days = three days;* שְׁנֵי הַמְּאֹרֹת[5] *the two l.*

    b. שֶׁבַע שָׁנִים[6] *seven years;* שִׁבְעָה פָרִים[7] *seven bullocks.*

---

[1] Gen. 27:45.   [3] Gen. 27:44.   [5] Gen. 1:16.   [7] Num. 23:1, 29.
[2] Ex. 12:49.   [4] Josh. 2:22.   [6] Gen. 5:7.

c. אֵילִם שִׁבְעָה[1] *seven rams;* מַעֲלוֹת שֶׁבַע[2] *seven steps.*

3. שְׁנֵים עָשָׂר אֲנָשִׁים[3] *twelve men;* פָּרִים שְׁנֵים עָשָׂר[4] *twelve bullocks;* אַחַד עָשָׂר יוֹם[5] *eleven days;* שֵׁשׁ עֶשְׂרֵה נֶפֶשׁ[6] *sixteen souls.*

4. שִׁבְעִים בָּנִים[7] *seventy sons;* אַמּוֹת עֶשְׂרִים[8] *twenty cubits;* אַרְבָּעִים לַיְלָה[9] *forty nights;* שִׁבְעִים נֶפֶשׁ[10] *seventy souls.*

5. אַרְבָּעִים וּשְׁנֵי יְלָדִים[11] *forty-eight cities;* עָרִים אַרְבָּעִים וּשְׁמֹנֶה[12] *forty-two children;* שְׁלֹשִׁים וְשָׁלֹשׁ שָׁנָה[13] *thirty-three years;* חָמֵשׁ שָׁנִים וְשִׁבְעִים שָׁנָה[14] *seventy-five years.*

6. מֵאָה נְבִיאִים[15] *a hundred prophets;* מֵאַת אֲדָנִים[16] *a hundred sockets;* רִמּוֹנִים מֵאָה[19] *a hun-* מֵאַת שָׁנָה[18] *a hundred years;* מֵאָה־שָׁנָה[17] *dred pomegranates;* עֹלוֹת[21] *or* אֶלֶף עֹלוֹת[20] אֶלֶף *a thousand burnt-offerings.*

7. *a.* הָאַרְבָּעִים[22] *the forty;* הָעֶשְׂרִים[23] *the twenty;* הָאֶחָד[24] *the one.*

   b. חֲמֵשֶׁת הָאֲנָשִׁים[25] *the five men;* אֵת אַרְבָּעִים הַיּוֹם[26] *the forty days;* הַשְּׁלֹשָׁה וְהַשִּׁבְעִים וְהַמָּאתַיִם[27] *the two hundred and seventy-three;* הַחֲמִשִּׁים וּמָאתַיִם אִישׁ[28] *the two hundred and fifty men.*   [*month.*

8. *a.* בַּשָּׁנָה הָרִאשֹׁנָה[29] *in the first year;* בַּחֹדֶשׁ הַתְּשִׁיעִי[30] *in the ninth*

   b. בִּשְׁמֹנֶה עֶשְׂרֵה[31] *or* בִּשְׁנַת שְׁמֹנֶה שָׁנָה[32] *in the eighteenth year;* בְּאַרְבָּעִים שָׁנָה[33] *in the fortieth year.*

   c. בִּשְׁנַת אַרְבַּע[34] *in the fourth year;* שְׁנַת־הַשֶּׁבַע[35] *the seventh year.*

9. *a.* שְׁנַיִם שְׁנַיִם[36] *two by two;* אֶחָד לַשֵּׁבֶט[37] *one for each tribe.*

   b. פַּעֲמַיִם[38] *twice;* שָׁלֹשׁ רְגָלִים[39] *or* שָׁלֹשׁ פְּעָמִים[40] *three times;* אַחַת[41] *once;* שֶׁבַע עַל־חַטֹּאתֵיכֶם[42] *seven times for your sins;* שִׁבְעָתַיִם[43] *seven times;* אַרְבַּעְתָּיִם[44] *four times.*

1 2 Chron. 13:9.	12 2 Kgs. 2:24.	23 Gen. 18:31.	34 Zech. 7:1.
2 Ezek. 40:22.	13 2 Sam. 5:5.	24 Eccles. 4:9.	35 Deut. 15:9.
3 Deut. 1:23.	14 Gen. 12:4.	25 Judg. 18:17.	36 Gen. 7:9.
4 Ezr. 8:35.	15 1 Kgs. 18:4.	26 Deut. 9:25.	37 Deut. 1:23.
5 Deut. 1:2.	16 Ex. 38:27.	27 Num. 3:41.	38 Num. 20:11.
6 Gen. 46:18.	17 Gen. 17:17.	28 Num. 16:35.	39 Ex. 23:17.
7 2 Kgs. 10:1.	18 Gen. 11:10.	29 2 Chron. 29:3.	40 Ex. 23:14.
8 2 Chron. 3:4.	19 2 Chron. 3:16.	30 Jer. 36:9.	41 1 Kgs. 10:22.
9 Gen. 7:4.	20 1 Kgs. 3:4.	31 2 Chron. 34:8.	42 Lev. 26:18.
10 Ex. 1:5.	21 2 Chron. 1:6.	32 2 Kgs. 22:3.	43 Gen. 4:15.
11 Josh. 21:39.	22 Gen. 18:29.	33 Deut. 1:3.	44 2 Sam. 12:6.

c. חֲצִי *one-half;* שְׁלִישִׁית *one-third;* שְׁתֵּי יָדוֹת *two-thirds;* אַרְבַּע יָדוֹת *four-fifths;* תֵּשַׁע יָדוֹת *nine-tenths.*

The various constructions of the numerals may be classified as follows :

1. אֶחָד is an adjective, and follows the substantive which it modifies.[a]

2. The numerals from *two* to *ten* are used with *plural* nouns and may stand in one of three constructions :—

    a. Before the noun and in *annexion* with it (§ 8. 2. *a*).

    b. Before the noun, with the noun in apposition (§ 6. 2. and Rem. *b*).

    c. After the noun, and in apposition with it (§ 6. 1. *e*).[b c]

3. The numerals from *eleven* to *nineteen* are used with plural nouns,[d] and usually stand *before* the noun (§ 6. 2. and Rem. *b*), though sometimes after it (§ 6. 1. *e*).

4. The numerals from *twenty* to *ninety* may be followed by the substantive (in apposition, cf. § 6. 2. and Rem. *b*), or may be preceded by the substantive and stand in apposition with it (§ 6. 1. *e*). In the former case the substantive is generally in the singular,[e] in the latter it is always in the plural.

5. Numerals made up of tens and units vary greatly in usage. They generally follow a plural noun, though sometimes they precede it. The common nouns cited below (Remarks *d, e*) generally stand in the singular, if the numeral precedes. Frequently the substantive is used twice, in the singular with the *ten*, in the plural with the *unit.*

6. The numerals מֵאָה *hundred,* מָאתַיִם *two hundred,* together with the words for *three hundred, four hundred,* etc., and אֶלֶף *thousand,* אַלְפַּיִם *two thousand* admit the same constructions as the numerals *two* to *ten* (see above 2. *a.-c*).[f] The substantive, except in the case of those named in Remarks *d, e* (below), is in the plural.

7. In the use of the article with numerals, it may be noted that,

    a. A numeral standing alone receives it, as would any other noun.

    b. When the numeral is in the construct, the article is written with the following substantive; when it is in the absolute, the article may be prefixed to the numeral, or to the substantive, or to both.

8. In reference to the use of ordinals, it may be noted that,

    a. Those from *one* to *ten* are treated as ordinary adjectives.

    b. Above *ten,* the cardinals are used as ordinals, following in *annexion* with the noun, or preceding it in *apposition.*

    c. In dates, the cardinals from *one* to *ten* also are often used instead of the ordinals.[g]

9. *a.* Distributives are expressed by the repetition of the numeral, or by the use of the preposition לְ.

b. Numeral adverbs are expressed by forms of פַּעַם *time*, רֶגֶל *foot*, יָד *hand*, by feminine forms of the cardinals, by dual formations.

c. Fractions are expressed by specific words (e. g., חֲצִי *one-half*), by the feminine form of the ordinals, by use of the word יָדוֹת, etc.

REMARKS.

(*a*) אֶחָד is sometimes used as a substantive in annexion with a following word, e. g., 2 Sam. 13:13; Job 2:10.

(*b*) This construction is comparatively rare and late.

(*c*) Nouns designating weights and measures are frequently omitted after the numeral, which, however, is masculine or feminine according to the gender of the omitted noun; e. g., Gen. 24:22; 1 Sam. 10:4; Ruth 3:15.

(*d*) Certain common nouns stand in the singular with the numerals *eleven* to *nineteen:* אִישׁ *man*, אֶלֶף *thousand*, אַמָּה *cubit*, יוֹם *day*, כֶּסֶף *silver*, נֶפֶשׁ *soul*, שָׁנָה *year*, שֶׁקֶל *shekel*; e. g., Num. 1:44; Deut. 1:2; Hos. 3:2; Gen. 46:18.

(*e*) But except in the case of the nouns just mentioned in Rem. *d*, and a few others denoting *weight* or *measure*, such as בַּת *bath*, כִּכָּר *talent*, כֹּר *cor*, גֵּרָה *gerah*, the numerals from *twenty* to *ninety*, even when they precede the substantive, usually take a noun in the plural; e. g., Num. 11:25; Ezek. 40:17.

(*f*) These words, however, with the exception of מֵאָה, having no construct, cannot stand in *annexion* with a following substantive.

(*g*) In dates the nouns יוֹם *day*, חֹדֶשׁ *month* are frequently omitted; e. g., Gen. 8:5; Ex. 12:3; Deut. 1:3.

REFERENCES FOR STUDY.

II. Use of Tenses and Moods.

16. THE TENSES, IN GENERAL.

1. *a.* אֶל־הָאִשָּׁה אָמַר[1] *unto the woman he said.*

   b. זָקַנְתִּי מִהְיוֹת לְאִישׁ[2] *I am too old to be to a husband.*

   c. דָּרַךְ כּוֹכָב מִיַּעֲקֹב[3] *a star shall proceed from Jacob,* etc.

2. *a.* אָז יָשִׁיר־מֹשֶׁה[4] *then sang* (proceeded to sing) *Moses.* [*answering him.*

   מֹשֶׁה יְדַבֵּר וְהָאֱלֹהִים יַעֲנֶנּוּ[5] *Moses kept speaking and God kept*

   יִמְצָאֵהוּ בְּאֶרֶץ מִדְבָּר[6] *he found him in a desert land.*

   b. אֶרְאֶנּוּ וְלֹא עַתָּה[7] *I see him but not now.*

   וְכָל־בְּכוֹר בָּנַי אֶפְדֶּה[8] *but all the first-born of my sons I redeem.*

   שִׂפְתֵי חֲכָמִים תִּשְׁמוּרֵם[9] *the lips of the wise preserve them.*

   c. עַתָּה תִרְאֶה אֲשֶׁר אֶעֱשֶׂה[10] *now thou shalt see what I shall do.*

   מָחָר יַעֲשֶׂה יְהוָה הַדָּבָר הַזֶּה[11] *to-morrow Yahweh will do this thing.*

   מִכֹּל עֵץ־הַגָּן אָכֹל תֹּאכֵל[12] *from every tree of the garden thou mayest eat.*

   בַּעֲבוּר תִּהְיֶה־לִּי לְעֵדָה[13] *that they may be to me for a testimony.*

The Hebrew has, strictly speaking, *two* tenses. These, however, do not correspond to the tenses of the Indo-European languages. The following general statements, based chiefly on the examples cited above, although also in part upon a larger induction, will present, briefly, the peculiarities of the Hebrew tenses:

1. The *Perfect*, used alike of actions or states belonging to the sphere of the past, present, or future, represents the action or state as actually completed (finished), or as conceived of by the writer or speaker as completed. Hence it may be used

---

[1] Gen. 3:16.   [5] Ex. 19:19.   [8] Ex. 13:15.   [11] Ex. 9:5.
[2] Ruth 1:12.   [6] Deut. 32:10.   [9] Prov. 14:3.   [12] Gen. 2:16.
[3] Num. 24:17.   [7] Num. 24:17.   [10] Ex. 6:1.   [13] Gen. 21:30.
[4] Ex. 15:1.

a. Of actions belonging to the *past,* and so finished.

b. Of actions or states in the *present,* but regarded as finished.

c. Of actions or states that are yet to happen, but which, for the sake of effect, the writer or speaker describes as having actually taken place or existed.

2. The *Imperfect,* used alike of actions or states belonging to the sphere of the past, present or future, represents the action or state as actually incomplete (unfinished), or as conceived of by the writer or speaker as incomplete. Hence it may be used

a. Of actions belonging to the *past,* but regarded by the writer as incipient or frequentative.

b. Of actions in the *present,* regarded as happening or likely to happen.

c. Of actions in the *future,* and so, whether the idea be that of mere futurity, or of possibility, obligation, purpose or condition, in the strictest sense *unfinished.*

GENERAL REMARKS.

(1) The tense, therefore, has in itself no indication of the *order* of time; it merely assigns to the action or state a given characteristic, viz., completeness, or incompleteness. The *order* of time, i. e., the sphere of time (whether past, present, or future) of each action or state must be determined from the context.

(2) The Imperfect may perhaps better be described as representing an action as *coming,* or *becoming,* i. e., as in movement. The Perfect, on the other hand, is the tense of *rest.* The former represents the thing as *doing,* the latter represents it as *done.*

(3) The names "Past" and "Future" not only fail to convey the true meaning of the tenses, but carry with them an entirely false conception. The names "Aorist" and "Subsequent" are far better;[1] yet also they fail to cover the respective usages of these tenses. The terms "Perfect" and "Imperfect," while not entirely satisfactory, seem, upon the whole, to be the best. They are, however, to be used in the sense described, viz., "finished," "unfinished."

(4) No effort to translate literally the Hebrew tenses will be successful. It is incorrect to say, e. g., that the literal rendering of Gen. 2:5 is *and a mist will go up,* etc. The future idea is no more a necessary element in the *Imperfect* tense than in the *Perfect.* Every attempt to follow rigidly the so-called past and future rendering will fail.

---

[1] Suggested by Prof. Wm. G. Ballantine, D. D., in October HEBRAICA, 1885, pp.53-55.

(5) This peculiarity often appears also in the Greek, e. g., πεῖσαι differs from πείθειν, and μὴ πείσῃς from μὴ πεῖθε not as to the sphere of time to which they belong, but as to the character of the act. Both are indefinite as to date; the former, however, is momentary, the latter, continuous.

(6) The distinction indicated by the tenses is not necessarily a real one. It may exist only in the mind of the writer or speaker. He is at liberty, therefore, upon one occasion to describe the action as it really is, upon another, as he for any reason may conceive it to be. Still further, in describing events belonging to the past he may either represent them as they really are, viz., *finished*, or he may, for the sake of rhetorical effect, represent them as taking place before his eyes. In the same series, one event may be described in one way, the second in the other way. In the representation of events belonging to the sphere of the future, the same liberty may be exercised. At times this is puzzling; but, in most cases, the context is a sure guide.

(7) There is danger, of course, that in our effort to analyze the various possible uses of the tenses, we may force into them some significations which they were never intended to convey. Prof. Driver, however, has truly said: "In itself the Perfect (for example) enunciates simply the completion of an act: it is by way of accommodation to the usage of another language that, eliciting its special force from the context, we make the meaning more definite by exhibiting it explicitly, as occasion demands, under the form of an aorist, a perfect, or a present."

17. The Perfect, Used of Past Events.

1. בָּרָא א'' אֵת הַשָּׁמַיִם וְאֵת הָאָרֶץ¹ *God created the heaven and the* [*earth.*

וְכוּשׁ יָלַד אֶת־נִמְרֹד² *and Cush begat Nimrod.*

וּבְנֵי יִשְׂרָאֵל פָּרוּ³ *and the children of Israel were fruitful.*

שָׁלֹשׁ שָׁנִים מָלַךְ בִּי''⁴ *three years reigned he in Jerusalem.*

2. עָזְבוּ אֶת־יְהוָֹה⁵ *they have forsaken Yahweh.*

לָמָּה נָפְלוּ פָנֶיךָ⁶ *why hath thy countenance fallen?*

אֲשֶׁר שָׁתוּ עָלָי⁷ *who have set themselves against me.*

מָלְאוּ מָתְנַי חַלְחָלָה⁸ *my loins have become (= are) full of anguish.*

3. אֶת־שׁוֹר מִי לָקַחְתִּי⁹ *whose ox have I taken?*

אִם־עָשִׂיתִי זֹאת¹⁰ *if I have (ever) done this.*

1 Gen. 1:1.   4 1 Kgs. 15:2.   7 Ps. 3:7.   9 1 Sam. 12:3.
2 Gen. 10:8.   5 Isa. 1:4.   8 Isa. 21:3.   10 Ps. 7:4.
3 Ex. 1:7.   6 Gen. 4:6.

[1] תַּאֲוַת לִבּוֹ נָתַתָּה לּוֹ *thou hast given him the desire of his heart.*

4. [2] מְלַאכְתּוֹ אֲשֶׁר עָשָׂה *his work which he had made.*

[3] חֲטָאתֶם לַיהוָה אֱלֹהֵיכֶם *ye had sinned against Yahweh your God.*

[4] כִּי לֹא אָכַל לֶחֶם *for he had not eaten bread.*

The Perfect, designating that which is finished, is used of past events. Here may be distinguished,

1. The *historical* perfect (employed in simple narration), which denotes an action or state completed at or during a particular period in the past. This period, long or short, is fixed by the context. There is no reference to other events.

2. The *present* perfect (or Greek perfect), which denotes an action (not a state) completed in the past, but viewed in relation to the present; in other words, an action resulting in a state.[a] [b]

3. The *indefinite* perfect, which denotes an action completed at some point in the past, which "the speaker is not able or desirous to specify more closely."[c]

4. The *pluperfect*, which denotes a finished action, viewed in relation to some other past action, either already mentioned, or yet to be mentioned.

REMARKS.

(a) This perfect is frequently to be rendered as a present, though the past should be used wherever it is possible.

(b) The difference between this and the historical [perfect is an important one. The whole interpretation of a passage will turn on the choice made.

(c) While the exact moment is not specified, the limits within which it must fall are often seen from the context.

REFERENCES FOR STUDY.

---

[1] Ps. 21:3.   [2] Gen. 2:2.   [3] Deut. 9:16.   [4] 1 Sam. 28:20.

18. The Perfect, Used of Present Events.

1. הֲרִמֹתִי יָדִי אֶל־יְהוָה[1] *I lift up my hand to Yahweh.*

וְאֹתוֹ צִוֵּיתִי לִהְיוֹת נָגִיד[2] *and him I appoint to be prince.*

וְעַתָּה שָׁלַחְתִּי אִישׁ־חָכָם[3] *and now I send a wise man.*

2. לֹא יָדַעְתִּי[4] *(I have perceived = I have come to know =) I know not.*

זָכַרְנוּ אֶת־הַדָּגָה וגו׳[5] *we remember the fish,* etc.

קָטֹנְתִּי מִכֹּל הַחֲסָדִים[6] *I am too small for all the mercies,* etc.

3. יָדַע שׁוֹר קֹנֵהוּ[7] *an ox knoweth his owner.*

יָבֵשׁ חָצִיר נָבֵל צִיץ[8] *grass withereth, flower fadeth.*

מִשָּׁמַיִם י׳ הִבִּיט רָאָה אֶת־[9] *from heaven Y. looks down; he sees,* etc.

The Perfect, as designating that which is *finished*, is used of events which, indeed, are regarded as completed, yet sustain so close a relation to the present as in many cases to be regarded as belonging to the sphere of the present. Here belong,

1. The *perfect of the immediate past*, which denotes an action finished *at* the moment or *just before* the moment of speaking, and is generally best rendered by our present.

2. The *stative perfect*, used of verbs expressing a physical or mental state (see *Elements*, § 58. Note 3);[a][b] here the state or condition is one which, although entered into in the past, or the result of some past activity, is regarded as existing at the time of speaking, and is, consequently, best rendered by the present.[c]

3. The *perfect of experience*, used to express truths which have been established by experience, and, hence, generally accepted.[d][e]

REMARKS.

(a) Compare the Latin *novi, memini*, and the Greek οἶδα.

(b) The most common verbs in this class will be found below in the "References for Study."

(c) It is not to be supposed that the Perfect of these verbs is limited to this usage. They may have, according to the demands of the context, the other uses of the perfect.

(d) With this use of the Perfect may be compared the gnomic aorist of the Greek.

(e) The Imperfect is likewise employed to express general truths, but from a different point of view (§ 21. 3).

---

1 Gen. 14:22.
2 1.Kgs. 1:35.
3 2 Chron. 2:12.
4 Gen. 4:9.
5 Num. 11:5.
6 Gen. 32:11.
7 Isa. 1:3a.
8 Isa. 40:7.
9 Ps. 33:13.

REFERENCES FOR STUDY.

19. The Perfect, Used of Future Events.

1. הַשָּׂדֶה נָתַתִּי לָךְ[1] the field I give (= will give) thee.

לְזַרְעֲךָ נָתַתִּי אֶת־הָא' הַזֹּאת[2] to thy seed I will give this land.

יָדַעְתִּי כִּי הוֹשִׁיעַ י'[3] I know that Yahweh will save.

2. a. לָכֵן גָּלָה עַמִּי[4] therefore my people shall go into captivity.

דָּרַךְ כּוֹכָב מִיַּעֲקֹב[5] a star shall proceed from Jacob, etc.

הָעָם....רָאוּ אוֹר גָּדוֹל[6] the people....shall see a great light.

b. וְחָלַף בִּיהוּדָה שָׁטַף וְעָבַר עַד־צַוָּאר יַגִּיעַ[7] and he shall sweep onward into Judah; he shall overflow and pass through; he shall reach even to the neck.

כִּי־כוֹכְבֵי הַשָּׁמַיִם....לֹא יָהֵלּוּ אוֹרָם חָשַׁךְ הַשֶּׁמֶשׁ[8] for the stars of heaven....shall not give their light, the sun shall be darkened, etc.

c. וְלֹא יַשְׁחִיתוּ....כִּי־מָלְאָה הָאָרֶץ דֵּעָה אֶת־י'[9] and they shall do no harm....for the earth shall be filled with the knowledge of Y.

כִּי־אֲרֻבּוֹת מִמָּרוֹם נִפְתָּחוּ[10] for the windows of heaven shall be opened.

כִּי־שָׁמַע י' קוֹל בִּכְיִי[11] for Y. shall hear the voice of my weeping.

3. כִּי־נְתָנָם יְהֹוָה בְּיָדֵנוּ[12] for Y. will have given them into our hand.

לֵךְ כִּי שְׁלָחֲךָ יְהֹוָה[13] go, for (then) Y. will have sent thee.　　[ten.

וּמוֹלַדְתְּךָ אֲשֶׁר־הוֹלַדְתָּ[14] and thine issue which thou shalt have begot-

---

[1] Gen. 23:11.　　　[5] Num. 24:17.　　　[9] Isa. 11:9.　　　[12] 1 Sam. 14:10.
[2] Gen. 15:18.　　　[6] Isa. 9:1.　　　[10] Isa. 24:18.　　　[13] 1 Sam. 20:22.
[3] Ps. 20:7.　　　[7] Isa. 8:8.　　　[11] Ps. 6:9 (cf. 10).　　[14] Gen. 48:6.
[4] Isa. 5:13.　　　[8] Isa. 13:10.

עַד־עֵת....יְלֵדָה [1] *until the time when she....shall have brought forth.*

4. לוּ הַחֲיִתֶם אוֹתָם לֹא הָרַגְתִּי אֶתְכֶם [2] *if you had kept them alive, I should not have killed you.*

לוּלֵי יְ' צְ' הוֹתִיר לָנוּ....כִּסְדֹם הָיִינוּ [3] *except Y. of hosts had left us a very small remnant, we should have been as Sodom, etc.*

אִם־לֹא הֲבִיאֹתִיו אֵלֶיךָ....וְחָטָאתִי [4] *if I do not bring him (= shall not have brought) back to thee....then I will bear the blame.*

The Perfect, as designating that which is finished, or conceived of as finished, is frequently used of events which belong to the sphere of the future.[a] Here are to be noted,

1. The *perfect of certainty*, used of actions in the future, which the speaker or actor has fully determined to perform; this occurs especially in the statement of promises, decrees, and contracts.

2. The *prophetic perfect*, really an extension of the Perfect of *certainty;* this use of the tense portrays boldly and expressively the confidence of the speaker as to the certain occurrence of a yet future event. There may be distinguished,

a. Cases in which the Perfect is the first verb of a series, the remaining verbs being Perfects of a similar character, or Imperfects with a future meaning.

b. Cases in which the series of verbal forms, while composed chiefly of Imperfects, contains here and there a Perfect which has been inserted "to give variety to the scene, or to confer particular emphasis upon individual traits in it."

c. Cases in which the Perfect is used after כִּי in assigning a reason for something which, though still future, is deemed *certain.*

3. The *future-perfect*, which denotes a finished action, viewed in relation to some other action still in the future.[b]

4. The *conditional perfect*, used in certain forms of conditional sentences (§ **48.** 6, 7), in which the fulfillment or non-fulfillment of the condition is thus vividly expressed. [c] [d]

REMARKS.

(*a*) The ease with which the Hebrew writer passed from one tense to the other is paralleled only by the difficulty which the modern translator finds in expressing the force of the change.

(*b*) The auxiliaries *shall have*, or *will have* do not always furnish the best rendering of this construction, there being many cases in which, especially after conjunctions,

1 Mic. 5:2.   2 Judg. 8:19.   3 Isa. 1:9.   4 Gen. 43:9.

the ordinary rendering (*has* or *have*) is entirely sufficient; e. g., כִּי נִרְאָה (Isa. 16:12; Gen. 28:15; 2 Kgs. 4:24).

(c) That the Perfect may also be used to express a *wish*, i. e., as a Precative, is claimed by some grammarians. In accordance with this usage, the following passages are by some explained: Isa. 26:15; 43:9; Ps. 4:2; 7:7; 10:16; 22:22; 31:6; 57:7; 71:3; 116:16; Job 21:16; 22:18, and a few others. But expositors do not agree on the cases in which this force exists; and nearly every case cited by any writer can be satisfactorily explained in another way.

(d) Of interest, likewise, are those cases in which the Perfect is used in interrogation (1) after such phrases as עַד מָתַי *till when?* עַד אָנָה *up to where?* e. g., Ex. 10:3; Ps. 80:5; and (2) where the speaker desires to represent a thing as highly improbable; e. g., Gen. 18:12; 21:7; Deut. 5:23; Judg. 11:13.

REFERENCES FOR STUDY.

20, THE IMPERFECT, USED OF PAST EVENTS.

1. *a.* יֹאבַד יוֹם אִוָּלֶד בּוֹ[1] *perish the day on which I was born.*

תְּהֹמֹת יְכַסְיֻמוּ[2] *the depths covered them.*

יִמְצָאֵהוּ בְּאֶרֶץ מִדְבָּר[3] *he found him in a desert land.*

---

[1] Job 3:3.   [2] Ex. 15:5.   [3] Dt. 32:10.

b. אָז יָשִׁיר־מֹשֶׁה[1] *then sang (proceeded to sing) Moses.*

וְכֹל שִׂיחַ הַשָּׂדֶה טֶרֶם יִהְיֶה בָא[2] *and no shrub of the field was yet in the earth.*

אָז יִמָּלֵא שְׂחוֹק פִּינוּ[3] *then our mouth was filled with laughter.*

2. וְכֵן יַעֲשֶׂה שָׁנָה בְשָׁנָה[4] *and so he did year by year.*　[*throng.*

בְּבֵית אֱלֹהִים נְהַלֵּךְ בְּרָגֶשׁ[5] *we used to go to the house of God in a*

חֶרֶב שָׁאוּל לֹא תָשׁוּב רֵיקָם[6] *Saul's sword never returned empty.*

The Imperfect, designating that which is *unfinished* (developing, moving), is used of events which belong to the sphere of the *past*. Here may be distinguished :[a]

1. The *incipient* (strictly so called) *imperfect*, which represents the action so designated as *beginning* or *in movement*. This usage,

　　a. Is most common in poetic and prophetic diction, when, presenting the action in the most vivid and lively manner, it is equivalent to our *historical present.*[b c d]

　　b. Is common in prose with certain particles which mark the point in the past at which the action described was still unconcluded. These particles are אָז *then*, טֶרֶם, בְּטֶרֶם *not yet.*[e]

2. The *frequentative imperfect*, used to express repeated acts, habits or customs.[f g h]

REMARKS.

(*a*) Certain exceptional cases of the Imperfect used of past time are Gen. 37:7; Ex. 8:20; Deut. 32:35; 2 Sam. 15:37; 23:10; 1 Kgs. 7:8b; 21:6; 2 Kgs. 13:20; Jer. 52:7; Ezek. 9:4; Job 6:17; Ps. 56:4.

(*b*) This Imperfect is frequently used in poetry immediately after a Perfect, to indicate the "rapid and instantaneous manner in which the second action is conceived as following the first," e. g., Ex. 15:12, 14; Hab. 3:10; Ps. 37:14f.; 74:14; 77:17.

(*c*) Just as a prophetic Perfect may be inserted in a series of Imperfects (§ 19. 2. *b*), so an Imperfect may be inserted in a series of Perfects, and the description thus be rendered more lively and forceful, e. g., Isa. 9:10; Joel 2:3 ff.; Nah. 2:5.

(*d*) This Imperfect is also frequently used in *descriptions* instead of the more commonly employed participle, e. g., Gen. 2:10; and in circumstantial clauses, e. g., 2 Sam. 15:37.

(*e*) אָז is found sometimes with the Perfect; טֶרֶם also, but rarely; e. g., Gen. 4:26; 24:15; Ex. 4:26; 15:15; 1 Sam. 3:7a; Ps. 90:2.

(*f*) The frequentative use of the Imperfect has its origin as follows: the Imperfect characterizes an action or state as uncompleted. The action thus characterized, may, indeed, be one which has not begun; but, *if begun*, and in the sphere of the past, it must, unless it be a continuous action, be one which is *repeatedly exercized*. A mere continuous action (see *h* below) is expressed by the Participle.

---

1 Ex. 15:1.　　3 Ps. 126:2.　　5 Ps. 55:15.　　6 2 Sam. 1:22.
2 Gen. 2:5.　　4 1 Sam. 1:7.

(*g*) The incipient and frequentative Imperfect denote actions which are unfinished; they differ, however, in that the former is used only of single acts, the latter of several.

(*h*) The difference between the usage of the Participle and Imperfect is important: the former represents an action as *continuing without interruption*; the latter as *occurring repeatedly*. In many cases the difference may be difficult to perceive; a close study, however, will invariably show that there is a distinction, it being impossible to substitute one for the other without a change of meaning. "While the Imperfect multiplies an action, the Participle prolongs it; the one presents a series of units, the other, a continuous line."* Cf. Gen. 29:2; 1 Sam. 2:13 f.; 1 Kgs. 10:22.

REFERENCES FOR STUDY.

Gen. 2:10	1*a*.	1 Kgs. 3:4; 5:28	2
Gen. 6:4	2	Isa. 1:21	2
Gen. 19:4; 24:45	1*b*.	Isa. 6:2	1*a*.
Gen. 30:38; 31:39	2	Isa. 7:23	2
Ex. 1:12	2	Isa. 23:7	2
Ex. 15:6, 7, 15	1*a*.	Isa. 26:11	2
Ex. 19:19	2	Isa. 43:17	1*a*.
Num. 9:16–23	2	Isa. 45:4	1*a*.
Num. 23:7	1*a*.	Isa. 51:2	1*a*.
Deut. 32:16, 17	2	Hab. 3:3, 7	1*a*.
Josh. 8:30; 10:12; 22:1	1*b*.	Ps. 7:16	1*a*.
Josh. 23:10	2	Ps. 18:4, 7, 21	1*a*.
Judg. 2:1	1*a*.	Ps. 30:9	1*a*.
Judg. 2:18	2	Ps. 42:5	2
Judg. 5:8, 26, 29	1*a*.	Ps. 69:5	1*b*.
Judg. 6:5	2	Ps. 95:10	2
1 Sam. 2:22	2	Ps. 99:6 f.	2
1 Sam. 3:3, 7b	1*b*.	Ps. 104:6–8	1*a*.
1 Sam. 9:9	2	Job 4:12; 10:10 f.	1*a*.
2 Sam. 15:37	1*a*.		

21. The Imperfect, used of Present Events.

1. לֵאמֹר מַה־תְּבַקֵּשׁ¹ *saying: What art thou seeking?*

   הִנֵּה תִרְאוּ אִישׁ מִשְׁתַּגֵּעַ² *so, ye see (the) man is mad.*

   יִתְיַצְּבוּ מַלְכֵי־אֶרֶץ³ *kings of the earth set themselves.*

2. "עַל־כֵּן יֵאָמַר וגו'⁴ *therefore it is said, etc.*

   וְכָל־בְּכוֹר בָּנַי אֶפְדֶּה⁵ *and all the first-born of my sons I redeem.*

   נַפְשִׁי יְשׁוֹבֵב יַנְחֵנִי⁶ *my soul he restoreth, he guideth,* etc.

   אֶת־יִרְאֵי יְהוָה יְכַבֵּד⁷ *those who fear Yahweh, he honoreth.*

---

* Driver's *Use of the Tenses in Hebrew*, 1881, pp. 41, 42.

1 Gen. 37:15.　　　3 Ps. 2:2.　　　5 Ex. 13:15.　　　7 Ps. 15:4.
2 1 Sam. 21:15.　　4 Gen. 10:9.　　6 Ps. 23:3.

3. כַּאֲשֶׁר תַּעֲשֶׂינָה הַדְּבֹרִים[1] *just as bees do.*

הָאָדָם יִרְאֶה לַעֵינַיִם וי״ יִרְאֶה לַלֵּבָב[2] *man looketh on the appearance, but Y. looketh on the heart.*

הַדֶּלֶת תִּסּוֹב עַל־צִירָהּ[3] *the door turneth on its hinges.*

אִישׁ־דָּמִים···יְתָעֵב י״[4] *the bloody man Y. abhorreth.*

4. בִּנְיָמִין זְאֵב יִטְרָף[5] *Benjamin is a ravening wolf.*   [*man?*

מִי־אַתְּ וַתִּירְאִי מֵאֱנוֹשׁ יָמוּת[6] *who art thou that thou fearest mortal*

The Imperfect, as designating that which is *unfinished* and so *developing* and *moving*, is used of actions or states which belong to the sphere of the *present*. Here we may, for convenience, distinguish,

1. The *incipient* (strictly so called) *imperfect*, which gives more *force* and *vividness* to the action, or represents it as taking place (or beginning to take place), while the words are being spoken.[a]

2. The *definite frequentative*, used of *particular* facts which are accustomed to occur more or less frequently within certain limits of time.

3. The *indefinite frequentative*, used in the statement of facts which may and do occur at any time, and of truths universally admitted.[b]

4. The *adjectival imperfect*, coming strictly under the *indefinite frequentative*, which, with an omitted relative, serves to denote a general attribute of the object with which it is connected.

REMARKS.

(*a*) It is not unusual for such an Imperfect to be found in a series of Perfects, referring strictly to the present, thus rendering the style more vivid, as well as more varied; e. g., Isa. 2:8; 9:10; 10:4, 28. Cf. § 20. R. c.

(*b*) The use of the Imperfect to express "general truths" is to be distinguished from the similar usage of the Perfect of experience (§ 18. 3). The Imperfect emphasizes the idea that the fact or truth is one liable at any time to occur; the Perfect, that it is a permanent and established one, as shown by past experience. The occasional occurrence of both usages in the same verse is sometimes merely for variety, though frequently very significant. Cf. Ps. 2:1 f.; 5:6; 6:7; 7:13 f.; 22:16; 23:5; 26:4, 5; 38:12; Prov. 4:17; 12:12; 28:1; Job 3:17; 11:20.

REFERENCES FOR STUDY.

Gen. 22:14	2	Josh. 7:12	2
Gen. 37:15	1	Judg. 14:10	2
Ex. 18:15	2	1 Sam. 9:6	2
Num. 24:17	1	1 Sam. 24:13	3
Deut. 28:49	3	2 Sam. 5:8b	2
Deut. 32:11	4	Isa. 1:23	2

---

[1] Deut. 1:44.   [3] Prov. 26:14.   [5] Gen. 49:27.   [6] Isa. 51:12.
[2] 1 Sam. 16:7.   [4] Ps. 5:7.

22. THE IMPERFECT, USED OF FUTURE EVENTS.

1. כִּי־יִרְאוּ אֹתָךְ הַמִּצְרִים¹ *when the Egyptians shall see thee.*

בַּמָּה אֵדַע כִּי אִירָשֶׁנָּה² *whereby shall I know that I shall, etc.*

וְהוּא יִהְיֶה פֶּרֶא אָדָם³ *and he will be a wild-ass of men.*

וְאִם־הָרֵעַ תָּרֵעוּ...תִּסָּפוּ⁴ *but if ye do evil, ye will be swept away.*

2. a. תִּשְׁמַע חֲלוֹם לִפְתֹּר⁵ *thou canst understand a dream to interpret it.*

יָדַעְתִּי כִּי־דַבֵּר יְדַבֵּר הוּא⁶ *I know that he can speak well.*

בָּקָר אֲשֶׁר לֹא־יִסָּפְרוּ⁷ *oxen which could not be counted.*

b. מִכֹּל עֵץ־הַגָּן...תֹּאכֵל⁸ *from every tree... thou mayest eat.*

יָשׁוּב הָרֹצֵחַ⁹ *the murderer may return.* [*thou shalt eat.*

3. a. עַל־גְּחֹנְךָ תֵלֵךְ וְעָפָר תֹּאכֵל¹⁰ *upon thy belly thou shalt go and dust*

לֹא תִּרְצָח....לֹא תִּגְנֹב¹¹ *thou shalt do no murder...thou shalt not*

b. וְאַתָּה תִּמְשָׁל־בּוֹ¹² *but thou shouldst rule over him.* [*steal.*

וְאָנֹכִי...אֵשֵׁב עִם־הַמֶּלֶךְ¹³ *and I ought to sit with the king.*

הַכְמוֹת נָבָל יָמוּת אַבְנֵר¹⁴ *was Abner to die as a fool dieth.*

c. יְדַבֶּר־נָא עַבְדֶּךָ¹⁵ *let now thy servant speak.*

d. אַל־יֶחֱטָא הַמֶּלֶךְ בְּעַבְדּוֹ¹⁶ *let not the king sin against his servant.*

לָמָּה תַכֶּה רֵעֶךָ¹⁷ *why shouldst thou smite thy neighbor?*

מִי אָנֹכִי כִּי אֵלֵךְ¹⁸ *who am I that I should go?*

---

1 Gen. 12:12.	6 Ex. 4:14.	11 Ex. 20:14.	15 Gen. 44:18.
2 Gen. 15:8.	7 1 Kgs. 8:5.	12 Gen. 4:7.	16 1 Sam. 19:4.
3 Gen. 16:12.	8 Gen. 2:16.	13 1 Sam. 20:5.	17 Ex. 2:13.
4 1 Sam. 12:25.	9 Num. 35:28.	14 2 Sam. 3:33.	18 Ex. 3:11.
5 Gen. 41:15.	10 Gen 3:14.		

4. *a.* קְחוּ לָכֶם תֶּבֶן מֵאֲשֶׁר תִּמְצָאוּ¹ *take for you straw whence ye may find it.*   [brother.

רוֹצֵחַ אֲשֶׁר יִרְצַח אֶת־רֵעֵהוּ² *the murderer who might slay his*

b. אִם־תִּתֶּן־לִי אֶת־חֲצִי בֵיתְךָ לֹא אָבֹא עִמָּךְ³ *if thou wouldst give me half thy house, I would not go in with thee.*

אִם־יוּכַל אִישׁ לִמְנוֹת אֶת־עֲפַר הָאָרֶץ גַּם זַרְעֲךָ יִמָּנֶה⁴ *if a man could number the dust of the earth, thy seed also could be numbered.*

c. אֲשֶׁר לֹא יִשְׁמְעוּ⁵ *that they may not understand.*

לְמַעַן אֲשֶׁר לֹא־יִקְרַב⁶ *that there may not come near.*

פֶּן־יִשְׁלַח יָדוֹ⁷ *lest he put forth his hand.*

The Imperfect, as designating that which is unfinished, finds its fullest and largest use in describing events which are yet within the sphere of the future.   Here we may distinguish:

1. The *future imperfect*, corresponding to our *future*. This is merely an extension of the *incipient* Imperfect (§§ **21. 1; 22. 1**), since future actions are conceived of as events which are to *begin* at some future time.[a]

2. The *potential imperfect*, which denotes

   a. Possibility and *capability*, usually best expressed by the auxiliaries *can*, *may*, or if the action is viewed from the stand-point of the past, by *could*, *might*.

   b. Permission and *concession*, to be rendered in the same way.[b]

3. The *imperative imperfect*, used in presenting ideas which are also expressed by the Imperative, or which are practically equivalent to those expressed by the Imperative :—

   a. Command, *prohibition;* the latter may be expressed *only* by the Imperfect, the Imperative never being used with a negative (§ **24. 1.** *a.*).

   b. Obligation, *necessity;* the exact rendering in these cases must be determined by the demands of the context, e. g., *I must sit, I ought to sit, I am to sit, I should sit.*

   c. Entreaty, *deprecation;* these may be distinguished from *command*, and *prohibition*, by noting the position of the speaker and his relation to the person or persons addressed.   With this belongs the use of the Imperfect in

---

1 Ex. 5:11.   3 1 Kgs. 13:8.   5 Gen. 11:7.   7 Gen. 3:22.
2 Deut. 4:42.   4 Gen. 13:16.   6 Num. 17:5.

    d. Questions implying *deprecation* or *entreaty;*[c] [d] or perhaps only greater courtesy than would have been expressed by the Perfect.[e]

4. The *subjunctive imperfect;* under which may be classified loosely three or four general usages :

    a. In expressions of *indefiniteness* and *uncertainty* (compare § 23. 2, above);

    b. In certain forms of conditional sentences (§ 48. 4, 7. *a*) ;

    c. In *final* sentences after conjunctions, e. g., בַּעֲבוּר ,לְמַעַן (§ 47. 4. *b*).[f]

REMARKS.

(*a*) It may be sufficient to say that the Imperfect is used to denote future events because they are in the strictest sense incomplete.

(*b*) The cases belonging under the *potential* Imperfect are to be regarded as Indicatives, since they express independent ideas (cf. § 23. 4. *a*).

(*c*) Compare Josh. 9:8 and Gen. 16:8.

(*d*) After מדוע ,למה, אִיךְ.

(*e*) Compare the use of the Perfect in Gen. 40:15; Isa. 43:22.

(*f*) On the use of the Imperfect with ן to express purpose, see § 24. 1. *e*, and 2. *d*.

REFERENCES FOR STUDY.

23. THE JUSSIVE, IMPERATIVE AND COHORTATIVE.

1. *a.* וַיֹּאמֶר אֱ׳ יְהִי־אוֹר¹ *and God said: Let there be light.*

כַּבֵּד אֶת־אָבִיךָ וְאֶת־אִמֶּךָ² *honor thy father and thy mother.*

תִּשְׁמֵט יָדֶךָ³ *let thy hand release it.*

וְדָם נָקִי אַל־תִּשְׁפְּכוּ⁴ *and shed not innocent blood.*

b. יָגֵל יַעֲקֹב⁵ *Jacob will (be permitted to) rejoice.*

יֵרֶא פַרְעֹה אִישׁ⁶ *let Pharaoh look out a man.*

וַיֹּאמֶר לוֹ רוּץ⁷ *and he said to him: Run.*

יְבַקְשׁוּ לַאדֹנִי הַמֶּלֶךְ נַעֲרָה⁸ *let them seek for my lord...a maiden.*

c. שִׁפְטוּ־נָא בֵּינִי וּבֵין כַּרְמִי⁹ *judge now between me and my vineyard.*

אַל־נָא יִחַר לַאדֹנִי¹⁰ *let not the Lord be angry.*

יֵשֶׁב־נָא עַבְדְּךָ¹¹ *let thy servant remain, I pray.*

d. יְבָרֶכְךָ י׳ מִצִּיּוֹן וּרְאֵה בְּטוּב יְרוּשָׁלָ͏ִם¹² *Yahweh bless thee out of Zion and see thou the good of Jerusalem.*

יַמְטֵר עַל־רְשָׁעִים פַּחִים¹³ *upon the wicked, he shall rain snares.*

זֹאת עֲשׂוּ וִחְיוּ¹⁴ *If ye do this, then ye shall live.*

e. תָּשֶׁת־חֹשֶׁךְ וִיהִי לָיְלָה¹⁵ *appoint darkness—then shall be night.*

קַוֵּה לַיהוָה וְיֹשַׁע לָךְ¹⁶ *wait on Yahweh that he may save thee.*

2. *a.* וַאֲגַדְּלָה שְׁמֶךָ¹⁷ *and I will make great thy name.*

נֵלְכָה עַד־כֹּה¹⁸ *we will go thither.*

b. אָגִילָה וְאֶשְׂמְחָה¹⁹ *let me be glad and rejoice.*

נְנַתְּקָה....וְנַשְׁלִיכָה²⁰ *let us break asunder....and cast.*

c. אֶעֱלֶה־נָּא וְאֶקְבְּרָה²¹ *let me go up, I pray, and bury.*

נֵלְכָה־נָּא דֶּרֶךְ שְׁלֹשֶׁת יָמִים²² *we would fain go three days' journey.*

d. וְהָבִיאָה לִּי וְאֹכֵלָה²³ *and bring it to me and I will (that I may) eat.*

שְׁאַל מִמֶּנִּי וְאֶתְּנָה²⁴ *ask of me that I may give.*

1 Gen. 1:3.
2 Ex. 20:12.
3 Dt. 15:3.
4 Jer. 7:6.
5 Ps. 14:7.
6 Gen. 41:33.
7 2 Sam. 18:23.
8 1 Kgs. 1:2.
9 Isa. 5:3.
10 Gen. 18:30.
11 Gen. 44:33.
12 Ps. 128:5.
13 Ps. 11:6.
14 Gen. 42:18.
15 Ps. 104:20.
16 Prov. 20:22.
17 Gen. 12:2.
18 Gen. 22:5.
19 Ps. 31:8.
20 Ps. 2:3.
21 Gen. 50:5.
22 Ex. 3:18.
23 Gen. 27:4.
24 Ps. 2:8.

אִם־אֲדַבְּרָה לֹא־יֵחָשֵׂךְ כְּאֵבִי וְאַחְדְּלָה מַה־מִנִּי יַהֲלֹךְ [1] *though I*
speak, my grief is not assuaged, and though I forbear, what depart-
eth from me.

The simple Imperfect, in the majority of instances, is an *indicative*.
That it may also be used with the force of an *imperative* or *subjunctive*,
has been shown in § 22. 3. There are, however, certain special forms[a b c d]
of the Imperfect, the Jussive and Cohortative, which *always* convey
some such force. These forms, it may be said, express "a motion of the
will," and hence may be joined together under the head of "voluntative."
With the "voluntative" Imperfect, there may be classified for syntactical
purposes the *Imperative*. We may distinguish as follows:—

1. The *Jussive*, used of the *second* and *third* persons,[e] and the *Imperative*, used only of the second, denote, in general, a strong desire that
something should happen.[f] They may express

    a. A positive *injunction* or *command*; the Jussive, but not the Im-
        perative, may also express *prohibition*.[g h i j k]

    b. *Permission* to do a thing, *advice*, or *suggestion*.

    c. *Entreaty*, or simple *petition*.

    d. *Benediction*, *imprecation*, *threatening*.

    e. *Conditional* or *final ideas*.

2. The *Cohortative*, used only of the *first* person[l] (sg. or pl.), emphasizes the *direction* of the will, the intention or purpose.[m n] It is employed,
therefore,

    a. To mark a strong determination to do a given thing (expressed
        by *I will*).

    b. To indicate a self-excitement toward a certain line of conduct
        (expressed by *let me*).

    c. To express a *wish* or *request*.

    d. In subordinate *final* sentences (cf. 1. *e.* above), and in conditional
        sentences (§ 48. R (*i*)).

REMARKS.

(*a*) See *Elements of Hebrew*, § 72. 1, 2.

(*b*) While, therefore, the ordinary form of the Imperfect *may* have the force of an
Imperative or Subjunctive, the special forms *must* have that force. In many grammatical forms there is no possible way of distinguishing the ordinary and the special
form, e. g., יִקְטֹל may mean *he will kill, he shall kill, let him kill.*

(*c*) The shortened form of the *Jussive*, corresponding to the Arabic *Jussive*, is ac-
counted for by the fact that the form is one of command and hence pronounced
rapidly.

---

[1] Job 16:6.

(d) The special form of the Cohortative (marked by the syllable הָ‌) corresponds to the Arabic *Energetic*, the nature of which is indicated by its name.

(e) A few cases of the Jussive of the first person are found, e. g., Dt. 18:16; 1 Sam. 14:36.

(f) The Jussive and likewise the Imperative are often found in poetry where the ordinary form would have been expected. This anomalous usage is to be explained not upon the supposition that the mood has here lost its original force, but that the poet saw fit, for the sake of vividness and variety, to represent a given act under the form of a command, rather than in the usual manner. Cases of this usage in the second person are found in Ps. 41:3; 65:14; 98:7; 104:19; 114:3–7; Isa. 2:9; 13:2; 23:1, 4; 35:1 f.; 40:3, 9; 54:14; 57:14; 62:10. Cases of the same usage which may be said to be expressive of emotion in the third person, are found in Ps. 11:6; 12:4; 34:6; 50:3; 66:7; 72:8, 13, 16, 17; 85:14; 121:3; Jer. 46:6; 51:3; Zech. 9:5; 10:7.

(g) In prohibition, (1) in the second person, the ordinary Imperfect takes לֹא and means *thou shalt not*, the Jussive takes אַל and means *do not*; (2) in the third person, the ordinary Imperfect takes לֹא and means *he shall not*, the Jussive takes אַל and means *let him not*; rarely the Jussive takes אַל, e. g., לֹא תֹסֶף Gen. 4:12.

(h) The Cohortative Imperative (*Elements of Hebrew*, § 72. 3) emphasizes the earnestness of the request, marking it as especially impressive, e. g., Dt. 26:15; Ps. 6:5.

(i) When several verbal forms expressing *command* would follow in succession, three usages exist: (1) The use of successive Imperatives, e. g., Gen. 1:22; 22:2; Isa. 1:16; (2) the use of the Imperative for the first, and of ordinary Imperfects for the remaining forms, e. g., Dt. 33:7; (3) the use of the Imperative for the first and of the Perfect with Wâw Consecutive for the remaining forms, e. g., Gen. 6:14.

(j) When several successive commands are made, of which one or more are in the first or third persons, the latter must of necessity be expressed by the Imperfect, e. g., Gen. 24:56; Dt. 9:14; Jer. 51:9.

(k) The interchange of the Imperative and the Imperfect (2d pers.), in the expression of command, occurs without perceptible force; the only gain being that of variety.

(l) A few cases of the Cohortative of a third person occur: Isa. 5:19 (twice); Ezek. 23:20; Prov. 1:20; 8·3. In the last three cases it does not seem to have any significance.

(m) Notice is to be taken here of the fact that a form *like* that of the Cohortative occurs frequently with the Wâw Consecutive; it is not to be regarded, however, as a Cohortative; Gen. 32:6; 1 Sam. 2:28 and in all about ninety times.

(n) Cases in which the *volition* indicated by הָ‌ is so controlled by outward circumstances as almost to become an involuntary action are found in Ps. 42:5, 10; 55:3, 18; 77:4, 7; Job 10:1; Isa. 38:10; 59:10; Jer. 3:25. Perhaps in some cases the הָ‌ cohortative, like the הָ‌ directive, has entirely lost its original force, Ps. 88:16; Jer. 4:19, 21.

REFERENCES FOR STUDY.

24. THE IMPERFECT, WITH WAW CONSECUTIVE.

1. *a.*   ¹וַתֵּלֶךְ הָאִשָּׁה לְדַרְכּוֹ וַתֹּאכַל *and the wom. went her way and ate.*

²רָאִיתִי אֱ' פָּנִים אֶל־פָּנִים וַתִּנָּצֵל נַפְשִׁי *I have seen God face to face, and my life has been spared.*

³וְיִצְחָק בָּא....וַיֵּצֵא *and I. had come....and he had gone out.*

b. ⁴כֹּה אָמַר יְ'....וַאֹמַר....וַתְּמָאֵן *thus saith Y.: (Israel is my son), and I say, (Let my son go), and thou refusest (to let him go).*

⁵מָה־אָדָם וַתֵּדָעֵהוּ *what is man, and (yet) thou knowest him.*

⁶נָשַׁף בָּהֶם וַיִּבָשׁוּ *He bloweth upon them, and they wither.*

⁷מוֹרִיד שְׁאוֹל וַיָּעַל *He bringeth down to Sheol, and bringeth up.*

⁸בּוֹכֶה וַיִּתְאַבֵּל *he is weeping and mourning.*

⁹תְּגָרֶשׁ גּוֹיִם וַתִּטָּעֶהָ *Thou expellest the nations, and plantest it.*

c. ¹⁰כִּי־יֶלֶד יֻלַּד־לָנוּ וַתְּהִי הַמִּשְׂרָה עַל־שִׁכְמוֹ וַיִּקְרָא שְׁמוֹ וגו'' *for to us a child shall be born; and the dominion shall be upon his shoulder, and one shall call his name, etc.*

¹¹נֹצְרִים בָּאִים מֵאֶרֶץ הַמֶּרְחָק וַיִּתְּנוּ....קוֹלָם *watchmen come from a distance, and shall lift up their voice.*

REMARK.—In reference to the substitution of the Imperfect with Wāw Consecutive for the Perfect, three general statements may be made:

(1) In uninterrupted narrative in which the first verb is a Perfect, or some equivalent of the Perfect, the verbs following are *regularly* in the Imperfect[a] with Wāw Consecutive,[b] unless they are separated from the conjunction by intervening words.[c]

1 1 Sam. 1:18.   4 Ex. 4:22,23.   7 1 Sam. 2:6.   10 Isa. 9:5.
2 Gen. 32:31.   5 Ps. 144:3.   8 2 Sam. 19:2.   11 Jer. 4:16.
3 Gen. 24:62,63.   6 Isa. 40:24.   9 Ps. 80:9.

(2) The expression for *and-he-called* being, therefore, וַיִּקְרָא , the form וְקָרָא cannot be used in this sense ; see, however, § 26. 2.

(3) From the instances cited above, it will be seen that the introductory verbal form may, under certain circumstances, be an Imperfect, or a Participle ; in some cases even a noun is employed, and in others, *no governing word of any kind precedes.*

We may now consider the more important details :

1. The Imperfect with Wāw Consecutive is found, like the Perfect, for which it is a substitute,

    a. To describe events or conditions belonging to the sphere of the past (§ 17. 1–4), whether as a historical Perfect, a present Perfect, an indefinite Perfect, or a Pluperfect ;*d* in these cases it is the continuation of a Perfect.

    b. To describe events or conditions belonging to the sphere of the present (§ 18. 1–3), whether as a Perfect of the immediate past, a stative Perfect, or a Perfect of experience ; in these cases it is the continuation of a Perfect, or a Participle, or a nominal expression, or even an Imperfect which refers to the present.

    c. To describe events belonging to the sphere of the future ; it assumes here the usage of the prophetic Perfect (§ 19. 2). Two cases are, however, to be distinguished :

        (1) that in which the Imperfect with Wāw Consecutive, having this usage, is preceded by a prophetic Perfect.*e*

        (2) that in which it is not so preceded ; this occurs when the writer desires to introduce a prophetic Perfect for variety, but, at the same time, wishes to connect it with what precedes.*f*

REMARKS.

(*a*) On the form of the Imperfect which is thus used with the Wāw Consecutive, see *Elements of Hebrew*, § 73.

(*b*) Various theories have been presented in explanation of the form of the conjunction, ·וַ. Ewald's view, that the vowel and Dāghēš-forte were the relics of some particle like אֲ , seems most satisfactory.

(*c*) For the explanation of the use of the tense in this connection, Professor Driver says: "The Imperfect (from the point of view of the spectator) expresses what in German is called *Eintritt,* and represents action, as *eintretend*—two terms which may be rendered in English by *ingress* and *ingressive.* A *succession* of events need not invariably be regarded as a mere series of completed and independent wholes: each term may be conceived as having relations with the one preceding it ; it may be viewed as *stepping in* after it, as presenting itself to view through an entrance prepared by its forerunner. The date at which the ingress, or entry, is imagined to take place is determined by the ·וַ , which connects the new event with a point previously assigned in the narrative: the goal at which it sets out, the starting-point from which it takes its origin, and to which therefore it is *relative*, is fixed at the termination of the action denoted by the preceding verb."—*Hebrew Tenses*, p. 85.

(*d*) Two comparisons may be considered here with profit: (1) In Assyrian there are two forms of the Imperfect, differing only slightly from each other, and both etymologically connected with the Hebrew Imperfect; of these the first represents an action as continuing, whether in past, present, or future; the second is the usual narrative tense, equivalent to the Greek Aorist, e. g., iddin (= in-din), the etymological equivalent of יִתֵּן; always means *he gave*, while יִתֵּן has this meaning only when preceded by a Wāw Consecutive. (2) In Arabic, there are not a few cases in which the Imperfect is used in the sense of an Aorist, e. g., ya-qum, the etymological equivalent of יָקוּם, when preceded by the negative adverb lam means *he did not stand*; יָקֻם is so translated only when the Wāw Consecutive precedes.

(*e*) Some assert that an Imperfect with Wāw Consec. may be used as a Pluperfect without any preceding Perfect, e. g., וָאֶקְרָב, Isa. 8:3; וַיָּבֹא, 37:5; but this may well be doubted.

(*f*) Having introduced his thought by a *prophetic* Perfect, the writer may continue it in one of four ways: (1) by an Imperfect with Wāw Consecutive; (2) by changing abruptly to the Imperfect used in a future sense; (3) by a Perfect, the connective "and" being omitted; (4) by a Perfect, the connective "and" being separated by certain words from the verb.

(*g*) This is of course rare and limited to prophetic usage; according to Professor Driver (p. 114) the only cases are Isa. 2:9; 5:15f.; 9:10–15; 59:15b–17; Ezek. 28:16; 31:12; Jer. 4:16; 15:6b–7; 51:29; Ps. 64:8–10; 94:23; but some of these are doubtful.

2. *a.* וַיָּקָם קַיִן....וַיַּהַרְגֵהוּ[1] *and Cain rose up and slew him.*

וַיָּשֻׁבוּ וַיָּבֹאוּ אֶל־בֵּיתָם[2] *and they returned and came unto their house.*

b. אֶת־קוֹלְךָ שָׁמַעְתִּי וָאִירָא....וָאֵחָבֵא[3] *I heard thy voice in the garden, and so was afraid and hid myself.*

וָאֶקַּח אֹתָהּ לִי לְאִשָּׁה[4] *and so I took her to be my wife.*

c. הֲשָׁמַע עָם קוֹל א'....וַיֶּחִי[5] *did ever a people hear the voice of God, and yet live?*

אָהַבְתִּי אֶתְכֶם....וַאֲמַרְתֶּם[6] *I loved you..and yet ye say. [is dead.*

d. אִשָּׁה־אַלְמָנָה אָנִי וַיָּמָת אִישִׁי[7] *I am a widow, for my husband*

וַתִּקְרָא שְׁמוֹ מֹשֶׁה וַתֹּאמֶר[8] *and she called his name Moses, and said,* etc.

e. וַיְבָרֲכֵהוּ : וַיֹּאמֶר[9] *and he blessed him; and he said,* etc.

1 Gen. 4:8.   3 Gen. 3:10.   5 Dt. 4:33.   7 2 Sam. 14:5.
2 1 Sam. 1:19.   4 Gen. 12:19.   6 Mal. 1:2.   8 Ex. 2:10.
                     9 Gen 27:23,24.

וַיּוֹסִפוּ.....׃ וַיֹּאמֶר אֲלֵיהֶם[1] *and they hated him all the more; and he said, etc.*

f. קְדֹשׁ יִשְׂרָאֵל וַיִּבְחָרֶךָ[2] *the Holy One of Israel, who hath chosen thee.*

הַתְּלָאָה.....׃ וַיֵּרְדוּ אֲבֹתֵינוּ[3] *the travail.....how our fathers descended.*

g. וְהֶהָמוֹן אֲשֶׁר בְּמַחֲנֵה פְלִשְׁתִּים וַיֵּלֶךְ הָלוֹךְ[4] *and the sound which was in the camp of the P. (and it) went on continually.*

יַעַן מָאַסְתָּ אֶת־דְּבַר־י׳ וַיִּמְאָסְךָ[5] *because thou hast despised the word of Y., therefore he hath despised thee.*

אִם־לֹא יִשְׂבְּעוּ וַיָּלִינוּ[6] *if they are not satisfied, then they stay all night.*

2. The use of the Imperfect with Wāw Consecutive marks some kind of connection, or relation with that portion of the narrative which precedes. This relation may be that of

a. *Chronological sequence;* in this case the force is expressed by the simple conjunction *and.*

b. *Consequence;* in this case the force may be expressed by *and so.*

c. *Contrast;* in this case the force may be expressed by *and yet.*

d. *Accessory circumstance,* when something passed over is afterwards brought in; here the force of the conjunction may best be rendered by *for,* or *since.*

e. *Amplification,* when, after a general statement has first been made, the particulars of the case are added.

f. *Explanation* of a preceding expression or word; here the conjunction must be rendered by a relative pronoun, or by *that* or *how.*

g. *Apodosis,* the protasis being either a noun in the nominative absolute (§ 7.), or a complete conditional clause; here the conjunction must either be omitted, or rendered by some such word as *then* or *therefore.*[a,b,c]

REMARKS.

(a) In quite a number of cases the action expressed by the Imperfect with Wāw Consecutive is really parallel or synchronous with what goes before; e. g., Gen. 5:5; 1 Sam. 14: 25b,49; Isa. 39:1; 64:4.

1 Gen. 37:5,6.   3 Num. 20:14,15.   5 1 Sam. 14:19.
2 Isa. 49:7.   4 1 Sam. 15:23.   6 Ps. 59:16.

(b) In other cases the Imperfect with Wāw Consecutive introduces an amplification not of any particular preceding verb, but of the entire preceding narrative, considered as a whole; thus furnishing what is practically a parallel account; e. g., 1 Sam. 9:1; 1 Kgs. 7:13.

(c) It is only fair to ask how far some of these usages are to be explained as due to the combining, by a reviser or editor, of two or more distinct narratives into one.

3. a. וַיִּקְרָא א׳ לָאוֹר יוֹם וְלַחֹשֶׁךְ קָרָא לָיְלָה¹ and God called the light day, and the darkness he called night.

וַיִּבְרָא א׳....בְּצֶלֶם א׳ בָּרָא אֹתוֹ² and God created...., in the image of God created he him.

b. וַיַּרְעֵם בַּשָּׁמַיִם י׳ וְעֶלְיוֹן יִתֵּן קוֹלוֹ³ and Y. thundered in the heavens, and the Most High uttered his voice.

כִּי מָלְאוּ מִקֶּדֶם....וּבְיַלְדֵי נָכְרִים יַשְׂפִּיקוּ⁴ for they are filled from the east, and they strike hands with the children of strangers.

4. וַיְהִי בָּעֵת הַהוּא וַיֹּאמֶר א׳⁵ and it came to pass at that time that Abimelech said.

וַיְהִי מִקֵּץ יָמִים וַיָּבֵא ק⁶ and it came to pass at the end of days that Cain brought, etc.

וַיְהִי בִּימֵי אַמְרָפֶל....; עָשׂוּ⁷ and it came to pass in the days of Amraphel....they made war.

וַיְהִי הַשֶּׁמֶשׁ בָּאָה....וְהִנֵּה⁸ and it came to pass the sun had gone down....and behold.

5. כַּהֲרִימִי קוֹלִי וָאֶקְרָא⁹ as I lifted up my voice and cried.   [me.

הַצָּד־צַיִד וַיָּבֵא לִי¹⁰ that hath taken venison and brought it to

3. When for any reason one or more words intervene between the Imperfect and its conjunction,

a. In prose, the verb invariably goes back to the Perfect; for the whole force of the construction seems to rest upon the union of the verbal form and the conjunction; but

1 Gen. 1:5.   4 Isa. 2:6.   7 Gen. 14:1.   9 Gen. 39.18.
2 Gen. 1:27.   5 Gen. 21:22.   8 Gen. 15:17.   10 Gen. 27:33.
3 Ps. 18:4.   6 Gen. 4:3.

b. In poetry, the verb is frequently found still remaining in the Imperfect, thus adding vividness and force to the narrative, in accordance with the principle explained in § **20. 1.** *a.*

4. Notice is to be taken of the frequent occurrence of the preparatory formula וַיְהִי *and it happened, and it was*, to introduce adverbial and especially temporal clauses. This usage, while not universal, prevails largely in the earlier books. The following verb may be either Imperfect with Wāw Consecutive, a Perfect, or, when the context demands, an Imperfect. Frequently, also, the sentence is resumed by וְהִנֵּה, or by וְ with the subject of the verb.

5. The Imperfect with Wāw Consecutive is used to continue a sentence introduced by an Infinitive or Participle. This occurs, in contrast with the parallel usage of the Perfect, with Wāw Consecutive (§25. 5), when that which is described by the Infinitive or Participle is something real or definite, rather than contingent or indefinite.

REFERENCES FOR STUDY.

25. THE PERFECT, WITH WAW CONSECUTIVE.

1. *a.* ....וְהִשְׁקָה....יַעֲלֶה אֵד¹ *and a mist used to go up and water the....*

יָבֹאוּ בְּנֵי הָא'....וְיָלְדוּ לָהֶם² *the sons of God used to go in.... and they bore to them.* [*it....*

תִּזְרַע אֶת־זַרְעֲךָ וְהִשְׁקִיתָ³ *thou usedst to sow thy seed and water*

b. עַל־כֵּן יַעֲזָב־אִישׁ....וְדָבַק⁴ *therefore a man forsakes....and cleaves....*

תִּרְאֵנִי וּבָחַנְתָּ לִבִּי⁵ *thou seest me and triest my heart.*

תֶּאֱבַל הָא' וְאֻמְלַל כָּל־יוֹשֵׁב⁶ *the earth mourns, and every inhabitant fainteth.*

c. (1) וְא'....יִהְיֶה לְגוֹי גָּדוֹל וְנִבְרְכוּ בוֹ⁷ *and Abraham will become a great nation, and (all the nations of the earth) will be blessed in him.*

יִשָּׂא אֶת־רֹאשֶׁךָ וַהֲשִׁיבְךָ וְנָתַתָּ כוֹס־פַּרְעֹה בְּיָדוֹ⁸ *he will lift up thy head and restore thee, and thou wilt place the cup of Pharaoh in his hand.*

נָכוֹן יִהְיֶה הַר...בְּרֹאשׁ הֶהָרִים וְנִשָּׂא וְנָהֲרוּ...כָּל־הַגּוֹיִם⁹ *the mountain.....will be established at the top of the mountains, and will be lifted up ..., and all nations will flow.*

בֵּרַכְתִּי אֹתוֹ וְהִפְרֵיתִי...וְהִרְבֵּיתִי¹⁰ *I will bless him and make him fruitful and multiply him.*

הִנְנִי מֵבִיא אֶת־הַמַּבּוּל...וַהֲקִמֹתִי¹¹ *behold, I am going to bring the flood...., but I will establish, etc.*

(2) יְהִי מְאֹרֹת...וְהָיוּ¹² *let there be luminaries...and let them be.*

יֵלְכוּ וְקֹשְׁשׁוּ לָהֶם תֶּבֶן¹³ *let them go and gather themselves straw.*

1 Gen. 2:6. 5 Jer. 12:3. 8 Gen. 40:13. 11 Gen. 6:17,18.
2 Gen. 6:4. 6 Hos. 4:3. 9 Isa. 2:2. 12 Gen. 1:14.
3 Deut. 11:10. 7 Gen. 18:18. 10 Gen. 17:20. 13 Ex. 5:7.
4 Gen. 2:24.

¹אַל־נָא תִקְבְּרֵנִי בְמִ׳ וְשָׁכַבְתִּי *do not bury me in Egypt, but let me lie.*

²אֲלַקֳטָה־נָא וְאָסַפְתִּי *let me glean, now, and gather.*

³נִקְרְבָה...וְלַנוּ בַגִּבְעָה *let us draw near and lodge in Gibeah.*

(3) ⁴דַּבֵּר אֶל־בְּנֵי י׳ וְאָמַרְתָּ *speak unto the sons of Israel and say.*

⁵לֵךְ וְאָסַפְתָּ....וְאָמַרְתָּ *go and gather....and say.*   [*swarm.*

⁶הוֹצֵא אִתָּךְ וְשָׁרְצוּ *bring them forth with thee, and let them*

(4) ⁷לְמַעַן יִיטַב־לִי...וְחָיְתָה נַפְשִׁי *that it may be well with me ....and my soul may live.*

⁸לְמַעַן יֵלְכוּ וְכָשְׁלוּ....וְנִשְׁבְּרוּ וְנוֹקְשׁוּ וְנִלְכָּדוּ *that they may go and stumble....and be broken and snared and taken.*

⁹פֶּן־יִשְׁלַח יָדוֹ וְלָקַח...וָחַי *lest he put forth his hand and take and live.*

REMARK.—In reference to the substitution of the Perfect with Wāw Consecutive for the Imperfect, Imperative, etc. (cf. the corresponding construction § 24.), three general statements may be made :

(1) In uninterrupted narration in which the first verb is an Imperfect, an Imperative, or some expression possessing the characteristics of these forms, the verbs following are regularly in the Perfect[a] with Wāw Consecutive, unless they are separated from the conjunction[b] by intervening words.[c, d]

(2) The expression for *and-he-will-call* being therefore וְקָרָא, the form וְיִקְרָא cannot be used in this sense ; see, however, § 26. 2.

(3) From the instances cited above and below, it will be seen that the introductory verbal formula may be an Imperfect, Imperative, Participle ; that in some cases even a noun may be employed, and, in others, *no governing word of any kind precedes.*

We may now consider the more important details :

1. The Perfect with Wāw Consecutive is found (with a preceding Imperfect or equivalent) like the Imperfect (or Imperative, or Participle), for which it is a substitute,

   a. To describe events or conditions belonging to the sphere of the past (§ 20. 2), especially as a *frequentative* Imperfect.

1 Gen. 47:29.   4 Lev. 1:2.   6 Gen. 8:17.   8 Isa. 28:13.
2 Ruth 2:7.   5 Ex. 3:16.   7 Gen. 12:13.   9 Gen. 3:22.
3 Jud. 19:13.

b. To describe events or conditions belonging to the sphere of the *present* (§ **21.** 1–3), whether as an *incipient, definite frequentative,* or *indefinite frequentative* Imperfect.

c. To describe events belonging to the sphere of the *future* (§ **22.** 1–4); whether (1) after an Imperfect, Participle, or *prophetic* Perfect, as a *future* Imperfect; (2) after a jussive or cohortative Imperfect; (3) after an Imperative; (4) after a subjunctive Imperfect expressing purpose.*e,f*

REMARKS.

(*a*) On the form of the Perfect when thus used, and especially on the change of accent which takes place, see *Elements of Hebrew*, § 73.

(*b*) On the form of the conjunction when thus used see *Elements of Hebrew*, § 73.

(*c*) In explanation of this use of the Perfect three points may be considered: (1) that the idiom corresponds to and was called forth by the opposite construction of the Imperfect with Wāw Consecutive;* (2) that "the usage rests originally upon a 'play of the imagination,' in virtue of which an action, when brought into relation with a preceding occurrence as its *consequence,* from the character of inevitability it then assumes, is contemplated as actually completed;"† (3) "that the consciousness of this relation is to be conceived as essentially dependent upon union with Wāw, of which union the change of tone (where not hindered from taking place by external or accidental causes) is the inseparable criterion and accompaniment," the Wāw appearing really in this connection to possess a demonstrative significance, and being equivalent to *then* or *so* (cf. Gen. 3:5).‡

(*d*) In Assyrian the Perfect has been greatly narrowed (or has not been developed) in its usage, and presents no analogy to the construction under consideration. In Arabic the Perfect after the conjunction 'a d h a *when, as often as,* is said to take the meaning of the Imperfect.

(*e*) It is to be noted that the exact modal force of the preceding dominant verb, characterizes also the following Perfect with Wāw Consecutive; in other words, the particular auxiliary used in translating the first verb, *will, should, let,* must also be used with the second.

(*f*) The following is a list of particles given by Driver which govern a Perfect with Wāw Consecutive following an Imperfect:—(1) אוּלַי *perhaps,* Gen. 27:12; (2) אוֹ *or if,* 1 Sam. 26:10; (3) אָז *then,* 1 Sam. 6:3; (4) אֵיךְ *how?* Gen. 39:9; (5) אַל *not,* Jer. 17:21; (6) אִם *if,* Gen. 28:20,21; (7) אֲשֶׁר *so that,* Deut. 2:25; *when,* Lev. 4:22; *who so,* Gen. 24:14; (8) הֲ *inter.,* Ex. 2:7; (9) הֲלֹא *nonne?* 2 Kgs. 5:12; (10) הֵן *if,* Jer. 3:1; (11) טֶרֶם or בְּטֶרֶם *before (that),* Jer. 13:16; (12) כַּאֲשֶׁר *when,* Deut. 22:26; (13) כִּי *that,* Gen. 37:26; *when,* Ex. 21:20; (14) כִּי אִם *surely,* 1 Kgs. 20:6; (15) לֹא or בַּל *not,* Ex. 28:43; (16) כִּמְעַט *almost,* Gen. 26:10; (17) לוּ *if,* Ezek. 14:15; (18) לָמָה *why,* 2 Kgs. 14:10; (19) לְמַעַן *in order that,* Gen. 12:13; (20) מִי *expressing wish,* 2 Sam. 15:4; (21) מִי יוֹדֵעַ *perhaps,* 2 Sam. 12:22 (Qᵉri); (22) מָתַי *when,* Ps. 41:6; (23) עֵקֶב *in return for,* Deut. 7:12; (24) עַד or עַד אֲשֶׁר *until,* Ex. 23:30; (24) פֶּן *lest,* Gen. 3:22; · שֶׁ *that,* Eccl. 2:24. Only a few examples (the list is given, *Driver,* p. 162) occur of an Imperfect repeated after one of these particles, e. g., Num. 22:6; Isa. 40:27; Hos. 10:12.

---

* So nearly all grammarians.   † Olshausen, § 229a (cf. Driver, p. 141).
‡ Driver, p. 141.

2. *a.* ¹וַיִּתֵּן אֹתָם רָאשִׁים עַל־הָעָם....וְשָׁפְטוּ אֶת־הָעָם....אֶת־ הַדָּבָר הַקָּשֶׁת יְבִיאוּן אֶל־מֹשֶׁה *and he made them heads over the people....and they used to judge the people....but the weighty matters they used to bring....* [....*and judge.*

²וְהָלַךְ....וְסָבַב....וְשָׁפַט *and he would go....and come around*

b. ³הִרְחִיב יְ׳ לָנוּ וּפָרִינוּ בָאָרֶץ *Y. hath given enlargement to us, and we shall be fruitful in the land.*

⁴לֹא יָלַדְתְּ וְהָרִית וְיָלַדְתְּ *thou hast not borne, but thou shalt conceive and bear* [*your heart.*

c. ⁵וּמַלְתֶּם אֶת־עָרְלַת לְבַבְכֶם *therefore circumcise the foreskin of* ⁶וְאָמַרְתָּ אֲלֵהֶם *say unto them.*

⁷וְאָהַבְתָּ אֵת יהוה *therefore love thou Yahweh.*

⁸וּבָחַרְתָּ בַּחַיִּים לְמַעַן תִּחְיֶה *so choose life, that thou mayest live.*

d. ⁹הַמְדַבֵּר אֵלֶיךָ....וְהֵבֵאתוֹ אֵלַי *he that speaketh to thee...bring him to me.*

¹⁰כָּל־אֹכֵל חָמֵץ וְנִכְרְתָה הנ׳ *everyone eating leavened bread, that soul shall die.*

¹¹בְּיוֹם אֲכָלְךָ מִמֶּנּוּ וְנִפְקְחוּ עֵינֵיכֶם *in the day of your eating from it your eyes will be opened.*

¹²עֶרֶב וִידַעְתֶּם *at evening, then ye shall know.*

¹³בְּמוֹתִי וּקְרַבְתֶּם אֹתִי *when I die, ye shall bury me.*

¹⁴כִּי יִשְׁאָלְךָ בִנְךָ....וְאָמַרְתָּ *when thy son shall ask thee....thou shalt say.*

¹⁵אִם זְכַרְתַּנִי....וְעָשִׂיתָ־נָּא חֶסֶד *if thou rememberest me...then do me a kindness.* [*bring the man?*

3. ¹⁶וְהִנֵּה נֵלֵךְ וּמַה־נָּבִיא לָאִישׁ *but behold, (if) we go, what shall we* ¹⁷הֵן נִזְבַּח....וְלֹא יִסְקְלֻנוּ *if we sacrifice...., will they not stone us?*

---

1 Ex. 18:26.   6 Zech. 1:3.   10 Ex. 12:15.   14 Deut. 6:20,21.
2 1 Sam. 7:16.   7 Deut. 11:1.   11 Gen. 3:5.   15 Gen. 40:14.
3 Gen. 26:22.   8 Deut. 30:19.   12 Ex. 16:6.   16 1 Sam. 9:7.
4 Judg. 13:3.   9 2 Sam. 14:10.   13 1 Kgs. 13:31.   17 Ex. 8:22.
5 Deut. 10:16.

2. The Perfect with Wāw Consecutive is frequently found *without a preceding Imperfect* (or equivalent) *to introduce it.* Here we may distinguish several usages:

    a. When the Perfect (with Wāw Consecutive) is equivalent to a *frequentative* Imperfect; in such cases the verbal form, but for its connection with what precedes, would have been in the Imperfect.[a,b]

    b. When it is equivalent to an ordinary *future* Imperfect.

    c. When it is equivalent to an Imperative expressing a command or entreaty.

    d. When it is used in the apodosis of a conditional sentence, the protasis being expressed either by a Participle, an Infinitive, a finite verb (Perf. or Impf.), or a noun.[c, d]

3. When for any reason one or more words intervene between the Perfect and its conjunction, the verb goes back to the Imperfect.[e]

REMARKS.

(a) It will be noted that, in such passages, an Imperfect is frequently found in connection with the Perfect (with Wāw Consecutive), e. g., in Ex. 18:26, יביאון and ישפוטו .

(b) Notice also the series of Perfects in Josh. 15:3-11; 16:2,3,6,7,8; 17:9; 18:12-21, etc.

(c) Here) has a *demonstrative force;* cf. the use of *fa* in Arabic.

(d) Notice the use of the Perfect with Wāw *demonstrative* after a Participle, Judg. 7:17; 1 Kgs. 2:2; 18:11,12; 20:36; 2 Kgs. 7:9, etc.

(e) There are very few cases of this, nearly all being cited by Driver, p. 181.

4. *a.* וְהָיָה בְּעַנְנִי עָנָן....וְנִרְאֲתָה[1] *and it shall be when I bring clouds ....then shall be seen....*

    וְהָיָה בְּאַחֲרִית הַיָּמִים[2] *and it shall be in the end of days.*

b. וְהָיָה כְּבֹא מֹשֶׁה הָאֹהֱלָה יֵרֵד[3] *and it used to be when Moses entered the tent there would come down.*

    וְהָיָה אִם זָרַע י׳ וְעָלָה מִ׳[4] *and it used to happen when Israel had sown that Midian would come up.*

5. מַכֵּה אִישׁ וָמֵת[5] *the smiter of a man and he dies.*

    הַיּוֹצֵא וְנָפַל עַל הַכַּשְׂדִּים[6] *he that goeth forth and falleth upon..*

    בְּלֶכְתְּךָ וְנִפְלִינוּ[7] *in thy going forth with us and we are separated.*

    בְּהִנָּגֵף עַמְּךָ וְשָׁבוּ[8] *when thy people are smitten and turn.*

---

1 Gen. 9:14.   3 Ex. 33:7.   5 Ex. 21:12.   7 Ex. 33:16.
2 Isa. 2:2.   4 Jud. 6:3.   6 Jer. 21:9.   8 1 Kgs. 8:33.

4. Notice is to be taken of the frequent occurrence of the preparatory formula וְהָיָה (cf. וַיְהִי §24.), to introduce adverbial and especially temporal clauses. There may be distinguished,

a. The cases in which וְהָיָה has the force of a *future*.

b. The cases in which it has a *frequentative force*.

5. The Perfect with Wāw Consecutive is used to continue a sentence introduced by an Infinitive or Participle. This occurs, in contrast with the parallel usage of the Imperfect with Wāw Consecutive (§24. 5), when that which is described by the Infinitive or Participle is something contingent or indefinite rather than real or definite.

REFERENCES FOR STUDY.

26. THE PERFECT AND IMPERFECT WITH WAW CONJUNCTIVE.

1. *a.* הִקְשָׁה י' א' אֶת-רוּחוֹ וְאִמֵּץ אֶת-לְבָבוֹ[1] *Y. thy God hardened his spirit and made strong his heart.*

בָּנִים גִּדַּלְתִּי וְרוֹמַמְתִּי[2] *children I have made great and exalted.*

הֵמָּה כָּשְׁלוּ וְנָפָלוּ[3] *they stumbled and fell.*

---

[1] Deut. 2:30.   [2] Isa. 1:2.   [3] Ps. 27:2.

b. וַיְיַסְּדוּ הַבֹּנִים אֶת־הֵיכַל יהוה[1] *and the builders established the temple of Y.*

וָאֹמַר אָנִי טוֹבָה חָכְמָה מִגְּבוּרָה[2] *and I said, Wisdom is better than strength.*

c. וְהֶאֱמִן בַּיהוה וגו׳[3] *and he believed in Yahweh, etc.*

וְהוֹכִחַ אַבְרָהָם אֶת־אֲבִימֶלֶךְ[4] *and Abraham rebuked Abimelech.*

וְהִגַּדְתִּי לוֹ כִּי שֹׁפֵט אֲנִי אֶת־בֵּיתוֹ[5] *and I have told him that I will judge his house.*

2. a. דַּבֵּר....וְיָשֻׁבוּ וְיַחֲנוּ[6] *command....that they return and encamp.*

מַה־נַּעֲשֶׂה וְיִשְׁתֹּק הַיָּם[7] *what shall we do that the sea may be calm ?*

b. יִקָּווּ הַמַּיִם....וְתֵרָאֶה הַיַּ[8] *let the waters be collected....and the dry land appear.*

וְכָל הָעָם יִשְׁמְעוּ וְיִרָאוּ[9] *and all the people shall hear and fear.*

יַעֲלוּ וְיַכּוּ אֶת־הָעָי[10] *they shall go up and smite Ai.*   [sion.

הֵן יֵבֹשׁוּ וְיִכָּלְמוּ[11] *behold, they shall be ashamed and put to confu-*

הַשֹּׁחַד יְעַוֵּר פִּקְחִים וִיסַלֵּף דב׳[12] *the bribe blindeth the seeing and perverteth the words, etc.*

וְיִעֲפוּ נְעָרִים וְיִגָעוּ[13] *even youths faint and are weary.*

c. לְמַעַן יִרְאוּ וְיֵדְעוּ וְיָשִׂימוּ וְיַשְׂכִּילוּ[14] *that they may see and know and consider and understand.*

פֶּן־יֶאֱנַף וְתֹאבְדוּ[15] *lest he be angry and ye perish.*

There are cases in which, contrary to the principles set forth in §§ 24, 25. there is found the Perfect with Wāw Conjunctive instead of the Imperfect with Wāw Consecutive, or the Imperfect with Wāw Conjunctive instead of the Perfect with Wāw Consecutive. All such cases are to be regarded as exceptional. They may be loosely classified as follows:

1. Instead of the *Imperfect with Waw Consecutive* (וַ), there is used the Perfect with Wāw Conjunctive,

---

1 Ezra 3:10.   5 1 Sam. 3:13.   9 Deut. 17:13.   13 Isa. 40:30.
2 Eccl. 9:16.   6 Ex. 14:2.   10 Josh. 7:3.   14 Isa. 41:20.
3 Gen. 15:6.   7 Jon. 1:11.   11 Isa. 41:11.   15 Ps. 2:12.
4 Gen. 21:25.   8 Gen. 1:9.   12 Ex. 23:8.

a. When the second action is synonymous or simultaneous with the first, and is consequently to be represented as *co-ordinate* with it, the usual construction representing it as *subordinate.*

b. In the later books in which the influence of the Aramaic is felt.[a]

c. In instances of which no sufficient explanation can be given.[b]

2. Instead of the *Perfect with Waw Consecutive*, there is found the Imperfect with Wāw Conjunctive,

a. When the Imperfect is a voluntative, and, combining with **ו**, furnishes a most concise and elegant expression of *purpose* (§ 24. 1. *e*, 2. *d*).[c]

b. When, as in the case of the Perfects cited above (§ 26. 1. *a*), the second is to be treated as co-ordinate, being emphatic, or synonymous with the first,—whether used in the sense of a future or a frequentative.[d]

c. When the Imperfect follows another Imperfect introduced by a conjunction.[e]

REMARKS.

(*a*) The Imperfect with Wāw Consecutive continues even in the later books to be the prevailing construction except in the Book of Ecclesiastes, in which, according to Driver, it occurs only three times (1:17; 4:1,7). This construction, however, is not found in Aramaic.

(*b*) Some of these cases occur in the very earliest books.

(*c*) While in most cases the special form of the voluntative, i. e., the Jussive or Cohortative, is employed, in many the usual form of the Imperfect occurs.

(*d*) This is, of course, more frequent in poetry than in prose.

(*e*) These cases are few, cf. Driver, p. 162.

REFERENCES FOR STUDY.

Gen. 1:26; 9:27; 17:2; 22:17; 27:29,31..2*b.*
Gen. 28:6..................................1*c.*
Gen. 31:7..................................1*a.*
Ex. 24:7; 26:24...........................2*b.*
Dt. 2:30; 33:2,20..........................1*a.*
Judg. 3:23; 7:13...........................1*c.*
1 Sam. 1:12; 3:13..........................1*c.*
2 Sam. 6:16; 13:18.........................1*c.*
1 Kgs. 3:11*b*; 6:32,35; 11:10............1*c.*

Isa. 2:11; 40:12...........................1*a.*
Isa. 41:11,15,22; 42:6,14,21,23............2*b.*
Ezek. 9:7; 13:6,8; 25:12; 37:2; 41:3,8,13,
   15.....................................1*b.*
Amos 7:2,4*b*..............................1*c.*
Ps. 25:9; 37:40; 49:9; 73:8................2*b.*
Esth. 2:14; 3:12; 8:15; 9:23,24............1*b.*
Ezra 6:22; 8:30,36; 9:2....................1*b.*
Neh. 9:7,8; 12:39; 13:1,30.................1*b.*

27. THE PARTICIPLE.

1. *a.* רֹעֵה צֹאן[1] *keeper of a flock.*

יֹדְעֵי טוֹב וָרָע[2] *knowers of good and evil.*

יֹשְׁבֵי בֵיתֶךָ[3] *dwellers in thy house.*   [*of Cush.*

b. הַסֹּבֵב אֵת כָּל־אֶרֶץ כּוּשׁ[4] *the one that encompasseth all the land*

---

[1] Gen. 4:2.   [2] Gen. 3:5.   [3] Ps. 84:5.   [4] Gen. 2:13.

עֹשִׂים חֶסֶד וֶאֱמֶת[1] *doing kindness and truth.*

תְּשֻׁאוֹת מְלֵאָה[2] *full of noise.*

הַמְסֻכָּן תְּרוּמָה[3] *he that is impoverished of an oblation.*

2. *a.* וְהוּא יֹשֵׁב פֶּתַח־הָאֹהֶל[4] *and he was sitting in the door of the tent.*

וְהִנֵּה אֲנַחְנוּ מְאַלְּמִים[5] *and behold, we were binding sheaves.*

מֹשֶׁה הָיָה רֹעֶה אֶת־צֹאן יִתְרוֹ[6] *Moses was keeping Jethro's flock.*

הָיָה מֹשֵׁל בְּכָל־הַמַּמְלָכוֹת[7] *he was ruling over all the kingdoms.*

b. קוֹל דְּמֵי אָחִיךָ צֹעֲקִים אֵלַי[8] *the voice of thy brother's blood is crying unto me.* [ing.

הַגִּידָה־נָּא לִי אֵיפֹה הֵם רֹעִים[9] *tell me where they are shepherd-*

אֲשֶׁר אָנֹכִי מְלַמֵּד אֶתְכֶם[10] *which I am teaching you.*

אֵל זֹעֵם בְּכָל־יוֹם[11] *a God that hath indignation every day.*

זֹמֵם רָשָׁע לַצַּדִּיק[12] *the wicked plot against the just.* [earth.

c. אָנֹכִי מַמְטִיר עַל־הָאָרֶץ[13] *I am (about) to bring rain upon the*

הִנֵּה יָמִים בָּאִים[14] *behold, the days are coming.*

שָׂרַי אִשְׁתְּךָ יֹלֶדֶת לְךָ[15] *Sarai, thy wife, will bear thee a son.*

אֲשֶׁר אֲנַחְנוּ הֹלְכִים[16] *in which we are (about) to go.*

1. In respect to *government*, the Participle[a,b] may be

　a. A noun (construct) followed by another noun in the *genitive*,[c] or

　b. A *verb* governing the following noun as an accusative or by means of prepositions.[d,e]

2. In respect to *tense* or temporal function, the Participle is used in the description of

　a. A state (or action)[f] belonging to the sphere of the *past;* thus presenting some particular attribute or characteristic, or picturing vividly the particular circumstances under which a given event took place.[g]

　b. A state or action belonging to the sphere of the *present*, and thus represented as continuing, enduring, permanent.[h,i,j]

　c. A state or action belonging to the sphere of the *future*, thus

---

1 Gen. 24:49.　　5 Gen. 37:7.　　9 Gen. 37:16.　　13 Gen. 7:4.
2 Isa. 22:2.　　6 Ex. 3:1.　　10 Deut. 4:1.　　14 Jer. 23:5.
3 Isa. 40:20.　　7 1 Kgs. 5:1.　　11 Ps. 7:12.　　15 Gen. 17:19.
4 Gen. 18:1.　　8 Gen. 4:10.　　12 Ps. 37:12.　　16 Jud. 18:5.

represented as beginning, and hence *certain;* only the context determining whether there is reference to a near or to a remote future.[k]

3. *a.* רַק הָעָם מְזַבְּחִים בַּבָּמוֹת[1] *only the people kept sacrificing in the high places.*

b. מַה־נּוֹרָא הַמָּקוֹם הַזֶּה[2] *how fearful (timendus) is this place.*

4. *a.* דַּבֵּר....כִּי שֹׁמֵעַ עַבְדֶּךָ[3] *speak...., for thy servant heareth.*

b. וּלְבֵנִים אֹמְרִים לָנוּ עֲשׂוּ[4] *yet brick, they say to us, make.* [*discord.*

5. *a.* יָפִיחַ כְּזָבִים....וּמְשַׁלֵּחַ מְדָנִים[5] *who uttereth lies and letteth loose*

b. הַעֹזְבֶת....וְאֶת־בּ׳ א׳ שָׁכֵחָה[6] *who forsaketh...and the covenant of God forgetteth.*   [*the needy.*

מֵקִים....דָּל....יָרִים אֶבְיוֹן[7] *he raiseth up the poor....lifteth up*

c. מוֹרִיד שְׁאוֹל וַיָּעַל[8] *he bringeth down to Sheol and bringeth up.*

שְׂרָפִים עֹמְדִים....וְקָרָא[9] *seraphim were standing, and each kept calling.*

3. *a.* While, usually and properly, the Participle denotes a *fixed, continuous* state, it is sometimes found, instead of the Imperfect, marking a "fact liable to recur."

b. The passive Participle is often equivalent with Latin Participle in *dus.*

4. *a.* The subject of the Participle *generally* precedes it; but it sometimes follows, especially when the verbal idea is to be emphasized.

b. The subject of the Participle is occasionally omitted, and in such cases must be supplied from the context.

5. The Participle is found joined in one way or another with finite verbal forms, as follows:

a. Following an Imperfect.

b. Followed by a Perfect or Imperfect.

c. Followed by a Perfect or Imperfect with Wāw Consecutive (cf. the usage in §§ 24. 5 ; 25. 4*b*).

REMARKS.

(*a*) When the Participle is used as an adjective, it follows the law of the adjective (§ 10).

---

[1] 1 Kgs. 3:2.	[4] Ex. 5:16.	[6] Prov. 2:17.	[8] 1 Sam. 2:6.
[2] Gen. 28:17.	[5] Prov. 6:19.	[7] 1 Sam. 2:8.	[9] Isa. 6:2.
[3] 1 Sam. 3:9.			

84 HEBREW SYNTAX [§ 28.

(b) On the use of the Participles with the article, see § 4. 3. f.

(c) This construction is especially frequent in poetry.

(d) The Participle is sometimes followed by לְ (dative of *advantage or disadvantage*) rather than by an accusative, e. g., 1 Sam. 11: 9.

(e) Cases in which both constructions of the Participle (nominal and verbal) occur simultaneously are not infrequent, e. g., עֹשֶׂה שַׁחַר עֵיפָה Amos 4: 13.

(f) On the force of the Participle as compared with that of the Imperfect, see § 20. R. (h).

(g) Note the rarity in earlier books of the use of a Participle with a finite verb (e. g., Gen. 4:17; 37:2; 1 Sam. 2:11) as compared with the same usage in later books (e. g., Neh. 1:4; 2:13,15).

(h) The Participle, as well as the Perfect (§ 18. 3) and the Imperfect (§ 21. 3), may be used to express a general truth, e. g., Ps. 19:2; 29:5, but only in later Hebrew.

(i) Note also its frequent use as an appositive of a preceding substantive, e. g., Isa. 40:22,23.

(j) With use of the Participle for the present, compare the similar usage in Aramaic, where it is more common than the proper participial usage.

(k) In this usage the Participle is often preceded (for vividness) by הִנֵּה *behold*; though this particle is also employed when the Participle refers to the past or present, e. g., 1 Kgs. 19:5; 1 Sam. 14:33.

REFERENCES FOR STUDY.

28. THE INFINITIVE ABSOLUTE.

1. הַחֲרֵם כָּל־עִיר[1] *the destroying every city.*

הָרֹג בָּקָר וְשָׁחֹט צֹאן[2] *slaughtering oxen and killing sheep.*

---

[1] Deut. 3:6. [2] Isa. 22:13.

2. *a.* לֹא אָבוּ בִדְרָכָיו הָלוֹךְ[1] *they would not walk in his ways.*

רָאִיתִי[2]....נָאוֹף וְהָלוֹךְ בַּשֶּׁקֶר *I see committing adultery and walking in lies.*

b. וָאֶכֹּת אֹתוֹ טָחוֹן הֵיטֵב[3] *and I stamped it, grinding diligently.*

וָאִירָא הַרְבֵּה מְאֹד[4] *and I was very much afraid.*

The Infinitive absolute[a] partakes of both a nominal and a verbal character.[b] Like the verb[c] it may govern a noun in the accusative; like the noun it may be construed as a nominative, genitive, or accusative. Its more important usages may be classified as follows:

1. It may govern a dependent noun only in the accusative; it never stands in annexion.[d]

2. *a.* It may stand as an accusative,[e,f] governed by a finite verb, but the Infinitive construct is more frequently employed.

b. It may stand as an adverbial accusative, equivalent to an ordinary adverb.[g]

REMARKS.

(*a*) The Infinitive absolute differs from the Infinitive construct in being more stiff, and in being unable either to stand in annexion with a following word, or to be governed by a preceding preposition.

(*b*) "1. The Semitic Infinitive is really not an Infinitive in the sense of the term as used in Greek, Latin, German [and English] grammar; for it was originally, and has remained to the present day, a true noun, which contains in itself all the properties of the noun, and is construed as such in the sentence. The most which can be admitted is, that this noun sometimes gives up its capacity for inflection, and becomes an adverb; but never in any case does it pass over into the verb-system, in the manner which characterizes the proper Infinitive idea. 2. The Semitic *nomen actionis* expresses the abstract idea of being, acting, or suffering; and has been derived from the verb in the way in which verbal derivatives, with a concrete meaning, passed over into the abstract meaning. 3. This abstract verbal noun, through its derivation from the verb, has received the power of construction peculiar to the verb, so that it can subordinate another noun in the accusative, and attach to itself a subject in the nominative; while, on the other hand, it has no power whatever, in itself, of expressing any difference in tense, or in the kind of verb. 4. From the agreement in form among the different branches of the Semitic family of languages, it plainly follows that even the original Semitic language had already handed over the function of the abstract verbal noun to certain forms."[5]

(*c*) The Infinitive, like the Participle, is without tense, referring alike to past, present, or future, according to the demands of the context.

(*d*) The Infinitive absolute rarely has a subject, e. g., Ps. 17:5.

---

[1] Isa. 42:24.　　　[2] Jer. 23:14.　　　[3] Deut. 9:21.　　　[4] Neh. 2:2.
[5] Adolph Koch, *Der semitische Infinitif*, 1874.

(e) Sometimes also as a nominative, e. g., Isa. 32:17; 2 Chron. 31:10; and as a genitive, e. g., Isa. 14:23.

(f) The suffix governed by the Infinitive absolute must have את.

(g) The most common Infinitives thus used are הרבה, Gen. 15:1; הרחק, Gen. 21:16; הרק, Ex. 30:36; הפלא, Isa. 29:14; השכם, 1 Sam. 17:16; הכן, Josh. 3:17; הקף, Josh. 6:11; הערב, 1 Sam. 17:16. With the exception of מהר, Josh. 2:5, all forms thus used are in the Hîph'îl.

3. a. רָאוֹ רָאִינוּ כִּי הָיָה יְ עִמָּךְ[1] we saw for a certainty that Y. was with thee.

פָּקֹד פָּקַדְתִּי אֶתְכֶם[2] I will surely visit you.

נִשְׁאֹל נִשְׁאַל מִמֶּנִּי[3] he urgently besought me.

הָעֵד הֵעִיד בָּנוּ[4] he strictly charged us.

b. וַיִּשְׁפֹּט שָׁפוֹט[5] and he is always acting as judge.

בֵּרַכְתָּ בָרֵךְ[6] thou hast repeatedly blessed.

c. אוֹרוּ אָרוֹר[7] curse ye bitterly.

שִׁמְעוּ שָׁמוֹעַ....וּרְאוּ רָאוֹ[8] hear ye indeed....and see ye indeed.

d. וַיָּשֻׁבוּ הַמַּיִם....הָלוֹךְ וָשׁוֹב[9] and the waters kept continually receding.

הָלְכוּ הָלוֹךְ וְגָעוֹ[10] they went going on and lowing.

3. The Infinitive absolute[a] is used in connection with a finite verb[b] (generally of the same root[c] and stem[d]), as a sort of cognate or absolute accusative (§ 31. 4). Various cases arise:—

a. The Infinitive may *precede* the finite verb, and mark the *certainty* of the idea conveyed or *intensify* it.[e][f]

b. The Infinitive may *follow* the finite verb, and convey the idea of *repeated* or *continued* action.

c. The Infinitive may *follow* the finite verb, and, as when preceding it, *intensify* the idea.[g]

d. Two Infinitives may follow, one of which is frequently הָלַךְ, and the idea thus emphasized is that of *continuance*.[h]

REMARKS.

(a) The Infinitive construct is rarely employed for the Infinitive absolute, e. g., Ps. 50:21; Ruth 2:16; Neh. 1:7.

(b) Sometimes the finite verb is omitted, the Infinitive only remaining.

1 Gen. 26:28.	4 Gen. 43:3.	7 Judg. 5:23.	9 Gen. 8:3,5.
2 Ex. 3:7.	5 Gen. 19:19.	8 Isa. 6:9.	10 1 Sam. 6:12.
3 1 Sam. 20:6.	6 Num. 24:10.		

(c) In poetry the Infinitive is sometimes of a different (though cognate) root, e. g., Jer. 8:13; 48:9; Isa. 28:28.

(d) The Infinitive absolute is frequently in Qâl when the finite verb is of a different stem; e. g., in the Niph., Ex. 19:13; 21:20,22,28; Mic. 2:4; in the Pi'êl or Pû'âl, Josh. 24:10; Gen. 37:33; in the Hiph'il, 1 Sam. 23:22; in the Hith., Isa. 24:19. Cf. also Lev. 19:20; Ezek. 16:4.

(e) The particle גַּם is frequently employed to give additional emphasis; it stands between the verb and the infinitive; e. g., Gen. 31:15; 46:4; Num. 16:13.

(f) A negative, in such cases, generally stands between the Infinitive and the verb, e. g., Ex. 5:23; 34:7; Deut. 21:14; Nah. 1:3; Mic. 1:10; though sometimes before both verb and Infinitive, e. g., Gen. 3:4; Amos 9:8; Ps. 49:8.

(g) While the Infinitive, when it follows the verb, generally gives the idea of repetition or continuance, there are many cases in which this force is not allowed by the context, e. g., Gen. 31:15; Isa. 22:17; Jer. 22:10.

(h) In connection with הלך, used to express *continuance*, the second word, which then expresses the principal idea, may be not only an Infinitive absolute, but also a Participle, or verbal adjective, e. g., 1 Sam. 2:26; 14:19; 2 Sam. 3:1; 1 Chron. 11:9.

4. a. ¹אֶת־כָּל־זֶה רָאִיתִי וְנָתוֹן אֶת־לִבִּי *all this have I seen and applied my heart.*

²וַיִּתְקְעוּ בַּשּׁוֹפָרוֹת וְנָפוֹץ הַכַּדִּים *and they blew the trumpets and broke the pitchers.*

b. ³יוּמַת הָאִישׁ....רָגוֹם אֹתוֹ....כָּל־הָעֵדָה *let the man be put to death ...let all the congregation stone him.*

⁴לַגֵּר....תִּתְּנֶנָּה....אוֹ מָכֹר לְנָכְרִי *to the stranger thou shalt give it, or sell it to an alien.*   [watch, etc.

5. a. ⁵עָרוֹךְ הַשֻּׁלְחָן צָפֹה הַצָּפִית וגו'' *they prepare the table, set the*

b. ⁶אָכוֹל וְהוֹתֵר *ye shall eat and leave thereof.*

c. ⁷זָכוֹר אֶת־יוֹם הַשַּׁבָּת *remember the Sabbath day.*

⁸לָקוֹחַ אֶת־הַסְּפָרִים הָאֵלֶּה *take thou these documents.*

d. ⁹הַעֲלֵה....קָהָל וְנָתֹן....לְזַעֲוָה *I will bring up a company and deliver them to vexation.*

4. The Infinitive absolute is used to continue the verbal idea[a]
   a. Introduced by a Perfect, or an Imperfect with Wāw Consecutive.
   b. Introduced by an Imperfect referring to the future.

---

¹ Eccles. 8:9.   ⁴ Deut. 14:21.   ⁶ 2 Kgs. 4:43.   ⁸ Jer. 32:14.
² Judg. 7:19.   ⁵ Isa. 21:5.   ⁷ Ex. 20:9.   ⁹ Ezek. 23:46.
³ Num. 15:35.

5. The Infinitive absolute is, still further, used as a concise and vivid substitute for a finite verb;[b c] as,

a. For the Perfect in narration and description; cf. Latin Historical Infinitive.

b. For the Imperfect, referring to the future.

c. For the Imperative, when it is to be expressed emphatically.

d. For the Cohortative, in the way of exclamation.[a]

REMARKS.

(a) Especially frequent in later literature, when it was thought sufficient to express the distinction of *tense, number* and *person* in the first verbal form and allow it to be understood in the case of those following.

(b) For examples of its use where the subject is expressed, see Gen. 17:10; Ps.17:5; Prov. 17:12; etc.

(c) This usage is probably due to the ellipsis of the finite verb, e. g., אָכוֹל standing for זָכוֹר תִּזְכְּרוּ for זָכוֹר ; אָכוֹל תֹּאכֵלוּ.

(d) In none of these cases, or in those under 4 a, b, may the Infinitive have a negative.

REFERENCES FOR STUDY.

Gen. 8:7	3b.	1 Kgs. 22:30	5d.
Gen. 27:30; 43:3,20	3a.	2 Kgs. 4:43	5b.
Gen. 41:43	4a.	Isa. 5:5; 59:4	1
Gen. 46:4	3c.	Isa. 7:15; 22:13	2a.
Ex. 3:7	3a.	Isa. 42:20	4a.
Ex. 8:11	4a.	Isa. 59:4	5a.
Ex. 36:7	2b.	Jer. 2:2	5c.
Lev. 32:44	4b.	Jer. 7:13	2b.
Num. 16:13	3c.	Jer. 22:10	3b.
Num. 25:17	5c.	Ez. 1:14	5a.
Deut. 5:12	5c.	Hos. 4:2	5a.
Josh. 6:13	3d.	Amos 9:8	3a.
Judg. 5:23	3c.	Zech. 3:4; 7:5	4a.
Judg. 7:19	4a.	Zech. 12:10	5b.
Judg. 11:25	3a.	Job 15:3	5b.
1 Sam. 2:30; 9:6	3a.	Job 15:35	1
1 Sam. 2:26; 14:19	3d.	Eccl. 9:11	4a.
1 Sam. 2:27,28	4a.	Dan. 9:5	4a.
2 Sam. 3:1; 5:10	3d.	1 Chron. 11:9	3d.
2 Sam. 19:43	3a.		

29. THE INFINITIVE CONSTRUCT.

1. a. לֹא טוֹב הֱיוֹת הָאָדָם לְבַדּוֹ[1] *the being of man alone is not good.*

הַמְעַט מִכֶּם הַלְאוֹת אֲנָשִׁים[2] *is the wearying of men too little for you ?*

---

[1] Gen. 2:18.   [2] Isa. 7:13.

b. בְּיוֹם עֲשׂוֹת יְ׳ אֱלֹהִים[1] *on the day of Y. God's making,* etc.

לֹא־עֵת הֵאָסֵף[2] *not time for being gathered.*

c. לִבְעֲבוּר נַסּוֹת[3] *for the sake of trying = in order to try.*   [see.

וַתִּכְהֶיןָ עֵינָיו מֵרְאֹת[4] *and his eyes were weak so that he could not*

בְּהִוָּלֶד לוֹ אֶת־יִצְחָק[5] *when Isaac was born to him.*

d. לֹא אֵדַע צֵאת וָבֹא[6] *I know not (how) to go out or to come in.*

שָׂנֵאתִי עֲשֹׂה סְטִים[7] *I hate the doing of sin.*

2. *a.* הָקִים אֶת־הַמִּשְׁכָּן[8] *to set up the tabernacle.*

לְהָמִית צַדִּיק[9] *to destroy the righteous.*

לְמַעַן הָקִים אֹתְךָ[10] *in order to establish thee.*

b. (1) שֶׁבֶת אַחִים גַּם יָחַד[11] *the dwelling of brethren also together.*

אֵין מַיִם לִשְׁתּוֹת הָעָם[12] *there was no water for the people to*
drink.

בְּחֶמְלַת יְ׳ עָלָיו[13] *in Yahweh's sparing him.*

(בְּקָרְאִי אֹתִי) בְּקָרְאִי עֲנֵנִי[14] *in my calling, answer me (cf.*

(2) לָשׂוּם הַמֶּלֶךְ אֶל־לִבּוֹ[15] *that the king should take it to heart.*

מְשֹׁל בָּכֶם אִישׁ אֶחָד[16] *that one man should rule over you.*

c. בְּיוֹם עֲשׂוֹת יְ׳ א׳ אֶרֶץ[17] *in the day of Y. God's making earth,* etc.

דְּרֹשׁ אָחִיךָ אֹתוֹ[18] *thy brother's seeking it.*

בְּשִׂנְאַת יהוה אֹתָנוּ[19] *in Yahweh's hating us.*

בְּדַבֵּר אֶבְיוֹן מִשְׁפָּט[20] *when the needy speak justice.*

The Infinitive construct, like the Infinitive absolute, partakes of both a nominal and a verbal character. It is much more flexible than the Infinitive absolute and may, at one time, exercise both functions.

1. The Infinitive construct as a *noun*[a] may be used,

   a. As a nominative serving as the subject,

   b. As a genitive depending upon a preceding construct,

   c. As a genitive depending on a preceding preposition,[b]

   d. As an accusative, the direct object of a verb.

---

1 Gen. 2:4.	6 1 Kgs. 3:7.	11 Ps. 133:1.	16 Judg. 9:2.
2 Gen. 29:7.	7 Ps. 101:3.	12 Ex. 17:1.	17 Gen. 2:4.
3 Ex. 20:20.	8 Num. 9:15.	13 Isa. 47:9.	18 Deut. 22:2.
4 Gen. 27:1.	9 Gen. 18:25.	14 Ps. 4:2.	19 Deut. 1:27.
5 Gen. 21:5.	10 Deut. 29:12.	15 2 Sam. 19:20.	20 Isa. 32:7.

2. *a.* The Infinitive construct, likewise the verbal noun, which is really an Infinitive, governs as its direct object a noun which is construed as an accusative.[c,d]

   b. The Infinitive construct may have a subject, which will be

   (1) a noun placed immediately after it as *genitive*, or

   (2) a noun following it (not always immediately) as a *nominative.*[e,f,g]

   c. The Infinitive construct may be followed by two nouns, a subject and an object, in which case the former of the two is the subject (either genitive or nominative).[h,i]

REMARKS.

(*a*) While the Infinitive construct is in many respects a noun, it does not receive an article, cases like עֵת הַדַּעַת (Gen. 2:9) being rare and exceptional.

(*b*) בְּ with the Infinitive construct is equivalent to *while, when (quando);* כְּ, *as soon as, when (cum* with subjv.).

(*c*) The object of the Infinitive construct is never a genitive.

(*d*) Only the suffix of the first person may be appended as an accusative to the Infinitive; other suffixes, except occasionally the third plural, must have אֵת.

(*e*) In Arabic there are three possible constructions: (1) Infinitive, subj. in *gen.*, obj. in *acc.*; (2) Infinitive, obj. in *gen.*, subj. in *nom.*; (3) Infinitive, subj. in *nom.*, obj. in *acc.*

(*f*) Since the case-endings have been lost, it is often impossible to determine whether the subject is a genitive or nominative; but it may clearly be taken as a nominative (1) when the לְ prefixed to the inf. has pretonic ָ (e. g., 2 Sam. 19:20); (2) when a word stands between the Infinitive and the subject (see above).

(*g*) The subject is frequently omitted when it can be supplied from the context, e. g., Gen. 24:30; Isa. 5:2.

(*h*) Sometimes the object rather than the subject follows the Infinitive, e. g., Josh. 14:11; Isa. 5:24; 20:1.

(*i*) The Hebrew by the "combination of the verbal and nominal construction of the Infinitive construct is enabled to secure wonderful brevity," e. g., Gen. 39:18; Deut. 22:2.

3. *a.* זָכוֹר אֶת־יוֹם הַשּׁ' לְקַדְּשׁוֹ[1] *remember the Sabbath day to keep it holy.*   [*tell thee.*

   וָאִמָּלְטָה רַק־אֲנִי לְבַדִּי לְהַגִּיד לָךְ[2] *and only I have escaped to*

   b. וַיְהִי הַשֶּׁמֶשׁ לָבוֹא[3] *and the sun was about to go down.*

   יהוה לְהוֹשִׁיעֵנִי[4] *Yahweh is about to deliver me.*

   c. מֶה לַעֲשׂוֹת לָךְ[5] *what can be done for thee ?*

   הֲיֵשׁ לְדַבֶּר לָךְ[5] *can one speak for thee ?*

---

[1] Ex. 20:8.   [3] Gen. 15:12.   [4] Isa. 38:20.   [5] 2 Kgs. 4:13.
[2] Job 1:16.

d. וְאָדָם אַיִן לַעֲבֹד אֶת־הָאֲדָמָה¹ *and there was no man to till the g.*

עֵת לָלֶדֶת וְעֵת לָמוּת² *there is a time to be born and a time to die.*

e. אֲשֶׁר־בָּרָא א' לַעֲשׂוֹת³ *which God created while making.*

וַיְבָרֶךְ אֹתָם א' לֵאמֹר⁴ *and G. blessed them, saying.*

וַיְנַסּוּ־אֵל לִשְׁאָל־אֹכֶל⁵ *and they tempted God in asking for food.*

4. *a.* הֵחֵל הָאָדָם לָרֹב⁶ *men began to multiply.*

וַתֹּסֶף לָלֶדֶת אֶת־אָחִיו⁷ *and she added to bear his brother.*

b. וּוּכַל אִישׁ לִמְנוֹת⁸ *a man may be able to number.*

c. וַיִּשְׁאַל אֶת־נַפְשׁוֹ לָמוּת⁹ *and he asked for himself to die.*

לֹא־יִתֵּן אֶתְכֶם לַהֲלֹךְ¹⁰ *he will not permit you to go.*

3. The Infinitive construct with the preposition לְ,
   a. Is used primarily to express *purpose.*[a]
   b. May be rendered "is to," "is about to," in statements of time.[b]
   c. Is sometimes best expressed by "can" (= possibility).
   d. Denotes consequence, "that," "so that."
   e. Marks a concomitant circumstance (= gerund in *do*).[c]

   4. The Infinitive construct with the preposition לְ occurs when the Infinitive alone would have answered,[d]
   a. After verbs of *beginning, ceasing.*
   b. After verbs implying *ability,* or *possibility.*
   c. After verbs of *wishing, commanding, refusing.*

REMARKS.

(a) Cf. the more emphatic construction (1) with לְמַעַן, Deut. 8:3; 1 Kgs. 12:15; Isa. 30:1; Jer. 32:29; Mic. 6:5,16; (2) with לְבַעֲבוּר, 2 Sam. 17:14; 18:18.

(b) The use of לְ in לַעֲשׂוֹת, Isa. 5:2, till it should produce, is worthy of note.

(c) "It thus serves to characterize more closely the idea of the verb by stating the sphere in which the action moves;" the phrase is best translated by treating the Infinitive as the main verb, and the finite verb as an adverb.

(d) The Infinitive as subject sometimes has לְ, e. g., Prov. 21:9; 2 Sam. 18:11.

5. *a.* הָאֹמֵר לְכוֹרֶשׁ. וְלֵאמֹר לִירוּשָׁלַ͏ִם¹¹ *who says to C. . and says to J.*

אֶת־בְּנֵיכֶם יִקָּח וְשָׂם לוֹ בְּמֶרְכַּבְתּוֹ וְלָשׂוּם לוֹ שָׂרֵי אֲלָפִים¹²
your sons he will take and set them on his chariots, and will make them leaders of thousands.

---

1 Gen. 2:5.   4 Gen. 1:22.   7 Gen. 4:2.   10 Ex. 3:19.
2 Eccl. 3:2. 5 Ps. 78:18.   8 Gen. 13:16. 11 Isa. 44:28.
3 Gen. 2:3.   6 Gen. 6:1.   9 1 Kgs. 19:4. 12 1 Sam. 8:11,12.

b. עַל־רָדְפוֹ וְשִׁחֵת רַחֲמָיו¹ *because he pursued him and stifled his compassion.*

וַיְהִי כַּהֲרִימִי וָאֶקְרָא² *and it came to pass when I raised my voice and cried.* [eat.

6. אֲשֶׁר צִוִּיתִיךָ לְבִלְתִּי אֲכָל־מִמֶּנּוּ³ *of which I commanded thee not to* רַק חֲזַק לְבִלְתִּי אֲכֹל הַדָּם⁴ *only be strong not to eat the blood.*

5. The Infinitive construct sometimes
   a. Continues a sentence introduced by an Imperfect or Participle.
   b. Is continued by the Perfect or Imperfect with Wāw Consecutive (§§ 24. 5 ; 25. 5).

6. When the Infinitive is to be negatived, לְבִלְתִּי is employed.

REFERENCES FOR STUDY.

<table>
<tr><td>Gen. 4:13; 24:30</td><td>1c.</td><td>Isa. 10:32</td><td>3b.</td></tr>
<tr><td>Gen. 18:29</td><td>4a.</td><td>Isa. 13:19; 10:15</td><td>2c.</td></tr>
<tr><td>Ex. 14:12</td><td>1a.</td><td>Isa. 47:9</td><td>2b.</td></tr>
<tr><td>Ex. 14:12</td><td>2a.</td><td>Jer. 7:10</td><td>2a.</td></tr>
<tr><td>Ex. 32:29</td><td>5</td><td>Jer. 17:10; 19:12</td><td>5</td></tr>
<tr><td>Lev. 10:10,11</td><td>5</td><td>Hos. 9:13</td><td>3b.</td></tr>
<tr><td>Deut. 8:2; 11:4; 15:10; 25:17</td><td>1c.</td><td>Amos 8:4</td><td>5</td></tr>
<tr><td>Deut. 25:19</td><td>2b.</td><td>Mic. 6:8</td><td>1d.</td></tr>
<tr><td>Josh. 14:7</td><td>2c.</td><td>Ps. 32:9</td><td>3b.</td></tr>
<tr><td>1 Sam. 12:17; 14:33</td><td>3e.</td><td>Ps. 34:23</td><td>5</td></tr>
<tr><td>2 Sam. 14:25</td><td>3e.</td><td>Ps. 46:3; 76:10; 133:1</td><td>2b.</td></tr>
<tr><td>2 Sam. 17:14</td><td>1c.</td><td>Prov. 14:8; 16:12</td><td>1a.</td></tr>
<tr><td>2 Sam. 18:11</td><td>1a.</td><td>Prov. 26:2</td><td>3e.</td></tr>
<tr><td>1 Kgs. 12:15; 15:4</td><td>2a.</td><td>Job 33:17</td><td>2c.</td></tr>
<tr><td>1 Kgs. 13:4</td><td>2c.</td><td>2 Chr. 5:11; 20:6; 25:9</td><td>3c.</td></tr>
<tr><td>Isa. 5:24; 10:2</td><td>5</td><td></td><td></td></tr>
</table>

¹ Amos 1:11.   ² Gen. 39:18.   ³ Gen. 3:11.   ⁴ Deut. 12:23.

III. Verbal Government and Apposition.

30. THE OBJECT ACCUSATIVE.

1. ברא א' את השמים ואת הא'[1] *God created the heavens and the e.*

2. ידיכם דמים מלאו[2] *your hands are full of blood.*

אולי יחסרון....חמשה[3] *perhaps they....will lack five.*

3. לבשו כרים הצאן[4] *the pastures are clothed with flocks.*

אזרו חיל[5] *they gird themselves with strength.*

4. ישב הבית[6] *he remained in the house.*

ויבאו ארץ כנען[7] *and they came to the land of Canaan.*

לא יצא העיר[8] *he went not out of the city.*

5. גמלתני הטובה....גמלתיך הרעה[9] *thou hast rendered me good, I have rendered thee evil.* [tidings.

ארוצה נא אבשרה את המלך[10] *let me run and bring the king*

1. In Hebrew, as in other languages, transitive verbs govern their object in the accusative.[a] But aside from ordinary transitive verbs, certain other classes are so construed; these are

2. Verbs denoting *fullness* or *want*,[b] of which the most common are מלא *be full,* שבע *be satisfied,* שרץ *teem,* פרץ *overflow,* רוה *be satisfied,* חסר *be deficient,* שכל *be deprived.*

3. Verbs denoting *to clothe* and *unclothe*, of which the most common are לבש *put on,* עדה *adorn oneself,* עטה *cover,* עטף *wrap up,* כסה *cover,* צפה *overlay,* טוח *spread over,* עטר *crown,* אזר, חגר, *gird,* פשט *put off.*

4. Verbs denoting *to go*, or *come*, *to dwell*, of which the most common are בוא *go in,* יצא *go out,* הלך *go,* ישב, שכן, גור *dwell,* שכב *lie down.*

5. Verbs which were originally transitive and now resume their original force, or which were originally intransitive but have come to be con-

---

[1] Gen. 1:1.   [4] Ps. 65:14.   [7] Gen. 45:25.   [9] 1 Sam. 24:18.
[2] Isa. 1:15.   [5] 1 Sam. 2:4.   [8] 2 Kgs. 20:4.   [10] 2 Sam. 18:19.
[3] Gen. 18:28.   [6] Ruth 2:7.

ceived of as transitive ; [c] e. g., רִיב *defend before court,* עָנָה *answer,*
reply to, בִּשֵּׂר *bring good news to,* נָאַף *commit adultery with,* עָרַב
become surety for, גָּמַל , שִׁלֵּם *repay, retaliate,* מָרָה *rebel against.*

REMARKS.

(a) Many verbs originally construed with prepositions come, in later usage, to be
taken transitively, e. g., נָשַׁק, 2 Sam. 15:5; 1 Sam. 20:41; while many which were originally transitive come to prefer a preposition, e. g., קָרָא with ל, אֶל, בְּ, or אַחַר.

(b) In poetry also with verbs which gain this force only from the context, e. g.,
נָזַל, Jer. 9:17; נָטַף, Joel 4:18; Judg. 5:4; שָׁטַף, Isa. 10:22; עָלָה, Isa. 5:6; Prov. 24:31.

(c) Here may be noted that double usage in accordance with which there may be
employed either the noun alone or the noun with the preposition בְּ, e. g., Ps. 22:8 and
Job 16:4; Ps. 35:16 and Job:16:9. Cf. also the use of בְּ in Lam. 1:17; Ex. 7:20, where we
would certainly employ the accusative.

REFERENCES FOR STUDY.

31. THE DOUBLE ACCUSATIVE.

1. הֶרְאַנִי יְ׳ אֹתָךְ[1] *Y. hath shown thee to me.*

נַשְׁקֶה אֶת אָבִינוּ יַיִן[2] *let us cause our father to drink wine.*

2. וְחָגַרְתָּ אֹתָם אַבְנֵט[3] *and thou shalt gird them with priestly girdles.*

וַיִּטָּעֵהוּ שֹׂרֵק[4] *and he planted it with choice vines.*

3. וּמָלְאוּ אֶת הָאָרֶץ חָלָל[5] *and they shall fill the land with slain.*

דָּגָן וְתִירֹשׁ סְמַכְתִּיו[6] *with corn and new wine have I sustained him.*

4. הַיְלָדִים אֲשֶׁר חָנַן א׳ אֶת עַבְדֶּךָ[7] *the children whom God hath
granted thy servant.*

תּוֹרְךָ נוֹרָאוֹת יְמִינֶךָ[8] *thy right hand shall teach thee terrible things.*

שְׁאַל אֶת הַכֹּהֲנִים תּוֹרָה[9] *ask the priests for instruction.*

5. קָרָא שְׁמוֹ יַעֲקֹב[10] *he called his name Jacob.*

וַיַּחְשְׁבֶהָ לּוֹ צְדָקָה[11] *and he counted it to him for righteousness.*

6. וַיִּבֶן אֶת הָאֲבָנִים מִזְבֵּחַ[12] *and he built the stones into an altar.*

וַיִּיצֶר יְ׳ אֶת הָאָדָם עָפָר[13] *and Y. formed the man out of dust.*

---

1 2 Kgs. 8:13.	5 Ezek. 30:11.	8 Ps. 45:5.	11 Gen. 15:6.
2 Gen. 19:32.	6 Gen. 27:37.	9 Hag. 2:11.	12 1 Kgs. 18:32.
3 Ex. 29:9.	7 Gen. 33:5.	10 Gen. 27:36.	13 Gen. 2:7.
4 Isa. 5:2.			

7. ‏הכית את כל אויבי לחי‎[1] *thou hast smitten all my enemies on the* cheek-bone.   [*soul.*

‏וקבע את קבעיהם נפש‎[2] *and he will spoil their spoilers as to the*

Verbs which govern two accusatives may be classified as follows :[a,b]

1. The causative of stems which in the Qăl governed *one* accusative.

2. Verbs denoting *to clothe, cover; to plant, sow*, which have or are assigned a causative force even in Qăl.

3. Verbs denoting *to fill, satisfy, sustain*, and the opposite.

4. Verbs denoting *to give, bestow; to ask, answer, teach.*

5. Verbs denoting *to name, appoint, consider.*

6. Verbs denoting *to make into,*[c] *make out of, build, form*, etc.

7. Verbs which take, besides a direct object, a remote object which specifies more distinctly the object affected by the action, or the circumstances connected therewith.

REMARKS.

(a) Many of these verbs are also construed with prepositions.

(b) Verbs which in the active govern two accusatives, in the passive govern one.

(c) Here belong ‏נתן‎ ‏שים‎, ‏שות‎, ‏עשה‎, ‏בנה‎, etc.

REFERENCES FOR STUDY.

32. THE COGNATE ACCUSATIVE.

1. ‏עישב זרע זרע‎[3] *herb producing seed.*
‏ויחלם יוסף חלום‎[4] *and Joseph had a dream.*
‏הדבר דברתי‎[5] *have I spoken (even) a word ?*

2. ‏בכו בכי גדול‎[6] *they wept with a great weeping.*
‏נסו מנסת חרב‎[7] *they fled the flight of the sword.*
‏קבורת חמור יקבר‎[8] *he shall be buried with the burial of an ass.*

---

[1] Ps. 3:8.   [3] Gen. 1:29.   [5] 2 Sam. 7:7.   [7] Lev. 26:36.
[2] Prov. 22:23.   [4] Gen. 37:5.   [6] 2 Sam. 13:36.   [8] Jer. 22:19.

3. ‏קְנָאתִי גְדוֹלָה חֵמָה‏[1] *I am jealous in great anger.*

‏גָדוֹל קוֹל וַיִּזְעַק‏[2] *and he cried a loud voice.*

4. ‏רָאוּ וּרְאוּ....שָׁמוֹעַ שִׁמְעוּ‏[3] *hear a hearing....see a seeing.*

‏תִּמְלֹךְ הֲמָלֹךְ‏[4] *shalt thou indeed reign ?*

Any verb may take a noun of the same stem to define and explain the verbal idea. This is called the cognate accusative. Here may be distinguished:

1. Cases in which the accusative furnishes a concrete example of the action expressed by the verb, and is employed either to express special emphasis, or where in modern languages the verb would be a word of general significance (cf. the usage in Latin and Greek).

2. Cases in which the cognate accusative, followed either by an adjective or a genitive, furnishes additional information concerning the action of the verb.

3. Cases in which this accusative is *cognate* not in stem, but only in signification. Hence arises a number of common and concise expressions, used, for the most part, in poetry.

4. Cases in which this accusative expresses not the concrete, but the *abstract* idea of the verb. Here belongs the usage of the Infinitive absolute before and after a finite form (§ 28. 3).

REFERENCES FOR STUDY.

<table>
<tr><td>Num. 31:2</td><td>1.</td><td>Jer. 14:17; 20:11; 23:6; 30:14</td><td>3.</td></tr>
<tr><td>1 Sam. 4:5</td><td>2.</td><td>Jer. 30:14</td><td>2.</td></tr>
<tr><td>1 Sam. 20:17</td><td>1.</td><td>Hos. 10:4</td><td>1.</td></tr>
<tr><td>2 Sam. 12:16; 13:15</td><td>1.</td><td>Jon. 4:6</td><td>2.</td></tr>
<tr><td>1 Kgs. 2:16</td><td>1.</td><td>Zech. 1:14,15</td><td>2.</td></tr>
<tr><td>Isa. 5:1</td><td>2.</td><td>Zech. 1:2</td><td>1.</td></tr>
<tr><td>Isa. 5:6</td><td>1.</td><td>Prov. 17:27; 22:23</td><td>1.</td></tr>
<tr><td>Isa. 37:6</td><td>3.</td><td></td><td></td></tr>
</table>

33. THE ADVERBIAL ACCUSATIVE.

1. *a.* ‏הַשָּׂדֶה נֵצְאָ‏[5] *let us go out into the field.*

‏הַיָּמִין וְאִם....הַשְּׂמֹאל אִם‏[6] *whether to the left or to the right.*

‏הָעִיר פְּנֵי אֶת וַיִּחַן‏[7] *and he encamped before the city.*

b. ‏הָאֹהֶל פֶּתַח יֹשֵׁב וְהוּא‏[8] *while he sat at the entrance of the tent.*

‏לֶחֶם בֵּית אֲשֶׁר אָבִיו בְּקֶבֶר‏[9] *in his father's grave which was in Bethlehem.*

---

[1] Zech. 8:2.   [4] Gen. 37:8.   [6] Gen. 13:9.   [8] Gen. 18:1.

[2] 2 Sam. 19:5.   [5] 1 Sam. 20:11.   [7] Gen. 33:18.   [9] 2 Sam. 2:32.

[3] Isa. 6:9.

2. תְחִלַּת קְצִיר שְׂעֹרִים[1] *at the beginning of barley-harvest.*

וְהָגָה יוֹמָם וָלַיְלָה[2] *he meditates day and night.*

3. חָמֵשׁ עֶשְׂרֵה אַמָּה....גָּבְרוּ הַמַּיִם[3] *the waters rose fifteen cubits.*

לְשִׁבְתְּךָ עוֹלָמִים[4] *that thou mayest live forever.*

הָעִיר הַיֹּצֵאת אֶלֶף[5] *the city that goes forth a thousand.*

4. עָרוֹם יָנוּס[6] *he flees naked.*

וַיֵּלֶךְ אֲגַג מַעֲדַנֹּת[7] *and Agag came with confidence.*

אֵרֵד אֶל בְּנִי אָבֵל[8] *I will go down to my son mourning.*

יְמוּתוּ אֲנָשִׁים[9] *they shall die as men.*   [men.

5. מֵישָׁרִים תִּשְׁפְּטוּ בְּנֵי אָדָם[10] *ye shall judge righteously the sons of*

רָאִיתִי א׳ פָּנִים אֶל פָּנִים[11] *I have seen God face to face.*

נוֹרָאוֹת נִפְלֵיתִי[12] *I have been wonderfully distinguished.*

6. חֶרֶב תֵּאָכֵלוּ[13] *ye have been devoured by the sword.*

תָּבֹאוּ לֵרָאוֹת פָּנָי[14] *ye come in to be seen by my face.*

7. וְנִבְקַע הַר הַזֵּיתִים....גֵּיא גְדוֹלָה[15] *and the mount of Olives shall be* cleft (so as to become) *a large valley.*   [great fear.

וַתְּהִי יַד י׳ בָּעִיר מְהוּמָה גְ׳[16] *a. t. h. of Y. was on t. c. (so that there arose)*

8. *a.* חָלָה אֶת רַגְלָיו[17] *he was ill as to his feet.*   [than thou.

רַק הַכִּסֵּא אֶגְדַּל מִמֶּךָּ[18] *only as to the throne will I be greater*

b. נִתְרָאֶה פָנִים[19] *let us see one another in person.*

וַיִּשְׁתַּחוּ אַפַּיִם[20] *and he bowed himself down as regards the face.*

c. הוּא יְשׁוּפְךָ רֹאשׁ[21] *he will bruise thee in the head.*

בִּשְּׁלָם הַבָּשָׂר[22] *he cooked them as to the flesh.*

d. קוֹלִי אֶל י׳ אֶקְרָא[23] *I cry unto Y. with my voice.*

שְׁמִי י׳ לֹא נוֹדַעְתִּי[24] *by my name Y. I was not known.*

Many nouns have become adverbs;[a] many adverbial ideas are expressed by means of prepositions.[b] Aside from these cases, the accusative is used in an adverbial sense, to express,

1. Designations of *place*,
   a. In answer to the question *whither ?*[c]
   b. In answer to the question *where ?*[d]

1 2 Sam. 21:9.	7 1 Sam. 15:32.	13 Isa. 1:20.	19 2 Kgs. 14:8.
2 Ps. 1:2.	8 Gen. 37:35.	14 Isa. 1:12.	20 Gen. 19:1.
3 Gen. 7:20.	9 1 Sam. 2:33.	15 Zech. 14:4.	21 Gen. 3:15.
4 1 Kgs. 8:13.	10 Ps. 58:2.	16 1 Sam. 5:9.	22 1 Kgs. 19:21.
5 Amos 5:3.	11 Gen. 32:31.	17 1 Kgs. 15:23.	23 Ps. 3:5.
6 Amos 2:16.	12 Ps. 139:14.	18 Gen. 41:40.	24 Ex. 6:3.

2. Designation of *time*, in answer to the question *when?* but only in general statements.[e]

3. Designations of *extent, duration, amount*, in answer to the questions *how far? how long? how much?*

4. The *state* or *condition* of the subject at the time of the action described in the principal verb.

5. The particular *mode* or *manner* in which the action of the verb is performed.

6. Rarely the instrument by means of which the action was performed.

7. The *effect* or *consequence* of the action of the verb.

8. The particular object or part to which the state or condition described by the verb is limited; i. e., the accusative of specification;[f]

    a. With verbs which express a state or condition.

    b. With verbs which have a reflexive force.

    c. With verbs which have a direct object accusative.

    d. In poetry and with passive verbs.

REMARKS.

(*a*) E. g., אמנם , חנם , פתאם ; בטח Judg. 8:11, also לבטח .

(*b*) Cf. the various meanings local and temporal of ב , ל , מן , אל , etc.

(*c*) In these cases the accusative ending הָ is frequently employed (cf. *Elements of Hebrew*, § 121. 3); e. g., Gen. 14:10; 20:1.

(*d*) Here also the ending הָ is sometimes employed; e. g., 1 Kgs. 4:14.

(*e*) In particular statements prepositions (ב , ל , כ) are generally employed.

(*f*) Here belongs the construction of the numeral noted in §§ 15. 2. *c*; 6. 2. R. (*b*).

REFERENCES FOR STUDY.

34. THE ACCUSATIVE WITH את.

1. וְהָאָדָם יָדַע אֶת חַוָּה[1] and the man knew Eve.
   וַיַּרְא א' אֶת הָאוֹר[2] and God saw the light.
   יַעֲזָב אִישׁ אֶת אָבִיו[3] a man leaves his father.

2. וַיֵּדַע אֵת אֲשֶׁר עָשָׂה לוֹ[4] and he knew what he had done to him.
   אַךְ אֶת זֶה לֹא תֹאכְלוּ[5] yet this ye shall not eat.
   אֶת מִי אֶשְׁלַח[6] whom shall I send?

3. וַנַּחֲרֵם אֶת כָּל עִיר[7] and we destroyed every city.
   וַעֲבַדְתֶּם אֶת אֱלֹהִים אֲחֵרִים[8] and ye shall serve other gods.
   קַח....אֶת אֶחָד מֵהַנְּעָרִים[9] take one of the servants.

4. וְכִי יִגַּח שׁוֹר אֶת אִישׁ אוֹ אֶת אִשָּׁה וָמֵת[10] and if an ox gore a
   man or a woman, that they die.

5. וָאֶשְׁמַע אֶת מְדַבֵּר אֵלַי[11] and I heard him who spake unto me.

6. וַיְחַזֵּק חָרָשׁ אֶת צֹרֵף[12] and the carpenter encouraged the smith.
   לָעוּת אֶת יָעֵף דָּבָר[13] to sustain with words him that is weary.

7. מַצּוֹת יֵאָכֵל אֵת שִׁבְעַת הַיָּמִים[14] unleavened bread shall be eaten
   the seven days.   [nights.
   אֵת אַרְבָּעִים הַיּוֹם וְאֵת אַרְבָּעִים הַלַּ'[15] the forty days and forty
   וְאֵת בֵּית י' אֲנִי הֹלֵךְ[16] and I am going to the house of Y.

8. חָלָה אֶת רַגְלָיו[17] he was diseased in his feet.   [foreskin.
   בְּהִמֹּלוֹ אֵת בְּשַׂר עָרְלָתוֹ[18] in his being circumcised in the flesh of his

9. וְאֵת כָּל מִבְרָחָיו בְּכָל אֲגַפָּיו בַּחֶרֶב יִפֹּלוּ[19] and (as for) all his
   fugitives in all his bands (they) shall fall by the sword.
   וַיִּפְּלוּ....אֶלֶף אִישׁ אֵת כָּל אֵלֶּה אַנְשֵׁי חַיִל[20] and there fell 18,000
   men, all these men of valor.   [have pierced.

10. וְהִבִּיטוּ אֵלַי אֵת אֲשֶׁר דָּקָרוּ[21] and they will look unto me whom they
    אֵי חֲנִית הַמֶּלֶךְ וְאֶת צַפַּחַת הַמַּיִם[22] where is the king's spear and
    the cruse of water?   [Esau.

11. וַיֻּגַּד לְרִבְקָה אֶת דִּבְרֵי ע'[23] and were told to Rebekah the words of
    אַל יֵרַע בְּעֵינֶיךָ אֶת הַדָּבָר[24] let not the thing be evil in thine eyes.

1 Gen. 4:1.   7 Deut. 2:34.   13 Isa. 50:4.   19 Ezek. 17:21.
2 Gen. 1:4.   8 Jer. 16:13.   14 Ex. 13:7.   20 Judg. 20:44.
3 Gen. 2:24.   9 1 Sam. 9:3.   15 Deut. 9:25.   21 Zech. 12:10.
4 Gen. 9:24.   10 Ex. 21:28.   16 Judg. 19:18. 22 1 Sam. 26:16.
5 Lev. 11:4.   11 Ezek. 2:2.   17 1 Kgs. 15:23. 23 Gen. 27:42.
6 Isa. 6:8.   12 Isa. 41:7.   18 Gen. 17:25.   24 2 Sam. 11:25.

1. The sign אֵת is prefixed to substantives[a] in the accusative, especially when they precede the verb; but only when they are definite,[b] and rather before the names of *persons*[c] than the names of *things*.[d] Besides the general usage, the particle is employed,

2. With אֲשֶׁר, זֶה, and מִי, but never with מָה.

3. With כֹּל, אַחֵר, אֶחָד, which partake somewhat of the nature and usage of pronouns.[e]

4. With a singular noun (without the article), when it represents a whole species.[f]

5. With a participle (without the article) in the sense of *he who*.[g]

6. With a noun from which *in poetry* (§ 5. 4) the article has been omitted.

7. With some expressions of time and place[g] (§ 33. 1–3).

8. With the adverbial accusative of specification (§ 33. 8).[h]

9. With expressions in which there is a transition to something new, or when something not thought of before is added.[i]

10. With what is strictly speaking an oblique case, or after וְ[j] with a circumstantial clause, or with what is meant to be less distinct or independent.[k]

11. With the subject of passive verbs and of verbs which are neuter or intransitive.

REMARKS.

(a) For its use with pronominal suffixes, see § 11. 2. b.

(b) Whether definite in themselves, or by position, see § 4. 1, 2. The cases in which אֵת occurs with an indefinite noun are few, e. g., Ex. 2:1; 21:28; 2 Sam. 18:18; and these cases are suspicious.

(c) Yet here omitted frequently, especially in poetry; cf. Ex. 15 and Judg. 5.

(d) When the object is double it is sometimes expressed with both, sometimes with one; and at other times it is omitted, e. g., 1 Sam. 17:36; Gen. 2:19; Deut. 12:6; 14:12–18; Num. 12:5.

(e) Also with other numerals accompanied by nouns, e. g., 2 Sam. 15:16; 1 Kgs. 6:16.

(f) Compare Lev. 7:8; 20:14.

(g) This usage is very rare.

(h) Compare the use of אֵת with the nominative absolute (§ 7. 5).

(i) Compare with this the later use of לְ.

(j) Compare the use of the accusative in Arabic after *wa* in the sense of *together with*.

(k) Note the usage of אֵת in Zech. 8:17 and Deut. 11:2.

REFERENCES FOR STUDY.

35. THE ACCUSATIVE WITH THE PASSIVE.

1. יֵחָלֵק אֶת הָאָרֶץ[1] *the land shall be divided.*   [Esau.

וַיֻּגַּד לְרִבְקָה אֶת דִּבְרֵי עֵשָׂו[2] *and were told to Rebekah the words of*

וַיִּוָּלֵד לַחֲנוֹךְ אֶת עִירָד[3] *and Irad was born to Enoch.*

2. הָרְאָה אֶת הַכֹּהֵן[4] *it shall be shown to the priest.*

חֶרֶב תְּאֻכְּלוּ[5] *ye shall be made to devour the sword.*

לִשׁוֹנִי מֻדְבָּק מַלְקוֹחָי[6] *my tongue is made to attach itself to my jaws.*

3. נוֹרָאוֹת נִפְלֵיתִי[7] *I have been fearfully distinguished.*

הַמְסֻכָּן תְּרוּמָה[8] *impoverished of an oblation.*

4. וַתִּמָּלֵא הָאָרֶץ אֹתָם[9] *and the earth was filled with them.*

מַלְבָּשִׁים בְּגָדִים[10] *clothed with garments.*

The accusative is used with the passive as follows:

1. That which was the object of the active is often construed also as an object of the passive, though really a subject.

2. Verbs which in the active take two accusatives, in the pass. take one.

3. An adverbial accusative may remain with the passive.

4. Verbs of fullness and clothing may take in the passive an accusative.

REFERENCES FOR STUDY.

36. VERBAL APPOSITION AND SUBORDINATION.

1. הוֹאֶל נָא וְלִין[11] *be pleased now and lodge.*

וַיָּשָׁב וַיַּחְפֹּר[12] *and he returned and digged.*

וַיֹּסֶף וַיִּקַּח אִשָּׁה[13] *and he added and took a wife.*

---

[1] Num. 26:55.
[2] Gen. 27:42.
[3] Gen. 4:18.
[4] Lev. 13:49
[5] Isa. 1:20.
[6] Ps. 22:16.
[7] Ps. 139:14.
[8] Is. 40:20.
[9] Ex. 1:7.
[10] 1 Kgs. 22:10.
[11] Judg. 19:6.
[12] Gen. 26:18.
[13] Gen. 25:1.

¹וַיְהִי קוֹל הַשּׁוֹפֵר הוֹלֵךְ וְחָזֵק *and the sound of the trumpet was going and becoming strong.*

²לְמַעַן יִלְמְדוּ וְיָרְאוּ *that they may learn and fear.*

2. ³הָחֵל רָשׁ *begin, take possession.*

⁴יָשׁוּב יִלְטֹושׁ *he will return, will sharpen (= will again sharpen).*

⁵תַּרְבּוּ תְדַבְּרוּ *ye do much, ye speak (= ye speak much).*

⁶הוֹאִיל הָלַךְ *he was willing, he went (= he went willingly).*

3. *a.* ⁷לֹא אָבוּ הָלוֹךְ *they would not go.*

b. ⁸וַיּוֹסִפוּ עוֹד שְׂנֹא אֹתוֹ *and they added still to hate him.*

c. ⁹מִהַרְתָּ לִמְצֹא *thou hast hastened to find (found quickly).*

¹⁰הִרְבְּתָה לְהִתְפַּלֵּל *she did much to pray (prayed much).*

4. ¹¹לֹא יָדַעְתִּי אֲכַנֶּה *I know not to flatter.*

¹²חָפֵץ יַגְדִּיל *he desired to make great.*

¹³יָקוּם רוֹצֵחַ יִקְטֹל *the murderer rises to kill.*

5. ¹⁴כְּהֲתִמְּךָ שׁוֹדֵד *when thou shalt finish to destroy.*

¹⁵יֹדֵעַ מְנַגֵּן *one who knows how to play.*

When one verbal form is employed to define the idea expressed by another, whether indicating some attendant circumstance or characteristic, or describing what grows immediately out of the first, the following constructions are found:

1. Both verbs are finite, the second being joined to the first by וֹ (either conjunctive or consecutive); here both verbs may be Imperatives, the first a Perfect and the second an Imperfect with Wāw Consecutive, or the first an Imperfect and the second a Perfect with Wāw Cons.*a*

2. Both verbs are finite, there being no connective ;*a,c* this is more common in poetry.

3. The first verb is a finite form, and the second an Infinitive, either (1) Inf. abs., or (2) Inf. cons. without לְ, or (3) Inf. cons. with לְ.*b*

4. Both verbs are finite, the second being brought into *direct* subordination to the first by being placed in the Imperfect (*subjunctive*); this is rare and late.*d*

5. The second verb may be a Participle and thus describe the circumstances "more vividly than would either the (subjunctive) Imperfect, or the Infinitive."*e*

---

1 Ex. 19:19.

2 Deut. 31:12.

3 Deut. 2:24.

4 Ps. 7:13.

5 1 Sam. 2:3.

6 Hos. 5:11.

7 Isa. 42:24.

8 Gen. 37:5.

9 Gen. 27:20.

10 1 Sam. 1:12.

11 Job 32:22.

12 Isa. 42:21.

13 Job 24:14.

14 Isa. 33:1.

15 1 Sam. 16:16.

REMARKS.

(a) In this case the second verb agrees with the first in gender, and number, and generally in tense.

(b) On this use of the Infinitive absolute and construct, cf. §§ 28, 29.

(c) In the passages cited, the first verb qualifies the second; in Isa. 53:11 יִרְאֶה יִשְׂבָּע *he shall see satisfyingly,* and Jer. 4:5 קִרְאוּ מִלְאוּ *call ye with full voice,* the second qualifies the first.

(d) Examine Num. 22:6 and Isa. 47:1, in which there is an interesting change of number and person, with which this construction is closely connected.

(e) In 1 Sam. 3:2 an adjective is used instead of a Participle.

REFERENCES FOR STUDY.

IV. The Sentence.

37. THE SUBJECT AND PREDICATE.

1. יצאו¹ מן העם *some of the people went out.*

  הרבה נפל מן העם² *much of the people fell.*

  הנני מישחיתם³ *behold, I am about to destroy them.*

2. *a.* אז יאמרו בגוים⁴ *then they said among the nations.*

  לא תוסיפי יקראו לך⁵ *thou shalt no longer be called.*

  b. על כן קרא שמה בבל⁶ *therefore they called its name Babel.*

  אם יחרוש בבקרים⁷ *when one ploughs in the morning.*

  ויאמר אליו⁸ *and one shall say unto him.*

  c. יפל הנפל⁹ *anyone who falls.*

  יתהלל המתהלל¹⁰ *let him that glorieth glory.*

  d. עד באך¹¹ *as far as thy coming = until one comes.*

  בערכך נפשת ליהוה¹² *in thine estimating persons unto Y.*

3. *a.* ינוח לי¹³ *it will be quiet for me (= I will feel quiet).*

  מקטר¹⁴ *it is scattered as incense (= incense is offered).*

  b. חשכה¹⁵ *it has become dark;* תמטיר¹⁶ *it rains.*

  ותצר לישראל¹⁷ *and it was strait with Israel.*

In reference to the *subject* of a sentence, it may be noted that,

1. Aside from the noun, adjective and pronoun which may serve as subject, prepositional phrases, adverbs and pronominal suffixes (joined to particles) also perform this service.

2. When the subject is *indefinite* (German *man*, French *on*, Eng. *they*) various constructions are employed, viz. : [a]

  a. The verb in the *third person plural.*[b]

  b. The verb in the *third person singular*, in giving names, when the subject may be gathered from the nature of the verb, or from the context.

---

1 Ex. 16:27.	6 Gen. 11:9.	10 Jer. 9:23.	14 Mal. 1:11.
2 2 Sam. 1:4.	7 Amos 6:12.	11 Gen. 13:10.	15 Mic. 3:6.
3 Gen. 6:13.	8 Zech. 13:6.	12 Lev. 27:2,3.	16 Amos 4:7.
4 Ps. 126:2.	9 Deut. 22:8.	13 Job 3:13.	17 Judg. 10:9.
5 Isa. 47:1.			

c. The verb with a Participle of the same for subject.

d. The pronoun of the second person singular, in the formula עַד בָּאָךְ, and in legal phraseology.

3. When the subject is *impersonal* (where in English we use *it*) there is employed,

    a. The verb (or participle) in the third singular, and when active, generally masculine; when passive, always masculine; but

    b. The verb in the third singular *feminine* in description of material phenomena, and also elsewhere.

4. *a.* צַדִּיק יְהוָה¹ *Yahweh is righteous.*

    יְהוָה הַצַּדִּיק² *Yahweh is the righteous one.*

   b. מִשְׁפְּטֵי י׳ אֱמֶת³ *the judgments of Y. are truth* (= *true*).

    עֵינַיִךְ יוֹנִים⁴ *thine eyes are doves* (= *like doves' eyes*).

   c. בַשָּׁמַיִם כִּסְאוֹ⁵ *his throne is in heaven.*

    הֲשָׁלוֹם אֲבִיכֶם⁶ *is your father in health?*

    אַתֶּם הַמְעַט מִכָּל הָעַמִּים⁷ *ye are the least of all the peoples.*

4. Aside from a verb, the *predicate* may be,

    a. An adjective, which is undefined, unless it is desired for special reason to prefix the article.

    b. A noun, a construction frequently employed because of the want of adjectives.

    c. A prepositional phrase, adverbial accusative, or adverb.

5. *a.* קָצִיר הַיּוֹם⁸ *harvest* (*is*) *to-day;* צַדִּיק י׳⁹ *Y.* (*is*) *righteous.*

   b. הַדָּם הוּא הַנֶּפֶשׁ¹⁰ *the blood is the soul;* דָוִד הוּא הַקָּטָן¹¹ *D. was* (*or is*) *the youngest;* מָה הֵמָּה אֵלֶּה¹² *what are these?* (cf. Zech. 4:4).

    אַתָּה הוּא הָאֱלֹהִים¹³ *thou art God.*

   c. אִישׁ הָיָה בְאֶרֶץ עוּץ¹⁴ *there was* (*lived*) *a man in the land of Uz.*

    וְהַנָּחָשׁ הָיָה עָרוּם¹⁵ *and the serpent had become subtile.*

   d. יֵשׁ תִּקְוָה¹⁶ *there is hope;* יֵשׁ אִתָּךְ¹⁷ *it is with thee.*

    אֵין יוֹסֵף¹⁸ *no Joseph;* תֶּבֶן אֵין נִתָּן¹⁹ *straw is not given.*

    הִנֵּנִי²⁰ *behold me;* הִנֵּה בָאֹהֶל²¹ *she is in the tent.*

---

1 Ps. 11:7.
2 Ex. 9:27.
3 Ps. 19:10.
4 Cant. 1:15.
5 Ps. 11:4.
6 Gen. 43:27.

7 Deut. 7:7.
8 1 Sam. 12:17.
9 Ps. 11:7.
10 Deut. 12:23.
11 1 Sam. 17:14.

12 Zech. 4:5.
13 2 Sam. 7:28.
14 Job 1:1.
15 Gen. 3:1.
16 Job 11:18.

17 Prov. 3:28.
18 Gen. 37:29.
19 Ex. 5:16.
20 1 Sam. 3:4.
21 Gen. 18:9.

5. The subject and predicate may be united in various ways :

a. They may stand together, with no connecting word of any kind.*c*

b. They may be joined by means of the pronoun of the third pers. ; whether the circumstance is one of past or present time, and whether the subject is first, second or third person. At first expressing *existence* only in the most general way, it comes to be equivalent to our verb *to be*, and is especially used when both subject and predicate are definite.*d,e* Cf. § 7. 6, 7.

c. The verb היה may be employed ; but this always expresses the idea of *becoming, existing*, and is therefore never identical with the substantive verb *to be.f*

d. Certain particles, viz., יש *existence*, אין *non-existence*, הנה *see, behold*, are employed. These were originally nouns, but in usage have come to be practically equivalent to our copula.

REMARKS.

(*a*) On the use of כל, דבר, איש to express the indefinite subject, § 14. 2. *b.*

(*b*) A paraphrastic mode of expression to express the same force as that conveyed by the *third person plural* is seen in the use of the passive, with which the accusative is joined, e. g., יִתֶּן אֶת הָאָרֶץ = *let them give the land;* cf. Gen. 17:5; 27:42; Amos 4:2, etc. (§ 35. 1).

(*c*) "An external sign for connecting the two main constituents of a proposition, when the predicate is not to be a verb—in other words, a *copula*—is really unnecessary; because the mode in which the discourse is delivered by the living voice is of itself sufficient to indicate the separation, in meaning, between the two different halves of the sentence; and, in Hebrew, a special word for this purpose is, in actual fact, very rarely used. The Indo-Germanic languages begin pretty early to use the verb *to be* for this sign, when the predicate did not consist of a more complete verb, and thus the substantive verb came to be the mere copula in a sentence, whereas the Semitic languages properly do not yet know of any such usage, and have, in this respect also, remained much more simple."*

(*d*) But also in later Hebrew frequently when the subject is indefinite.

(*e*) Cf. the use of הוא in Nah. 2:9; Isa. 18:2,7.

(*f*) Cf. the use of לא היה = *he is not.* Gen. 42:11; Isa. 15:6; 23:13.

(*g*) For an interesting use of הפך *to turn* and סבב *become*, see Lev. 13:3,4; Jer. 31:21.

REFERENCES FOR STUDY.

---

* *Ewald*, Hebrew Syntax, pp. 134,135.

38. ORDER OF WORDS IN A SENTENCE

1. *a.* בְּרָא אֱלֹהִים אֵת הַשָּׁמַיִם¹ *God created the heaven.*

וַיֹּאמֶר הַנָּחָשׁ אֶל הָאִשָּׁה² *and the serpent said unto the woman.*

b. גָּדוֹל אַתָּה וְגָדוֹל שְׁמֶךָ³ *great thou art and great is thy name.*

יְהוָה אֱלֹהֶיךָ הוּא אֱלֹהִים⁴ *Yahweh, thy God, is God.*

c. וַיהוָה עָנָה בִי⁵ *seeing that Y. hath testified against me.*

וְרֹאשׁוֹ מַגִּיעַ בַּשָּׁמַיְמָה⁶ *and the top (was) reaching to heaven.*

2. *a.* בְּרָא א׳ אֵת הַשָּׁמַיִם¹ *God created the heaven.* [*name.*

b. הִשְׁכִּיחוּ אֶת עַמִּי שְׁמִי⁷ *they have caused my people to forget my*

c. אֶתֶּן לְךָ עֲשֶׂרֶת כֶּסֶף⁸ *I will give thee ten pieces of silver.*

וַיְבָרֶךְ אֹתָם אֱלֹהִים⁹ *and God blessed them.*

1. The usual order of words, so far as concerns the two principal members, is as follows :

 a. Predicate, subject, when the predicate is a *verb.*[a]

 b. Predicate, subject, when the predicate is an *adjective* ;[b] but subject, predicate, when the predicate is a *noun.*[c]

 c. Subject, predicate, in what are called descriptive or circumstantial clauses.[d]

2. *a.* The usual order of words, so far as concerns the three principal members, is predicate, subject, object (direct or indirect) ;[e] and

 b. If there are two objects, that one comes first which is the more important ; but

 c. When the object (direct or indirect) is a pronoun, it is likely immediately to follow the predicate.[f]

---

[1] Gen. 1:1. [4] Deut. 4:35. [6] Gen. 28:12. [8] Judg. 17:10.
[2] Gen. 3:4. [5] Ruth 1:21. [7] Jer. 23:27. [9] Gen. 1:22.
[3] Jer. 10:6.

REMARKS.

(*a*) In Hebrew, the *act* was more important than the agent, and was consequently placed first.

(*b*) Compare the position of the adjective when attributive, viz., after the noun (§ **10. 2.** *a.*).

(*c*) This order, which is always followed when neither subject nor predicate is to be emphasized, indicates at once which is subject and which is predicate.

(*d*) "By putting the *subject* first, and the predicate afterwards, the action, its development, and its progress do not come into the foreground, as in ordinary narrative discourse; but the *person* is placed first, by himself, in order to be immediately thereafter more fully described and depicted as he is; and the whole proposition, in a manner quite the opposite of the usual narrative style, presents us with a harmonious and placid picture of something continuous, permanent,—just as the speaker conceives it."*

(*e*) Furthermore it may be said, additions in the form of an adjective, genitive or adverb *follow* the particular word which they modify. There are, of course special rules for the Infinitive absolute (§ 28.) and negatives (§ 37.).

(*f*) There is a growing tendency to insert small words and expressions between the more important members, e. g., זאת Ex. 14:5; כאר Jer. 18:13; לו Ps. 7:14; היה Job 1:1.

3. *a.* ¹ומעיל קטן תעשה לו אמו *and a little robe his mother made for him.*

²המת לי' בעיר יאכלו הכלבים *him that dieth of J. in the city shall the dogs eat.*

b. ³אחי אנכי מבקש *my brethren I am seeking.*   [*thing.*

⁴דבר גדול הנ' דבר אליך *had the prophet bid thee (do) a great*

c. ⁵ואתה בריתי תשמר *and thou my covenant shalt keep.*

⁶ויהוה פתהן יערה *Y. will lay bare their secret parts.*

d. ⁷וכתב האלת האלה הכהן *and the priest shall write these curses.*

⁸שכלה נשים חרבך *thy sword has made women childless.*

3. From the usual order (see above), there are sometimes found variations, e. g.,

a. *Object, predicate, subject*, which emphasizes the object.

b. *Object, subject, predicate*, which likewise emphasizes the object; this is the usual construction when the predicate is a participle, but elsewhere rare.

c. *Subject, object, predicate*, which emphasizes the subject, and "in prose confers upon the phrase a poetical coloring by transferring the predicate to the end."

¹ 1 Sam. 2:19.   ³ Gen. 37:16.   ⁵ Gen. 17:9.   ⁷ Num. 5:23.
² 1 Kgs. 14:11.   ⁴ 2 Kgs. 5:13.   ⁶ Isa. 3:17.   ⁸ 1 Sam. 15:33.
* *Ewald*, Hebrew Syntax, pp. 152, 153.

d. Predicate, object, subject, which emphasizes the subject; this is rare except when the object is a pronominal suffix (see § **38. 2.** *c*).

REFERENCES FOR STUDY.

39. EMPHASIS.

1. לֵךְ וִיהוָה יִהְיֶה עִמָּךְ[1] *go, and Yahweh be with thee.*

   אֵת הָאֲרִי הִכָּה עַבְדְּךָ[2] *the lion thy servant smote.*

   בַּחֲלוֹמִי הִנְנִי עֹמֵד[3] *in my dream, behold, I stood.*

2. a. אֶת הָעָם הֶעֱבִיר אֹתוֹ[4] *the people, he made them to pass over.*

   b. בְּיוֹם אֲכָלְכֶם וְנִפְקְחוּ[5] *in the day of your eating, then shall be, etc.*

   c. וּפִילַגְשׁוֹ....וַתֵּלֶד גַם הוּא[6] *and his concubine, she also bare.*

3. וַתִּרְאֵהוּ אֶת הַיֶּלֶד[7] *and she saw him, the boy.*

   אָנֹכִי נָתַן לָהֶם לִבְנֵי יִשְׂ[8] *I give to them, the children of Israel.*

4. a. וָאִמָּלְטָה רַק אֲנִי[9] *and I only am escaped.*　　　[own enemies.

   b. בִּי אָנִי[10] *in me;* בְּכַפּוֹ גַם הוּא[11] *in his mouth also;* אֹיְבִי לִי[12] *mine*

5. a. צֶדֶק צֶדֶק תִּרְדֹּף[13] *that which is altogether righteous thou shalt, etc.*

   אֶרֶץ אֶרֶץ אֶרֶץ שִׁמְעִי[14] *O earth, earth, earth, hear.*

   b. לֹא כִּי קָנוֹ אֶקְנֶה מֵאוֹתְךָ[15] *nay, but I will buy from thee.*

   הָקֵם הֵקִימוּ אֶת הַשֹּׁמְרִים[16] *they had but just set the watch.*

   הֲמָלֹךְ תִּמְלֹךְ[17] *wilt thou actually reign?*

   אָמַרְתִּי יָצֹא יֵצֵא[18] *I thought he will certainly go out.*

6. הֲדָם הוּא[19] *the blood itself;* אֲדֹנָי הוּא[20] *the Lord himself.*

7. לֶךְ לְךָ[21] *get thee;* נָס לוֹ[22] *he betook himself to flight.*

---

[1] 1 Sam. 17:37.	[7] Ex. 2:6.	[13] Deut. 16:20.	[18] 2 Kgs. 5:11.
[2] 1 Sam. 17:36.	[8] Josh. 1:2.	[14] Jer. 22:29.	[19] Lev. 17:11.
[3] Gen. 41:17.	[9] Job 1:15.	[15] 2 Sam. 24:24.	[20] Isa. 7:14.
[4] Gen. 47:21.	[10] 1 Sam. 25:24.	[16] Judg. 7:19.	[21] Gen. 12:1.
[5] Gen. 3:5.	[11] 2 Sam. 17:5.	[17] Gen. 37:8.	[22] Isa. 31:8.
[6] Gen. 22:24.	[12] Ps. 27:2.		

The language has various methods of marking emphasis, some of which have already been treated in other connections. The more important may be grouped as follows:

1. The word to be emphasized is placed, out of the usual order, at the head of its clause (§ 38. 3).

2. The word or phrase is placed independently at the beginning, without grammatical connection with what follows, and is afterwards resumed

    a. By a pronoun or another noun.[a]

    b. By Wāw, either conjunctive (rare) or consecutive (with Perfect or Imperfect).[b]

    c. By both Wāw and a pronoun.

3. The idea is expressed first by a pronoun and then by a noun.[c]

4. When a pronoun is to be emphasized, it is repeated either in the form of a separate pronoun, or of a pronominal suffix.[d]

5. *a.* The word, a noun, is simply repeated, sometimes twice.[e,f]

    b. The word, a verb, is written twice; once (generally first) in the form of the Infinitive absolute; a usage (§ 28. 3) found in the expression of (1) antithetic, (2) restrictive, (3) emphatic interrogative, and (4) emphatic declarative sentences.

6. The word to be emphasized is followed by the pronoun הוא (not ההוא = *that*, or *the same*), in the sense of αὐτός, *ipse*.

7. The use of the "ethical" dative marks the action as of special importance to the agent.[g]

REMARKS.

(*a*) See § 7. 1-4.

(*b*) See § 25. 2. *d*.

(*c*) This is rare and confined mostly to later writers.

(*d*) See § 11. 1. *a.*; in later writers, however, this construction does not seem to be especially emphatic.

(*e*) Note the repetition of series of words in Ex. 28:34; Num. 17:21; Hos. 8:11; Ezek. 1:20,21; Isa. 53:7; Zech. 12:12-14.

(*f*) See also § 6. 3. *a.*

(*g*) "This mode of expression indicates a special partition in the action by the agent or speaker, a certain earnestness or zeal with which he acts; it occurs as an expression of heartiness more in the diffuse and easy-going popular style, both in poetry and unimpassioned prose."*

REFERENCES FOR STUDY.

* *Ewald*, Hebrew Syntax, 173.

40. AGREEMENT OF NUMBER AND GENDER.

1. ‏הארץ היתה תהו ובהו‏[1] *the earth was a waste and an emptiness.*

‏פקודי י' ישרים‏[2] *the statutes of Y. are right.*

2. *a.* ‏ותהי שם המגפה גדולה‏[3] *and the slaughter there was great.*

‏ותפקחנה עיני שניהם‏[4] *and the eyes of both of them were opened.*

‏היו אנשים נכלמים‏[5] *the men were ashamed.*

b. ‏בא עליך רעה‏[6] *there comes upon thee evil.*

‏לא יסג כלמות‏[7] *reproaches do not depart.*

‏ישר משפטיך‏[8] *right are thy judgments.*

‏חזק ממנו המלחמה‏[9] *the war was too strong for him.*

3. ‏עיני תראינה‏[10] *my eyes shall see.*

‏ידיכם דמים מלאו‏[11] *your hands are full of blood.*

The general principles of agreement may be reduced to three :

1. When the *subject* precedes, the predicate agrees with it in gender and number.[a]

2. When the *predicate* precedes, two constructions are possible :

a. The predicate may agree with the subject in gender and number ; or,

b. The predicate may assume the *primary form*, viz., third masculine singular, whatever be the number or gender of the following subject.[b]

3. When the subject is *dual*, the predicate generally stands in the plural (though sometimes in the feminine singular.)[c]

[1] Gen. 1:2.	[4] Gen. 3:7.	[7] Mic. 2:6.	[10] Mic. 7:10.
[2] Ps. 19:9.	[5] 1 Chron. 19:5.	[8] Ps. 119:137.	[11] Is. 1:15.
[3] 2 Sam. 18:7.	[6] Is. 47:11.	[9] 2 Kgs. 3:26.	

4. *a.* עלתה ארמנותיה סירים[1] *her palaces grow up with thorns.*

תשטף ספיחיה[2] *its floods wash away.*

בהמות שדה תערוג[3] *the beasts of the field pine.*

תתחדש נעוריכי[4] *thy youth is renewed.*

b. ויראו איש ישראל[5] *and the men of Israel saw.*

בית שמש קצרים[6] *(men) of Beth-shemesh were reaping.*

כי תקראנה מלחמה[7] *when wars arise.*

כל הארץ בוכים[8] *the whole land was weeping.*

5. *a* ויהיו כל ימי אדם[9] *and all the days of Adam were.*

ותשא כל העדה[10] *and all the congregation lifted up.*

b. קול דמי אחיך צעקים[11] *hark! thy brother's blood crieth out.*

קול צפיך נשאו קול[12] *hark! thy watchers lift up the voice.*

c. רב שנים ידיעו חכמה[13] *multitude of years shall teach wisdom.*

קשת גבורים חתים[14] *the bow of the strong is broken.*

עיני גבהות אדם שפל[15] *the eyes of man's pride are cast down*

6. ויבוא נח ובניו[16] *and there went in Noah and his sons.*

ותדבר מרים ואהרן[17] *and there spoke Miriam and Aaron.*

מתו שאול ובניו[18] *Saul and his sons died.*   [pursued.

ויואב ואבישי אחיו רדף[19] *and Joab and Abishai his brother*

7. *a* מברכיך ברוך[20] *blessed be (every one of) those who bless thee.* [death.

מחלליה יומת[21] *(any one of) those who profane it shall be put to*

b שוררי...אין בפיהו נכונה קרבם הוות[22] *my enemies, there is no faithfulness in his mouth, their inward part (is) depths.*

בפיו יברכו ובקרבם יקללו[23] *with his mouth they bless, but they curse inwardly.*

c. ונשא נס לגוים ושרק לו[24] *and he will lift up his banner to the nations and will hiss to it.*

d. אקים את סכת ד'....פרציהן והרסתיו אקים ובניתיה[25] *I will raise up the tabernacle (f.) of David and close up their (f.) breaches, and his ruins I will raise up and I will build her.*

---

1 Is. 34:13.	8 2 Sam. 15:23.	15 Is. 2:11.	21 Exod. 31:14.
2 Job 14:19.	9 Gen. 5:5.	16 Gen. 7:7.	22 Ps. 5:9,10.
3 Joel 1:20.	10 Num. 14:1.	17 Num. 12:1.	23 Ps. 62:5.
4 Ps. 103:5.	11 Gen. 4:10.	18 1 Sam. 31:7.	24 Is. 5:26.
5 Jud. 9:55.	12 Is. 52:8.	19 2 Sam. 20:10.	25 Amos. 9:11.
6 1 Sam. 6:13.	13 Job 32:7.	20 Num. 24:9.	
7 Exod. 1:10.	14 1 Sam. 2:4.		

The exceptions to the general principles given above, arising from an adherence to the *sense* rather than the *form*, may be classified as follows :

4. *a.* The predicate may be *feminine singular* when the subject, designating *lifeless objects, animals, members of the body, abstract ideas* (see under § **2.** 2. *b, c.*) is *plural.*[d]

b. The predicate may be *plural*, when the subject is a collective noun, though *singular.*[e]

5. When the subject is a nominative in the construct relation with a genitive,

a. The predicate always agrees with the genitive, if the nominative is כֹּל *all.*

b. The predicate often agrees with the genitive, if the nominative is קוֹל *voice.*

c. The predicate in poetry may agree with the genitive whenever it is desired to lay upon it special emphasis.[f,g]

6. When the subject consists of two or more nouns joined by וְ, whether preceding or following the predicate, the latter may agree with one and be understood with the other, or may be in the plural and thus agree with them taken together.

7. There is frequently found change from one number to the other; here belong

a. Cases in which an individual subject is generalized or the opposite.

b. Cases in which both individualizing and, later, generalizing take place.

c. Cases in which, after speaking of a multitude, the writer suddenly limits himself to one of that number.

d. Cases in which several changes take place in the same verse, which may only be explained by supposing a desire for variety, or by special considerations characteristic of that verse.

REMARKS.

(a) Cf., however, (1) Isa. 21:2; Gen. 35:26; Hos. 10:6; where what seems to be a subject, with which the predicate though following does not agree, is really an accusative with a passive verb; and (2) Gen. 4:7; Eccl. 2:7 (cf. 1 Kgs. 2:21), etc., in which the predicate, disagreeing with its subject, is a participle used as a substantive.

(b) The adjective will then be singular masculine; though the number of instances in which the adjective follows this usage is not proportionately so great as in the case of the verb.

(c) Cf. עֵינָיו קָמָה (1 Sam. 4:15).

(d) Here the feminine is treated as neuter; cf. the Greek construction, according to which a neuter plural subject takes a singular predicate.

(e) On the use of the plural of אדון, בעל (Ex. 21:29), etc., see § 3. 2. c.

(f) This is the principle everywhere operating when the nominative is a numeral (3 to 10, 100, 1000) in the construct.

(g) Cf. also the use of מבחר in Ex. 15:4.

REFERENCES FOR STUDY.

V. Kinds of Sentences.

41. NEGATIVE SENTENCES.

1. *a.* (1) עוֹד אֵלָיו שׁוּב יָסְפָה וְלֹא[1] *and she returned unto him no more.*

עוֹד בָּשָׂר כָּל יִכָּרֵת לֹא[2] *all flesh shall not again be cut off.*

(2) תִּגְנֹב לֹא....תִּרְצָח לֹא[3] *thou shalt do no murder...thou shalt not steal.*

b. לִי אוֹיְבַי יַעַלְצוּ אַל אֵבוֹשָׁה אַל[4] *let me not be ashamed, let not my enemies triumph over me.*

מְרִיבָה תְהִי נָא אַל[5] *pray, let there be no strife.*

עוֹד אֵלַי דַּבֵּר תּוֹסֶף אַל[6] *speak to me no more.*

c. שְׁלָחָנִי יְהוָה לֹא[7] *(it is) not Y. (but some one else that) sent me.*

2. *a.* יִצְמָח טֶרֶם הַשָּׂדֶה עֵשֶׂב כָּל[8] *no herb of the field had yet, etc.*

b. תֶחֱטָאוּ לְבִלְתִּי[9] *in order that ye may not sin.*

c. נִרְאָה אֶבֶן אֵין[10] *no stone was seen.*

d. לוֹ הִגִּיד בְּלִי עַל[11] *because he did not make known to him.*

e. יִמּוֹט בַּל לְעוֹלָם צַדִּיק[12] *the righteous shall never be removed.*

מָנַעְתָּ בַּל שׂ׳ שׁ׳ אֲרֶשֶׁת[13] *the desire of his life thou hast not withheld.*

אָרֶץ וְיָרְשׁוּ יָקֻמוּ בַל[14] *that they may not rise and possess the land.*

f. אָפֵס יִהְיוּ שָׂרֶיהָ וְכָל[15] *and all her princes were no more.*

1. The most commonly used negatives are לֹא and אַל:

a. לֹא is the *objective,* unconditional negative (= οὐ, οὐκ), and is used,

　(1) with the Perf. and Impf. (Indicative) in ordinary declarative sentences;[a]

　(2) with the Imperfect in prohibitory sentences.

b. אַל is the *subjective,* dependent negative, and is used with the Imperfect (Jussive), to express dissuasion, deprecation.[b]

c. The position of לֹא and אַל is immediately before the predicate; but they may stand also before another word when that particular word is to be specially emphasized.[c,d]

---

[1] Gen. 8:12.　　[5] Gen. 13:8.　　[9] Ex. 20:20.　　[13] Ps. 21:3.
[2] Gen. 9:11.　　[6] Deut. 3:26.　　[10] 1 Kgs. 6:18.　　[14] Isa. 14:21.
[3] Ex. 20:14.　　[7] Num. 16:29.　　[11] Gen. 31:20.　　[15] Isa. 34:12.
[4] Ps. 25:2.　　[8] Gen. 2:5.　　[12] Prov. 10:30.

2. With the *Perfect and Imperfect* there are found, besides לֹא and אַל, also the following negatives:

a. טֶרֶם *not yet*, sometimes with the Perfect, but more often with the Imperfect in a past sense (cf. § **20. 1.** *b*).

b. לְבִלְתִּי[e] *in order that....not*, very rare, and with an ellipsis of אֲשֶׁר.

c. אַיִן *nothing, there is not;* with this negative the verbal form is generally a Participle (§ **45. 3**); but rarely a finite form is found.

d. בְּלִי[e] *not* (cf. בִּלְתִּי), generally after a preposition, but in poetry also alone in the sense of לֹא.

e. בַּל *not*, shorter form of בְּלִי, found only in poetry, and not different from לֹא.

f. אֶפֶס *no more;* like אַיִן, originally a noun; its more common use is to indicate restriction, limitation.

3. אֵינֶנּוּ שֹׁמֵעַ[1] *he is not hearing;* אֵינֶנִּי נֹתֵן[2] *I do not give.*
אֵין שַׂר בֵּית הַסֹּהַר רֹאֶה אֶת כָּל מְאוּמָה[3] *the keeper of the prison looked not to anything.*
וְתֶבֶן אֵין נִתָּן[4] *straw is not given.*

4. *a.* לִשְׁמֹר וּלְבִלְתִּי סוּר[5] *to keep...and not to turn aside.* [eat from it.
אֲשֶׁר צִוִּיתִיךָ לְבִלְתִּי אֲכָל מִמֶּנּוּ[6] *which I commanded thee not to*

b. אֵין עִמְּךָ לְהִתְיַצֵּב[7] *it is not possible to stand before thee.*
אֵין עֲרָךְ אֵלֶיךָ[8] *there is no comparing unto thee.*

c. בְּלֹא רְאוּת[9] *without seeing.*

d. מֵעֲבֹר[10] *that they go not over;* מֵרְאוֹת[11] *that he could not see.*

5. *a.* עַם נָבָל וְלֹא חָכָם[12] *a people foolish and unwise.*
לֹא עֵץ[14] *a no-wood.* לֹא אֱלֹהִים[13] *a no-god;*

b. עֲצוּמִים וְאֵין מִסְפָּר[15] *strong and without number.*
אֵין אִישׁ[16] *there is no man at all;* אֵין יוֹסֵף[17] *Joseph is gone.*
אָדָם אֵין צַדִּיק[18] *no man whatever is just.*

c. מַכַּת בִּלְתִּי סָרָה[19] *chastisement without ceasing.*   [of Gideon.
אֵין זֹאת בִּלְתִּי אִם חֶרֶב גִּדְעוֹן[20] *this is no other than the sword*

---

1 Jer. 7:16.   8 Ps. 40:6.   14 Isa. 10:15.
2 Ex. 5:10.   9 Num. 35:23.   15 Joel 1:6.
3 Gen. 39:23.   10 Num. 32:7.   16 Gen. 31:50.
4 Ex. 5:16.   11 Gen. 27:1.   17 Gen. 37:29.
5 Deut. 17:19,20.   12 Deut. 32:6.   18 Eccl. 7:20.
6 Gen. 3:11.   13 Deut. 32:21.   19 Is. 14:6.
7 2 Chron. 20:6.   20 Judg. 7:14.

d. יִשְׂגֶּה אָחוּ בְלִי מָיִם[1] *can the reed-grass grow without water ?*

מִגּוֹי[2] *so as not to be a nation;* מִמֶּלֶךְ[3] *so as not to be king.*

3. With the *participle* אֵין is used almost exclusively; this is in accordance with the original use of אֵין as a negative of substantives (see 5. below), and with the nominal nature of אֵין itself, which is never lost. This combination furnishes the prevailing form for expressing a negative present, though not of course restricted to this use.*f*

4. With the *infinitive* there are found,

    a. בִּלְתִּי with the preposition לְ, the usual negative of the Inf.

    b. אֵין לְ and אֵין, but only in late writers.

    c. בְּלֹא *without,* with the force of a preposition.

    d. מִן *from, so as not, lest,* after verbs which imply *restraint, hin-drance,* etc.

5. With *nouns* there are found, ·

    a. לֹא, which gives an opposite meaning, like *un-, in-, im-;* this usage occurs in the case of substantives as well as of adjectives.

    b. אֵין (cf. 3. above), equivalent to *without,* or *un-, in-, im-.*

    c. בְּלֹא = בִּלְתִּי, *without, except.*

    d. בְּלִי *without, un-, in-.*

    e. מִן *so as not to be,* the Inf. הֱיוֹת being supplied in thought.

6. אֵין כֶּסֶף לֹא נֶחְשָׁב לִמְאוּמָה[4] *silver was not at all regarded for anything* (cf. ch. 9:20).

מֵאֵין יֹשֵׁב[5] *without* (= *so that there is*) *no inhabitant.*

הֲמִבְּלִי אֵין אֱ' בְּיִשְׂרָאֵל[6] *is it because there is no god in Israel ?*

7. לֹא בְמוֹתוֹ יִקַּח הַכֹּל[7] *he will take nothing in his death.*

לֹא יוּמַת אִישׁ בַּיּוֹם הַזֶּה[8] *no man shall be put to death this day.*

8. אַל תַּרְבּוּ....יֵצֵא עָתָק[9] *multiply not....let no arrogance go forth.*

לֹא לָנֶצַח יִשָּׁכַח....תֹּאבַד[10] *not forever shall be forgotten....shall perish.*

6. More than one negative is sometimes employed in order to intensify the negative. This occurs chiefly in the case of מִן with אֵין or בְּלִי, and seldom with the more common negatives.

7. To express *nothing, no one,* the negative is combined with כֹּל or אִישׁ.*h* (§ 14. 2. *d.*)

---

1 Job 8:12.   4 1 Kgs. 10:21.   7 Ps. 49:18.   9 1 Sam. 2:3.

2 Jer. 48:2.   5 Isa. 5:9.   8 1 Sam. 11:13.   10 Ps. 9:19.

3 1 Sam. 15:23.   6 2 Kgs. 1:3.

8. In the case of two successive negative sentences, especially when, as in poetry, they are parallel, the negative may be omitted from the second, the influence of the first being deemed sufficient.

REMARKS.

(a) A few cases exist of לֹא with the Jussive, e. g., Gen. 24:8; 1 Sam. 14:36.

(b) On the other hand אַל is thought by some to stand occasionally in a declarative sentence, e. g., Ps. 41:3; 50:3; Jer. 14:17, though with a stronger force than would have been conveyed by לֹא.

(c) For the use of לֹא and אַל, without a verb, 1 Kgs. 2:30; 11:22; Gen. 19:18; Ruth 1:13.

(d) לֹא cannot stand before a Participle (when used as a verb), an Infinitive absolute, or an Infinitive construct. Note cases in which, through the influence of לֹא, a Participle passes into a finite verb, Ex. 9:20,21; 13:21,22; 1 Sam. 1:13; 2 Sam. 3:34; Hos. 1:6; Ps. 37:21.

(e) The י of בִּלְתִּי and בְּלִי is the old archaic genitive ending.

(f) For cases in which this combination is used of the past, see Gen. 39:23; Jer. 32:33; of the future, Jer 37:14.

(g) Cf. זוּלָתִי, which is used particularly before a single word; בִּלְתִּי, before a proposition.

(h) It is only when כָּל = omnis that this combination may be found; when כָּל = totus, the לֹא negatives the idea of wholeness.

REFERENCES FOR STUDY.

42. INTERROGATIVE SENTENCES.

1. ‏זֶה חַסְדְּךָ אֶת רֵעֶךָ‏ [1] *is this thy kindness to thy friend?* [Y.

‏גַם בְּעֵינַי יִפָּלֵא נְאֻם יְ‏ [2] *shall it also be marvelous in my eyes? saith*

‏כִּי לֹא כֵן בֵּיתִי עִם אֵל‏ [3] *for is not my house so with God?*

2. *a.* ‏הֲתֵלְכִי עִם הָאִישׁ הַזֶּה‏ [4] *wilt thou go with this man?*

‏הֲשָׁלוֹם אֲבִיכֶם‏ [5] *is your father well?* [house?

b. ‏הֲנִגְלֹה נִגְלֵיתִי אֶל בֵּית אָבִיךָ‏ [6] *did I plainly appear to thy father's*

c. ‏הֲשֹׁמֵר אָחִי אָנֹכִי‏ [7] *am I my brother's keeper?*

‏הַאַתָּה תִּבְנֶה לִּי בַיִת‏ [8] *wilt thou build me a house?* (cf. 1 Chr. 17:4).

d. ‏לִרְאוֹת הֲקַלּוּ הַמָּיִם‏ [9] *to see whether the waters had abated.*

3. ‏הֲלוֹא אִם תֵּיטִיב שְׂאֵת‏ [10] *is there not a lifting up, if thou doest well?*

‏הֲלֹא זֶה הַדָּבָר אֲשֶׁר דִּבַּרְנוּ‏ [11] *is not this the thing which we told thee?*

4. *a.* ‏הֲנֵלֵךְ אֶל רָ׳ גִּ׳ אִם נֶחְדָּל‏ [12] *shall we go to Ramoth-gilead, or shall*
we forbear? [heard?

‏הֲלוֹא יָדַעְתָּ אִם לֹא שָׁמַעְתָּ‏ [13] *hast thou not known, or hast thou not*

b. ‏דִּרְשׁוּ....אִם אֶחְיֶה‏ [14] *enquire....if I shall recover.*

‏נִרְאֶה אִם פָּרְחָה הַגֶּפֶן‏ [15] *let us see whether the vine has budded.*

1. A sentence is sometimes found to be interrogative, though lacking an interrogative particle. In such cases the arrangement of the words, or the tone of voice in the pronunciation of the sentence, was sufficient to indicate the interrogative force.[a]

2. The interrogative particle ‏הֲ‏ (Lat. *an*, Greek *ἦ*) is employed[b]

a. In questions, the answer to which is entirely doubtful.

b. In questions which are equivalent to a strong affirmative assertion.

c. In questions equivalent to denial, or which call for a negative reply.

d. In indirect questions, equivalent to *whether.*

3. The interrogative particle ‏הֲלֹא‏ (Lat. *nonne*) is employed when it is certain that an affirmative answer is expected.[c]

4. The interrogative particle ‏אִם‏ (strictly *if*) is employed,

a. To introduce the second member of a double interrogative sentence; here the compound form ‏וְאִם‏ (cf. *sive*) is more common.[d]

b. To introduce an indirect question depending upon some preceding thought (cf. the use of ‏הֲ‏ above).[e]

---

[1] 2 Sam. 16:17.
[2] Zech. 8:6.
[3] 2 Sam. 23:5.
[4] Gen. 24:58.
[5] Gen. 43:27.
[6] 1 Sam. 2:27.
[7] Gen. 4:9.
[8] 2 Sam. 7:5.
[9] Gen. 8:8.
[10] Gen. 4:7.
[11] Ex. 14:12.
[12] 1 Kgs. 22:15.
[13] Isa. 40:28.
[14] 2 Kgs. 1:2.
[15] Cant. 7:13.

5. *a.* (1) מִי הַמַּחֲנֶה[1] *who is (what persons are in) the camp?* מִי שְׁמֶךָ[2]
who is thy name?

   (2) מִי הוּא זֶה מֶלֶךְ הַכָּבוֹד[3] *who then is the king of glory?*

   (3) מִי יַשְׁקֵנִי מַיִם[4] *who will (O that some one would) give me,* etc.

b. (1) מָה אֵלֶּה[5] *what (= of what kind or character) are these?*

   (2) מַה תְּרִיבוּן עִמָּדִי[6] *wherefore do ye strive with me?*

   (3) מַה יִּצְדַּק אֱנוֹשׁ עִם אֵל[7] *how can a man be just with God?*

   (4) מַה לָּנוּ חֵלֶק בְּדָוִד[8] *we have no portion in D.* (cf. 2 Sam. 20:1).

   (5) מַה לָּכֶם תְּדַכְּאוּ עַמִּי[9] *what mean ye (that) ye crush my people?*

c. אֵי זֶה הַדֶּרֶךְ הָלָךְ[10] *which way did he go?*   [*house also?*

6. *a.* מָתַי אֶעֱשֶׂה גַם אָ' לְבֵיתִי[11] *when shall I provide for mine own*

b. כַּמָּה יְמֵי שְׁנֵי חַיֶּיךָ[12] *how many are the days of the years of thy life?*

c. אֵיכָה נֵדַע אֶת הַדָּבָר[13] *how shall we know the word,* etc.? [*you?*

   אֵיכָה אֶשָּׂא לְבַדִּי טָרְחֲכֶם[14] *how can I alone bear the burden of*

   אֵיכָה הָיְתָה לְזוֹנָה קִ' נ'[15] *how hath the faithful city become a*
harlot!

d. לָמָּה תַכֶּה רֵעֶךָ[16] *why smitest thou thy fellow?*

   לָמָּה רָגְשׁוּ גוֹיִם[17] *why have the nations raged?*

e. מַדּוּעַ מִהַרְתֶּן בֹּא הַיּוֹם[18] *why have ye come so soon to-day?*

   מַדּוּעַ פְּנֵיכֶם רָעִים הַיּוֹם[19] *why are your countenances sad to-day?*

   5. In reference to interrogative pronouns the following points in addition to what has been said may be noted :

    a. מִי *who?*

      (1) always refers to *persons*, whatever may be the particular phraseology of the sentence ;

      (2) is frequently followed by הוּא or זֶה, and the sentence thus rendered more vivid and pointed ;

      (3) is employed in conveying an optative idea.

    b. מָה *what?*

      (1) always refers to the nature or character of an object, and the object *may*, of course, be a person.

      (2) introduces an expression of reproach or blame, and may be rendered *wherefore?*

1 Gen. 33:8.   6 Ex. 17:2.   11 Gen. 30:30.   16 Ex. 2:13.
2 Judg. 13:17.   7 Job 9:2.   12 Gen. 47:8.   17 Ps. 2:1.
3 Ps. 24:10.   8 1 Kgs. 12:16.   13 Deut. 18:21.   18 Ex. 2:18.
4 2 Sam. 23:15.   9 Isa. 3:15.   14 Deut. 1:12.   19 Gen. 40:7.
5 Zech. 1:9; 4:4,13.   10 1 Kgs. 13:12.   15 Isa. 1:21.

(3) introduces an objection, or an interrogation implying impossibility, and may be rendered by *how?*

(4) has come in a few cases to be equivalent to a negative, and may be rendered *not.*

(5) with לְךָ or לָכֶם, is used in expressions of strong reproof.

c. אֵי־זֶה *which?* differs from מִי and מָה in being an adjective, though always preceding the noun which it modifies.

6. Aside from interrogative particles and interrogative pronouns, there are many interrogative adverbs. Among others may be noted:

a. מָתַי *when?* sometimes compounded with לְ and עַד

b. כַּמָּה *how much? how long?*

c. אֵיכָה *how?* used to inquire as to the *manner* in which a given event is to take place; and also to introduce an expression equivalent to a negative, and to express wonder, lamentation.

d. לָמָה *wherefore, why?* used to ask for the *purpose* or *aim* of an action.

e. מַדּוּעַ (for מַה־יָדוּעַ, cf. τί μαθών), *why?* used to ask for the *ground* or *cause* of an action.

REMARKS.

(a) This is seen especially in questions arising from great emotion or anxiety, e. g., 1 Sam. 16:4; 2 Sam. 18:29; 2 Sam. 19:23; and also in questions which are connected by וְ, and are in antithesis with a preceding declarative statement, e. g., Judg. 11:23; Jon. 4:10,11; Job 10:8,9.

(b) In some cases הֲ is dropped for euphonic reasons from before words beginning with א or ה, e. g., Gen. 18:12; 1 Sam. 22:15; 2 Sam. 19:23; 1 Kgs. 1:24.

(c) For cases of הֲכִי *is it . . . that?* see Gen. 27:36; 29:15; 2 Sam. 9:1; 23:19.

(d) Here הֲ also may be used, e. g., Judg. 14:15.

(e) אִם is still further used after a preceding declarative statement in the sense of *or.*

REFERENCES FOR STUDY.

43. EXCLAMATORY AND OPTATIVE SENTENCES.

1. *a.* הַמֶּלֶךְ[1] *O king!* אֶרֶץ[2] *O earth!* הֲפָכְכֶם[3] *your perverseness!*
כֻּלָּם[4] *you all.*

b. בִּי אֲדֹנִי[5] *O my lord!* הוֹי הַשַּׁאֲנַנִּים[6] *O they who are at ease in*
Zion! אֲהָהּ לַיּוֹם[7] *alas for the day!*

2. *a.* שָׁלוֹם לָכֶם[8] *peace be to you!* בָּרוּךְ אַבְרָם[9] *blessed be Abram.*

b. חַי אָנִי[10] *as I live!* חַי יְהוָה[11] *as Yahweh liveth!*
עֵינֶיךָ הָרֹאוֹת[12] *by thine eyes which see!* אֵת הַדָּבָר[13] *by the word!*

c. חָלִילָה לְּךָ מֵעֲשֹׂת וגו״[14] *far be it from thee to do, etc.*

d. כְּצִדְקִי וּכְתֻמִּי עָלַי[15] *according to my righteousness and my integ-*
rity, upon me!   [*thee!*

3. *a.* לוּ יִשְׁמָעֵאל יִחְיֶה לְפָנֶיךָ[16] *would that Ishmael might live before*
לוּ שְׁמָעֵנִי[17] *O hear me!* לוּ מַתְנוּ[18] *O that we had died!* [*God!*

b. אִם תִּקְטֹל אֱלוֹהַּ רָשָׁע[19] *if thou wouldest but kill the wicked, O*

c. מִי יַשְׁקֵנִי מַיִם[20] *O that some one would give me water to drink.*
מִי יִתֵּן מוּתֵנוּ בְיַד י׳[21] *O that we had died by the hand of Y.*

1. In exclamations there occurs

a. A noun, with or without the article ;[a,b] or

b. A noun with an interjection, e. g., בִּי (with אֲדֹנִי), הוֹי, or
אֲהָהּ (with the dative).[c]

2. Under the head of exclamatory utterance may be classified also

a. Clauses or sentences which have no mark of exclamation.

b. The use of חַי in oaths, and certain other rare expressions (see
examples).

c. The common expression חָלִילָה *to the profane,* i. e., *far be it.*

d. Sentences which, for brevity and force, omit the verb *to be.*[d]

---

1 1 Sam. 23:20.	7 Joel 1:15.	12 Deut. 3:21.	17 Gen. 23:13.
2 Job 16:18.	8 Gen. 43:23.	13 Hag. 2:5.	18 Num. 14:2.
3 Isa. 29:16.	9 Gen. 14:19.	14 Gen. 18:25.	19 Ps. 139:19.
4 Job 17:10.	10 Num. 14:28.	15 Ps. 7:9.	20 2 Sam. 23:15.
5 Gen. 43:20.	11 1 Sam. 14:45.	16 Gen. 17:18.	21 Ex. 16:3.
6 Amos 6:1.			

3. In optative expressions there are found

   a. The particle לוּ *if, would that,* used with the Imperfect and Imperative, and, in wishes which cannot be realized, with the Perfect.

   b. The particle אִם *if,* cf. לוּ.

   c. The interrogative מִי with the Imperfect; and especially מִי יִתֵּן *who would give = would that.*[e]

REMARKS.

(*a*) The *distinctive* article (§ 4. 3. *e.* (2)) is generally employed in prose.

(*b*) Originally in exclamations the third person only was used; in the later writers the second begins to be employed.

(*c*) Here also belong words or expressions used in swearing, however introduced.

(*d*) It should not be forgotten that the Infinitive absolute is used in exclamatory style "(1) when the speaker is too full of his subject to mention the action in any other than an ejaculatory manner, and as briefly as possible, e. g., 2 Kgs. 4:43; Job 40:2; (2) in a kind of vehement and rapid description of a number of actions that excite astonishment or displeasure, e. g., Hos. 4:2; Isa. 21:5."* (Cf. § 28. 5.)

(*e*) מִי יִתֵּן is followed (1) by a verb with or without Wāw Consecutive, (2) by an Infinitive, (3) by a noun.

REFERENCES FOR STUDY.

Gen. 18:25; 44:7,17	2*c.*	Jer. 22:24	2*b.*
Gen. 30:34	3*a.*	Amos 5:18	1*b.*
Gen. 43:20; 44:18	1*b.*	Mic. 2:1	1*b.*
Num. 20:3	3*a.*	Ps. 4:7; 14:7; 55:7	3*c.*
Deut. 4:3; 11:7; 32:40	2*b.*	Ps. 45:2*c*; 57:6	2*d.*
Deut. 5:26; 28:67	3*c.*	Ps. 81:9; 139:19	3*b.*
Judg. 9:29	3*c.*	Ps. 81:14	3*a.*
1 Sam. 30:23	2*b.*	Prov. 24:11	3*b.*
2 Sam. 15:4	3*c.*	Job 6:8; 11:5; 13:5; 14:13; 29:2; 31:35	3*c.*
Isa. 3:6	2*d.*	Job 6:14; 12:5	2*d.*
Isa. 63:19b	3*a.*		

44. COPULATIVE SENTENCES.

1. *a.* "וַיִּקְרָא לַיַּבָּ' אֶרֶץ וּלְמִקְוֵה הַמַּיִם וגו'[1] *and he called the dry land earth, but the collection of waters he called seas.*   [not eat.

וּמֵעֵץ הַדַּעַת לֹא תֹאכַל[2] *but of the tree of knowledge thou shalt*

   b. כִּי אָדָם לְעָמָל יוּלָּד וּבְנֵי רֶשֶׁף יַגְבִּיהוּ עוּף[3] *but man is born to trouble as the sparks fly upward.*   [bullock.

   c. קַח אֶת פַּר הַשּׁוֹר....וּפַר הַשֵּׁנִי[4] *take the bullock, even the second*

הֲלֹא אֲנִי מַחְשֶׁה וּמֵעוֹלָם[5] *am I not silent, and that from of old?*

   d. יְרֵא אֱ' אַתָּה וְלֹא חָשַׂכְתָּ[6] *thou fearest God, and (=for) thou hast not withheld.*

---

1 Gen. 1:10.   3 Job 5:7.   5 Isa. 57:11.   6 Gen. 22:12.
2 Gen. 2:17.   4 Judg. 6:25.   * Ewald, *Hebrew Syntax,* pp. 201-203.

2. *a.* בחלומי¹ והנה-גפן לפני *in my dream, (and) behold a vine, etc.*

b. "לא תצא² עוד אתנו למ' ולא תכבה וגו *thou shalt not go out with us henceforth to battle, that thou quench not, etc.*

c. אם זכרתני....ועשית נא....חסד³ *if thou rememberest me, then do kindness, etc.*

3. ויך⁴ את המחנה והמחנה היה בטח *and he smote the camp, while the camp was quiet.*

ויבאו⁵......ולוט ישב בשער סדם *and they came while Lot was sitting in the gate of Sodom.* [*Hezekiah.*

4. *a.* בימי⁶ עזיהו יותם אחז יחז' *in the days of Uzziah, Jotham, Ahaz,*

b. בשר⁷ בנפשו דמו לא תאכלו *flesh in its soul, viz., its blood ye shall not eat.*

נקתה⁸ לארץ תשב *she shall be desolate, sit upon the earth.*

c. קדשו⁹ צום קראו עצרה אספו זקנים *sanctify a fast, call an assembly, gather the old men.*

d ותשמע¹⁰....את קול הרצין העם *and she heard the noise of the guard, the people.*

1. The conjunction ו *and* is by far the most common copulative conjunction, and serves to join together not only words but sentences.[a,b] It is universally employed except in cases where special emphasis is to be placed upon the conjunctive relation?[c] But besides its ordinary use as a connective it serves to join to a preceding clause or sentence

a. An *antithetical* clause (here rendered *but*), in which, however, the opposition is indicated not by the ו, but by the arrangement of the words, or by the logical relation of the clauses thus joined.[d]

b. A clause of *comparison* (here rendered *as*), peculiar to poetical style.

c. An *epexegetical* clause (here rendered *even, namely, and that too*), furnishing a more detailed explanation.

d. A clause of *consequence* or *cause* (here rendered *for, since*).[e]

2. Another class of usages in which ו may be called *demonstrative* includes the following:

a. Cases in which the ו follows a prepositional phrase and, in the sense of *then*, connects with it some act or state.

---

1 Gen. 40:9.
2 2 Sam. 21:17.
3 Gen. 40:14.

4 Judg. 8:11.
5 Gen. 19:1.
6 Isa. 1:1.

7 Gen. 9:4.
8 Isa. 3:26.

9 Joel 1:14.
10 2 Kgs. 11:13.

b. Cases in which the ן, with an Imperfect or Imperative, expresses *purpose* or *result* (§ **26.** 2*a*).

c. Cases in which the ן joins an apodosis to a preceding protasis, not only in conditional but also in causal and relative sentences.ᶠ

3. Still another usage of ן is that occurring in circumstantial clauses (§ **45.**), when it is translated *while, although, after*, etc.

4. Omission of ן (asyndeton), where it might be expected, is found

a. In lists, enumerations, etc.

b. In expressions added by way of explanation or correction.

c. In a climax, or in highly rhetorical statements.

d. In hurried, abrupt discourse, or where the rapidity of the action is to be emphasized.ᵍ

REMARKS.

(*a*) For examples in which ן has the force of *with*, see Gen. 3:24; Judg. 6:5; 1 Sam. 18:6; 25:42; 29:10; Isa. 13:9.

(*b*) For cases of hendiadys, see Gen. 1:14; 3:16; 2 Chron. 16:14; Job 10:17.

(*c*) The conjunctions employed when the connection is to be emphasized are אַף, גַם, e. g., 1 Sam. 25:43; 22:7; Exod. 10:25; Isa. 40:24; 41:26.

(*d*) The most common adversative conjunctions are (1) כִּי *but* (after a negative), e. g., Gen. 24:3; 45:8; 1 Kgs. 21:15; Exod. 1:19; Josh. 17:18; Ps. 44:8; (2) כִּי אִם *but if, but*, e. g., Ps. 1:2; Gen. 15:4; Josh. 17:3; 1 Sam. 8:19. Cf. also אַף כִּי = *how much more, how much less*, e. g., 1 Sam. 14:29f.; 1 Kgs. 8:27.

(*e*) Here also belongs the use of ן in exclamations, e. g., Joel 2:23; 2 Sam. 1:21; Jer. 20:12; and in oaths, e. g., Joel 4:20; Amos 9:5; Hos. 12:6; Jer. 29:23; Isa. 51:15; Deut. 32:31; Ps. 71:19 (so Ewald).

(*f*) For the use of Wāw Consecutive with Imperfect and Perfect, see §§ 24, 25.

(*g*) In many stereotyped phrases also ן is dropped, e. g., מדר דר (Exod. 17:16) for מדר ודר.

REFERENCES FOR STUDY.

45. CIRCUMSTANTIAL SENTENCES.

1. *a.* וימת¹....והוא שפט את י' ארבעים שנה *and he died, and he had judged (having judged) Israel forty years.*

אל תאחרו אתי ויהוה הצליח דרכי² *do not delay me, since Y. hath prospered my journey.*

למה תקראנה לי נעמי וי' ענה בי³ *why call ye me Naomi, Y. having testified against me ?*

b. וירא אליו י'....והוא יושב פתח האהל⁴ *and Y. appeared unto him....while he sat before the tent.*

סלם מצב ארצה וראשו מגיע השמימה⁵ *a ladder set up on the earth, the top of it reaching to heaven.*

ותעמדון תחת ההר וההר בער באש⁶ *and ye stood under the mountain, while the mount was burning with fire.*

c. לא יעשה אבי...ולא יגלה את אזני⁷ *my father will do nothing ....without disclosing it to me.*

הלאל ילמד דעת והוא רמים ישפוט⁸ *shall any teach God knowledge, seeing that he judges those that are high ?*

d. היה רעה....והוא נער⁹ *he was tending the sheep....being a boy.*

דברי שלום ורעה בלבבם¹⁰ *who speak peace, while evil is in their heart.*

We frequently find a clause which furnishes material subordinate to that of the principal clause of a sentence; or which describes the condition or circumstances attending the action of the principal verb. Such clauses are termed circumstantial or descriptive and may be considered under the following heads:

1. Circumstantial clauses *following* the principal clause and joined by means of ו (§ **44. 3**),

    a. With the verb in the *Perfect*, especially in sentences which have a pluperfect or perfect meaning, often rendered by the past participle.

    b. With the verb a *Participle*, almost always in clauses which are of a strictly descriptive character.

    c. With the verb in the *Imperfect;* less common than either the Perfect or Participle, and for the most part in negative sentences.ᵃ

    d. With no verbal form of any kind.

---

¹ 1 Sam. 4:18.	⁴ Gen. 18:1.	⁷ 1 Sam. 20:2.	⁹ Gen. 37:2.
² Gen. 24:56.	⁵ Gen. 28:12.	⁸ Job 21:22.	¹⁰ Ps. 28:3.
³ Ruth 1:21.	⁶ Deut. 4:11.		

2. a. ויחפש בגדול החל[1] *and he searched beginning with the eldest.*

כי ימצא חלל...לא נודע מי הכהו[2] *if one shall be found slain, it not being known who hath smitten him.*

b. מאחרי בנשף יין ידליקם[3] *who tarry late at night while wine inflames them.*

יסתירני...בצור ירוממני[4] *he will hide me...lifting me upon a rock.*

c. יצאו נצבים[5] *they went forth, taking their position* (cf. Ex. 33:8).

שבעים מ' בהנות..מקצצים היו מלקטים[6] *seventy kings, having their thumbs and great toes cut off, gathered, etc.*

d. ויט אהלה בית אל מים והעי מקדם[7] *and he pitched his tent, Bethel being on the west and Ai on the east.*　　　　[*his loins.*

ראיתי כל גבר ידיו על חלציו[8] *I saw every man his hands upon*

e. וישבו שלש שנים אין מלחמה[9] *and they remained three years* (in the condition of) *absence of war, i. e., without war.*

לא תראו פני בלתי אחיכם אתכם[10] *ye shall not see my face* (in the condition of) *the absence of your brother, i. e., except your brother be with you.*

ויתקעם בלב אב' עודנו חי[11] *and he thrust them into the heart of Absalom while he was still alive.*

ויהי אך יצא יצא י'....ועשו...בא[12] *and it happened, Jacob having only just gone out, that Esau, his brother, came in.*

ויהי השמש באה ועלטה היה[13] *and it happened, the sun having gone down, that there was darkness.*

והיה אתם תמרדו היום....ומחר....יקצף[14] *and it shall be, seeing ye rebel to-day...., that to-morrow he will be wroth, etc.*

3. a. "ויהי הם מריקים שקיהם והנה וגו'[15] *and it happened, as they were emptying their sacks, that behold, etc.*

b. הוא מוצאת והיא שלחה[16] *she was being brought forth, when she sent, etc.*

"המה עם בית מיכה והמה הכירו וגו'[17] *being by the house of Micah, they recognized the voice, etc.*

---

1 Gen. 44:12.　　6 Judg. 1:7.　　10 Gen. 43:3.　　14 Josh. 22:18.
2 Deut. 21:1.　　7 Gen. 12:8.　　11 2 Sam. 18:14.　　15 Gen. 42:35.
3 Isa. 5:11.　　8 Jer. 30:6.　　12 Gen. 27:30.　　16 Gen. 38:25.
4 Ps. 27:5.　　9 1 Kgs. 22:1.　　13 Gen. 15:17.　　17 Judg. 18:3.
5 Num. 16:27.

2. Circumstantial clauses *following* the principal clause, and not joined by וֹ,

    a. With the verb in the *Perfect* (cf. 1. *a* above).

    b. With the verb in the *Imperfect* (cf. 1. *b* above).

    c. With the verb a *Participle*, to be taken as an accusative of state or condition.[b]

    d. With no verbal form, the clause being strictly nominal.

    e. In expressions introduced by אֵין‎, בְּלִי‎, בִּלְתִּי‎, לֹא‎, etc.[c]

3. Circumstantial clauses *preceding* the principal clause; here arise two cases:

    a. Those in which the circumstantial clause, preceding the principal clause, is introduced and supported by the formula וַיְהִי‎ or וְהָיָה‎ (cf. §§ 24. 4; 25. 4).

    b. Those in which there is no such introductory formula, the two clauses appearing to be coördinate.[d]

REMARKS.

(*a*) Since לֹא‎ may not be used with a Participle, when this negative is to be employed, the finite form must be substituted.

(*b*) That this is really an accusative appears from the corresponding construction in Arabic.

(*c*) In common use these negatives have become equivalent to prepositions.

(*d*) In circumstantial clauses the subject generally stands first whether the predicate is a finite verbal form, a Participle, or a noun; exceptions occur (1) when הִנֵּה‎ or some such emphatic word comes first, which regularly precedes the verb, e. g., Gen. 8:13; 9:7; 1 Sam. 25:14; (2) in the case of לֹא‎, Ps. 44:18; (3) even in sentences without a verb, e. g., Ps. 60:3; Gen. 49:10; Isa. 6:6; Amos 7:7.

REFERENCES FOR STUDY.

46. RELATIVE SENTENCES.

1. *a.* כָּל רֶמֶשׂ אֲשֶׁר הוּא חַי[1] *every creeping thing which is living.*

b. הַנָּבִיא אֲשֶׁר שְׁלָחוֹ יְ'[2] *the prophet whom Y. hath sent.*

c. גּוֹי אֲשֶׁר לֹא תִשְׁמַע לְשֹׁנוֹ[3] *a nation whose language thou dost not understand.*   [come.

יְהוָה אֲשֶׁר בָּאת תַּחַת כְּנָפָיו[4] *Y. under whose wings thou hast*

d. אֲשֶׁר שִׁכַּנְתִּי שְׁמִי שָׁם[5] *where I fixed my name.*

אֲשֶׁר נִשְׁבּוּ שָׁם[6] *whither they were carried away.*

אֲשֶׁר יָצְאוּ מִשָּׁם פְּלִשְׁתִּים[7] *whence the Phil. have proceeded.*

2. *a.* הַמַּיִם אֲשֶׁר מִתַּחַת לָרָקִיעַ[8] *the waters which (were) under the, etc.*

הָאֲנָשִׁים אֲשֶׁר הָלְכוּ אִתִּי[9] *the men who went with me.*

חַסְדְּךָ אֲשֶׁר רָאִיתָ אֶת עָנְיִי[10] *the mercy of thee who hast looked on my affliction.*

b. הָאָדָם אֲשֶׁר יָצָר[11] *the man whom he had formed.*

c. עַד הַיּוֹם אֲשֶׁר בָּא[12] *till the day that he come.*

בַּמָּקוֹם אֲשֶׁר דִּבֶּר[13] *in the place that he spoke.*

הָעִבְרִיֹּת אֲשֶׁר שֵׁם הָאַחַת שִׁפְרָה[14] *the Hebrew women of whom the name of one was Shiphra.*

3. *a.* וַיִּשְׁלַח אֲשֶׁר עַל הַבַּיִת וַאֲשֶׁר עַל הָעִיר....אֶל יֵהוּא[15] *and sent he who was over the house, and he who was over the city to Jehu.*

b. מְשַׁח אֶת אֲשֶׁר אֹמַר[16] *anoint him whom I shall name.*

1 Gen. 9:3.	5 Jer. 7:12.	9 Gen. 14:24.	13 Gen. 35:13.
2 Jer. 28:9.	6 1 Kgs. 8:47.	10 Ps. 31:8.	14 Ex. 1:15.
3 Deut. 28:49.	7 Gen. 10:4.	11 Gen. 2:8.	15 2 Kgs. 10:5.
4 Ruth 2:12.	8 Gen. 1:7.	12 2 Sam. 19:25.	16 1 Sam. 16:3.

c. וַיֹּאמֶר לַאֲשֶׁר עַל בֵּיתוֹ[1] *and he said to him who was over his house.*

עִם אֲשֶׁר תִּמְצָא לֹא יִחְיֶה[2] *with whomsoever thou shalt find....*
he shall not live.

A relative clause may best be understood as the expansion of an adjective or participle. It is generally introduced by אֲשֶׁר (§ 13.), sometimes by זֶה or זוּ (§ 13. 4. *a*)[a,b]; yet in many cases no introductory particle is employed (see below). The principal usages of relative clauses may be classified as follows :

1. Relative sentences introduced by אֲשֶׁר, in which, since אֲשֶׁר is only a *particle* and not a *pronoun*, a special pronoun, pronominal suffix, or adverb, is employed to express the desired idea. The pronoun or pronominal suffix agrees with its antecedent in gender and number,[c] and takes that particular case which the relative particle would have, if a noun.[d] It may, therefore, be,

   a. The *subject* of the sentence.

   b. The direct *object* of the verb, i. e., an *accusative.*

   c. The *genitive* after a construct, or after a preposition.

   d. An adverb, viz., שָׁם, used in the sense of *where, whither, whence.*

2. Relative sentences introduced by אשר in which, for the sake of brevity, the special pronoun, pronominal suffix, or adverb referred to above, has been omitted. This is seen in sentences in which

   a. The relative particle has the force of *subject*, and especially, where the predicate is a finite verb including the pronominal idea.

   b. The relative particle has the force of an *accusative.*

   c. The relative particle as an *adverbial accusative* follows a substantive having some general signification of time, place, manner.

3. Relative sentences in which the relative particle includes its antecedent and is equivalent to *he who, those who*, etc. The particle, therefore, has here two constructions. Aside from its connection with the relative clause which it introduces, it has a relation to the principal sentence on which this relative clause depends ;[e] thus it may be

   a. The *subject* of this principal sentence.

   b. The *object* often with a prefixed אֵת.[f]

   c. The *genitive* after a preposition.[g,h]

4. *a.* גּוֹי אֵיתָן הוּא[3] *a nation that is lasting.*

   בְּאֶרֶץ לֹא לָהֶם[4] *in a land which is not theirs.*

   b. דֶּרֶךְ לֹא יָדְעוּ[5] *a way they know not.*

1 Gen. 43:16.   3 Jer. 5:15.   4 Gen. 15:13.   5 Isa. 42:16.
2 Gen. 31:32.

יוֹרֶנּוּ בְּדֶרֶךְ יִבְחָר¹ *he teaches him in a way he should choose.*

c. אִישׁ הָיָה בְאֶרֶץ עוּץ אִיּוֹב שְׁמוֹ² *a man lived in the land of Uz, whose name was Job.*

הַדֶּרֶךְ יֵלְכוּ בָהּ³ *the way in which they must go.*

d. יִתְרַת עָשָׂה⁴ *the gain that he made.* [ure.

אַדִּירֵי כָּל חֶפְצִי בָם⁵ *the excellent ones in whom is my whole pleas-*

e. יוֹם אִירָא⁶ *the day I fear;* עֵת נִשְׁבַּרְתְּ⁷ *the time thou wast broken.*

5. a. מְקוֹם לֹא יָדַע אֵל⁸ *the place (of him) who knows not God.*

שְׁלַח נָא בְּיַד תִּשְׁלָח⁹ *send now by the hand (of him whom) thou wilt send.* [ask.

נִדְרַשְׁתִּי לְלוֹא שָׁאָלוּ¹⁰ *I was inquired of by (those who) did not*

בִּלְעֲדֵי אֶחֱזֶה אַתָּה הֹרֵנִי¹¹ *what is beyond that which I see, teach thou me.*

4. Relative sentences without an introductory particle, especially when the antecedent is *indefinite;* this is found

a. When the relative, or the word to which the relative force is given, is a *subject.*

b. When the relative is the *object* of a verb.

c. When the relative is a *genitive.*

d. When the relative clause follows a noun in the *construct;* this is rare and poetical.

e. When the relative follows a noun, in the construct, which has some general signification of time, place, manner.

5. Relative sentences in which the relative particle, though including its antecedent and equivalent to *he who* (see 3 above), is omitted; this is, for the most part, poetical, though found rarely in late prose writers. The predicate generally stands first in the relative clause, and is thus brought into antithesis with the preceding sentence.

REMARKS.

(a) The pronouns מִי *who,* מַה *what* sometimes also have a relative force, e. g., Gen. 19:12; 1 Sam. 20:4; Isa. 50:8.

(b) On the use of the article in a relative sense with a Participle and, rarely, with a finite verb, see § 4. 3. *f.*

(c) For agreement also in person, where the antecedent is a pronoun, see Gen. 45:4; Num. 22:30; Isa. 41:8.

1 Ps. 25:12.	4 Jer. 48:36.	7 Ezek. 27:34.	10 Isa. 65:1.
2 Job 1:1.	5 Ps. 16:3.	8 Job 18:21.	11 Job 34:32.
3 Ex. 18:20.	6 Ps. 56:4.	9 Ex. 4:13.	

(d) This pronominal suffix is regularly separated from the relative by one or more words.

(e) Note the double construction seen, for example, in Gen. 38:10; 43:16; 49:1.

(f) Distinguish from this the use of אֶת אֲשֶׁר , in the sense of *the fact that, how,* etc., to subordinate as object an entire clause.

(g) Cf. the combinations עַל אֲשֶׁר , כַּאֲשֶׁר , בַּאֲשֶׁר , etc.

(h) Cf. the usage (late and rare) which allows אֲשֶׁר to be followed by a noun in the accusative, Jer. 14:1; 46:1; Ezek. 12:25; Amos 5:1.

REFERENCES FOR STUDY.

47. Subject, Object and Adverbial Clauses.

1. a. טוֹב אֲשֶׁר לֹא תִדֹּר[1] *it is better that thou shouldst not vow.*

   טוֹב כִּי תִהְיֶה לָּנוּ[2] *it is good that thou be to us,* etc.

   b. מִי הִגִּיד לְךָ כִּי עֵירֹם אַתָּה[3] *who told thee that thou wast naked ?*

   וַיֹּאמֶר כִּי יָשׁוּבוּן[4] *and he said that they should return.*

   c. וַיַּרְא אֱ׳ אֶת הָאוֹר כִּי טוֹב[5] *and God saw that the light was good.*

   d. מָה אַתֶּם אֹמְרִים אֶעֱשֶׂה[6] *what do ye think I should do ?*

2. a. שָׁאַל אֶת נַפְשׁוֹ לָמוּת[7] *he asked that his soul should die.* [through.

   וְלֹא הֶאֱמִין ס׳ אֶת יִ׳ עֲבֹר[8] *but Sihon trusted not Israel to pass*

---

1 Eccl. 5:4. 3 Gen. 3:11. 5 Gen. 1:4. 7 1 Kgs. 19:4.
2 2 Sam. 18:3. 4 Job 36:10. 6 2 Sam. 21:4. 8 Judg. 11:20.

b. אֵינָם יוֹדְעִים לַעֲשׂוֹת רָע[1] *they do not know that they do evil.*

c. כַּאֲשֶׁר יָרֵא....מַעֲשׂוֹת יוֹמָם[2] *since he feared to do it by day.*

כִּי יָרֵא לָשֶׁבֶת בְּצוֹעַר[3] *for he feared to dwell in Zoar.*

1. Dependent sentences are found,

a. With the force of a *subject*, introduced by אֲשֶׁר or כִּי.

b. With the force of an *object*, introduced by כִּי.

c. With the logical subject, attracted by the verb of the principal sentence and treated as its object.

d. With no introductory particle, the verb being directly attached to what precedes.

2. A more condensed method of expressing subject and object sentences is seen

a. In the use of an accusative with an Infinitive (cf. the Latin), after verbs of *wishing, allowing, commanding,* etc.

b. In the same usage, more particularly in later writers, after verbs of *hearing, seeing, knowing,* etc.

c. In the use of מִן and rarely לְ with the Infinitive after verbs of *fearing.*

3. *a.* אָנֹכִי שֹׁאֵל מֵאִתָּךְ לֵאמֹר לֹא תִרְאֶה אֶת פָּנַי[4] *I ask of thee, saying, "Thou shalt not see my face."*

וַתֹּאמְרוּ לוֹ כִּי מֶלֶךְ תָּשִׂים עָלֵינוּ[5] *and ye have said unto him, "Thou shalt set a king over us."*

וַיֹּאמֶר שָׁאוּל אֶל שְׁמוּאֵל אֲשֶׁר שָׁמַעְתִּי בְּקוֹל י'[6] *and Saul said to Samuel, "I have obeyed the voice of Y."*

b. שָׁמַעְתִּי עָלֶיךָ לֵאמֹר תִּשְׁמַע חֲלוֹם[7] *I have heard concerning thee, Thou hearest a dream,* etc.

יֵדְעוּ גוֹיִם אֱנוֹשׁ הֵמָּה[8] *let the nations know they are men.*

c. אָמַר אֶל גָּד לֵאמֹר לְדָוִיד כִּי יַעֲלֶה דָוִיד וגו'[9] *he commanded Gad to say to David that David should go up,* etc.

וַיהוה חָפֵץ דַּכְּאוֹ הֶחֱלִי אִם תָּשִׂים אָשָׁם נַפְשׁוֹ יִרְאֶה זֶרַע יַאֲרִיךְ יָמִים וגו'[10] *and Yahweh was pleased to bruise him, he put him to grief, (with the understanding that) if he himself should make an offering of guilt, he would see seed, he would prolong days,* etc.

d. יִקְרָא....לָדִין עַמּוֹ[11] *he cries....that he will judge his people.*

---

1 Eccl. 4:17. 4 2 Sam. 3:13. 7 Gen. 41:15. 10 Isa. 53:10,11.
2 Judg. 6:27. 5 1 Sam. 10:19. 8 Ps. 9:21. 11 Ps. 50:4.
3 Gen. 19:30. 6 1 Sam. 15:20. 9 1 Chron. 21:18.

וַיְקַו לַעֲשׂוֹת עֲנָבִים[1] *and he expected that it would produce grapes.*
וַיֹּאמְרוּ כָּל הַקָּהָל לַעֲשׂוֹת כֵּן[2] *and the whole congregation said they would do so.*

3. Under object sentences belongs also what is called direct and indirect discourse. In reference to this it may be noted that

a. Direct discourse is introduced by כִּי, לֵאמֹר, or אֲשֶׁר, which are then equivalent to quotation marks; this is the earlier form and is much more common than the indirect, which, in most cases, would have been employed in English.

b. The gradual introduction of indirect discourse is seen in cases (like those cited above), in which it is only *partly* indirect.

c. That while in the older literature direct discourse prevails, in later writings it becomes customary to employ the Imperfect, with or without כִּי; and that in extended discourse of this kind the voluntative Imperfect is largely used.*

d. That more frequently, however, there is found especially in later writers the construction of the Infinitive with לְ (cf. the Latin).

4. *a.* אֲשֶׁר לֹא תוּכַל לְהֵרָפֵא[3] *so that thou canst not be healed.*
מָה אֱנוֹשׁ כִּי תִזְכְּרֶנּוּ[4] *what is man that thou rememberest him.*

  b. (1) אֲשֶׁר יֵדְעוּן[5] *in order that they know.*   [*it holy.*
     (2) זָכוֹר אֶת יוֹם הַשַּׁ׳ לְקַדְּשׁוֹ[6] *remember the Sabbath day to keep*
     (3) לְמַעַן יַאֲמִינוּ[7] *in order that they may believe.*
     (4) בַּעֲבוּר תִּהְיֶה לִּי לְעֵדָה[8] *that they may be to me for a testimony.*
     (5) לַעֲלוֹת לְעַם יְגוּדֶנּוּ[9] *when it comes up against the people to invade them.*

  c. (1) אֲשֶׁר לֹא יִשְׁמְעוּ[10] *in order that they may not understand.*
     (2) אַל יִמְשְׁלוּ בִי[11] *that they may not rule over me.*
     (3) לְבִלְתִּי נְתָן זֶרַע לְאָחִיו[12] *so as not to give seed to his brother.*
     (4) וַיִּמְאָסְךָ מִמֶּלֶךְ[13] *and he hath rejected thee that thou mayest not be king.*
     (5) וְעַתָּה פֶּן יִשְׁלַח יָדוֹ[14] *and now, lest he put forth his hand.*

5. *a.* כִּי תַעֲבֹד אֶת הָאֲדָמָה[15] *when thou tillest the ground,* etc.

---

[1] Isa. 5:2.	[5] Josh. 3:7.	[9] Hab. 3:16.	[13] 1 Sam. 15:23.
[2] 1 Chron. 13:4.	[6] Ex. 20:8.	[10] Gen. 11:7.	[14] Gen. 3:22.
[3] Deut. 28:27.	[7] Ex. 4:5.	[11] Ps. 19:14.	[15] Gen. 4:12.
[4] Ps. 8:5.	[8] Gen. 21:30.	[12] Gen. 38:9.	

* Ewald, *Hebrew Syntax*, p. 232.

1 כי החרשתי בלו עצמי *when I kept silent, my bones wasted.*

b. 2 ויהי כאשר קרב *and as soon as he came nigh.*

c. 3 ויהי במלכו כשבתו *and it came to pass, when he began to reign,*
as soon as he sat upon, etc.　　　　　　　　　　　　　　　　[over.

d. 4 וילינו שם טרם יעברו *and they lodged there before they passed*

e. 5 שבי אלמנה עד יגדל *remain a widow until he be grown.*

6 עד אשר עברנו את נחל *until we passed over the brook.*

f. 7 אחר חלץ את האבנים *after he hath taken out the stones.*

7 אחרי הקצות את הבית *after he hath scraped the house.*

g. 8 מאז באתי אל פרעה *since I came unto Pharaoh.*

9 מאז דברך אל עבדך *since thou didst speak unto thy servant.*

h. 10 ויהי מדי צאתם *and as often as they went out.*

11 מדי אדבר *as often as I speak.*

4. The more common methods of expressing *consequence* and *purpose* are the following:

    a. Clauses indicating *result* or *consequence*, with Imperfect introduced by the particles אֲשֶׁר or כִּי.

    b. Clauses indicating *purpose* or *intention*,

        (1) with an Imperfect following אֲשֶׁר;

        (2) with an Infinitive following לְ;

        (3) with an Imperfect following לְמַעַן;

        (4) with an Imperfect following בַּעֲבוּר;

        (5) with an Imperfect not accompanied by an introductory particle.

    c. Clause of *negative purpose*,

        (1) with an Imperfect following אֲשֶׁר לֹא;

        (2) with an Imperfect following אַל (or בַּל);

        (3) with an Infinitive following לְבִלְתִּי;

        (4) with an Infinitive or noun governed by מִן;

        (5) with an Imperfect following פֶּן.

5. The more common methods of expressing *time* are as follows:

    a. Clauses with Perfect or Imperfect following כִּי *when, quum.*

    b. Clauses with Perfect or Imperfect following כַּאֲשֶׁר *as soon as, when.*

---

1 Ps. 32:3.	4 Josh. 3:1.	7 Lev. 14:43.	10 1 Sam. 18:30.
2 Ex. 32:19.	5 Gen. 38:11.	8 Ex. 5:23.	11 Jer. 20:8.
3 1 Kgs. 16:11.	6 Deut. 2:14.	9 Ex. 4:10.	

c. Clauses with Infinitive following בְּ or כְּ , the former = *while,
when;* the latter, *as soon as, when.*

d. Clauses with Imperfect, rarely Perfect, following טֶרֶם or בְּטֶרֶם
before.

e. Clauses with Perfect or Imperfect following עַד , עַד אֲשֶׁר *until*
(cf. also עַד כִּי , עַד אִם).

f. Clauses with finite verb, or Infinitive, following אַחַר , אַחֲרֵי
after (cf. אַחֲרֵי כֵן).

g. Clauses with finite verb or Infinitive after מֵאָז *since.*

h. Clauses with finite verb or Infinitive after מִדֵּי *as often as.*

REFERENCES FOR STUDY.

48.　CONDITIONAL SENTENCES.

1. *a.* דְּבַשׁ מָצָאתָ אֱכֹל דַּיֶּךָ[1] *if thou hast found honey, eat (only) enough
for thee.*

וְעָזַב אֶת אָבִיו וָמֵת[2] *and if he leaves his father, he will die.*

---

[1] Prov. 25:16.　　　　[2] Gen. 44:22.

b. אם אמצא חמשים צדיקים[1] *if I find fifty righteous.*

c. לו חכמו ישכילו[2] *if they had been wise they would understand.*

d. לולי י' צ' הותיר וגו'[3] *except Y. of hosts had left to us.*

e. כי תאמר בלבבך[4] *if thou shalt say in thy heart.*

f. לא ישוב כי אם הרוה[5] *it does not return unless it has watered.*

2. *a.* ....אם לא את שני בני תמית אם לא[6] *my two sons thou shalt kill if I
do not,* etc.   [*by me.*

אם....תשוב....לא דבר י' בי[7] *if thou return, Y. hath not spoken*

b. אם חטאתי ושמרתני[8] *if I sin thou watchest me.*

c. אם השמאל ואימינה[9] *if thou goest to the left, then I will go to
the right.*

d. כי עתה שלחתני[10] *for then thou hadst sent me away.*

1. The *protasis* of a conditional sentence may be introduced

a. Without an introductory conditional particle of any kind, in
which case the conditional idea is indicated by the logical relation of the
clause to that with which it may be connected (see below).

b. By the particle אִם[a] *if* (negative, אִם לֹא *if not, unless*), less
often הִנֵּה[b] *if*, used with the Perfect, Imperfect, Participle,[c] or Infinitive[d] (with suffix).

c. By the particle לוּ *if*, implying that the statement made is one
which is not true or cannot be fulfilled; it is used with the Perfect,
Imperfect, Participle, and in elliptical expressions with the Imperative.

d. By the particle לוּלֵי (= לוּ *if*, לֵי, = לֹא *not*), implying that
the condition has a real existence, used with the Perfect, Imperfect, or
Participle.

e. By the particle כִּי, properly *so let it be assumed, suppose that,
if*;[e,f]

f. By the particle כִּי אִם *but if, unless,*[g] always after a negative.

2. The *apodosis* of a conditional sentence may be introduced,

a. Without any introductory particle.

b. By Wāw Consecutive, the verb standing in the tense demanded
by the context.

c. By Wāw Conjunctive, a rare usage.

d. By כִּי עַתָּה, or כִּי אָז[h] *for now, in that case.*

---

1 Gen. 18:26.   4 Deut. 7:17.   7 1 Kgs. 22:28.   9 Gen. 13:9.
2 Deut. 32:29.   5 Isa. 55:10.   8 Job 10:14.   10 Gen. 31:42.
3 Isa. 1:9.   6 Gen. 42:37.

3. את שני בני תמית אם לא אביאנו[1] *my two sons thou shalt kill
if I do (shall) not bring him back.*

אם יהיה לבן חיל לא יפל וגו'[2] *if he shall become a worthy man,
there shall not fall, etc.*

a. אם אמצא....חמשים צדיקים....ונשאתי וגו'[3] *if I shall find
fifty righteous....then I shall pardon.*

b. ואם לא (תתן) לקחתי בחזקה[4] *and if thou wilt not give, I will
take it by force.*

4. אם יוכל איש למנות....זרעך ימנה[5] *if a man should be able to
number....thy seed might be numbered.*

כי תעלה בבל השמים...יבאו שדדים לה[6] *though Babylon
should mount to heaven....spoilers would come to her.*

5. אם בא לראות שוא ידבר[7] *if he (at any time) hath come to visit
me, he will speak falsehood.*

אם שנותי ברק חרבי....אשיב נקם[8] *if at any time I have whet my
glittering sword.....I will requite vengeance.*

a. אם לא הביאתיו....וחטאתי[9] *if I have not brought him back,
then I shall be guilty.*

b. יבש חציר....כי רוח י' נשבה בו[10] *grass will wither if the
breath of Y. hath blown upon it.*

6. אם הניא אביה....נדריה....לא יקום[11] *if her father shall have
disallowed her.....her vows....shall not stand.*

a. אם נטמאה ותמעל....ובאו[12] *if she shall have defiled herself,
and been faithless, then they shall come.*

7. לו החיתם אותם לא הרגתי אתכם[13] *if you had kept them alive, I
should not have killed you.*

לולי י' צ' הותיר לנו....כסדם היינו[14] *except Y. of hosts had left us
a very small remnant, we should have been as Sodom, etc.   [stand this.*

a. לו חכמו ישכילו זאת[15] *if they had been wise, they would under-
אם שכחנו שם אלהינו......הלא א' יחקר זאת[16] *if we had
forgotten the name of our God....would not God find this out?*

---

1 Gen. 42:37.   5 Gen. 13:16.   9 Gen. 43:9.   13 Judg. 8:19.
2 1 Kgs. 1:52.   6 Jer. 51:53.   10 Isa. 40:7.   14 Isa. 1:9.
3 Gen. 18:26.   7 Ps. 41:7.   11 Num. 30:6.   15 Deut. 32:29.
4 1 Sam. 2:16.   8 Deut. 32:41.   12 Num. 5:27.   16 Ps. 44:21,22.

As regards the usage of tense in conditional sentences the principles given in §§ 16.–24. hold good. It is only necessary, therefore, to classify the more important forms.

3. In the *first* form, the protasis presents distinctly a future case (as, *if I (shall) find him*), and the apodosis denotes what *will be* the result (as, *I will inform him*). The *Imperfect* is employed in both.[i,j,k] But in the apodosis there is found also

a. The Perfect with Wāw Consecutive instead of the Imperfect (§ 25. 1. *b*).

b. The Perfect of *certainty* which is equivalent to an Imperfect (§ 19. 1).

4. In the *second* form, the protasis presents a future case, but less distinctly (as, *if I should find him*); the apodosis denotes what *would* (or *might*) *be* the result. The Imperfect is employed in both.[l,m,n]

5. In the *third* form, the protasis presents a future case, but one of an entirely uncertain and indefinite character, and regarded from the stand-point of the past (as, *if I shall have at any time found him*); the apodosis denotes what *will be* the result in case this contingency is realized. Here the Perfect is found in the protasis[o] and the Imperfect in the apodosis; but in the apodosis there is also found

a. The Perfect with Wāw Consecutive instead of the Imperfect (§ 25. 1. *b*.).

b. The Perfect in the sense of the Future Perfect (§ 19. 3).

6. In the *fourth* form the protasis presents a case either strictly past, or past as viewed from a definite moment fixed in the context (as, *if I have in the past*, or *shall have at a particular time, found him*) the apodosis denotes what *will be* the result immediately or at the particular moment referred to. The Perfect[p] (either present perfect, § 17. 2, or perfect of the immediate past, § 18. 1, or future perfect, § 19. 3) is used in the protasis, the Imperfect in the apodosis; but in the apodosis there is also found

a. The Perfect with Wāw Consecutive instead of the Imperfect (§ 25. 1. *b*.).

7. In the *fifth* form, the protasis presents a case which is supposed not to have been fulfilled (as, *if I had found him*); the apodosis denotes what *would have been* the result if the supposed case had been realized (as, *I should have informed him*). The Perfect is used in both members.[q,r,s,t] But in the apodosis there is found

a. The *Imperfect* instead of the Perfect, when reference is made to the present (as, *I should now inform him*).

8. *a.* ‏ועזב את אביו ומת‏[1] *and (if) he leave his father, he will die.*

‏וראה כל העם וקם‏[2] *and (if) all the people saw, they stood up.*

b. ‏והביאה לי ואכלה‏[3] *and (if thou) bring it to me [and] I will eat.*

‏שמעו....אלי ואכלו טוב‏[4] *(if ye) hearken to me [and] (ye will) eat good.*

‏נקבה שכרך עלי ואתנה‏[5] *(if thou wilt) specify to me thy hire [and] I will give it.*

‏וארא ואין איש‏[6] *and (if) I looked, there was no man.*

c. ‏הנך הולך מאתי והכך האריה‏[7] *behold, thou goest from me and a lion shall slay thee.*   [avenged, etc.

‏כל הרג קין שבעתים יקם‏[8] *should any one kill Cain, he shall be*

9. *a.* ‏אם אקח מכל אשר לך‏[9] *(may he punish me) if I take of all that is thine = I will not take.*

‏אם לא כאשר דברתם....כן אעשה‏[10] *(God do so to me, and more also), if I do not do according to what ye have spoken = I will surely do it.*

b. ‏ועתה אם תשא חטאתם ואם אין מחני‏[11] *and now if thou wilt forgive their sin [it is well], but if not, blot me out.*

c. ‏לא אשלחך כי אם ברכתני‏[12] *I will not let thee go....yes, if thou bless me, (then I will let thee go).*

d. ‏לו הואלנו ונשב בעבר הירדן‏[13] *oh that we had been content and had remained beyond the Jordan.*

8. Certain classes of sentences, conditional in force, though not in form, may be grouped as follows:

a. Sentences containing two members, each of which has as its verb a Perfect with Wāw Consecutive (as, *and I used to find him, and inform him*, or *and I find him, and I inform him = and if I found him I should inform him*, or *and if I find him, I inform him*). This Perfect is a frequentative (§ 25. 1. *a*). The usage occurs in the sphere of past, present or future time.

b. Sentences containing two members, both of which have Imperatives; or one, an Imperative, the other a Jussive or Cohortative; or both, Jussives (as, *find him and inform him = if you find him, you shall*

1 Gen. 44:22.   5 Gen. 30:28.   8 Gen. 4:15.   11 Ex. 32:32.
2 Ex. 33:10.   6 Isa. 41:28.   9 Gen. 14:23.   12 Gen. 32:27.
3 Gen. 27:4.   7 1 Kgs. 20:36.   10 Num. 14:28.   13 Josh. 7:7.
4 Isa. 55:2.

inform him, or *find him and I will inform him*, or *let me find him and I will inform him*).ᵘ

c. Sentences with a participle (often preceded by הִנֵּה) in the protasis, an Imperfect, or Perfect with Wāw Consecutive in the apodosis.

9. In certain usages, one or the other member of the conditional is regularly omitted. This is seen in

a. In the expression of the oath, the apodosis, viz., *I lift my hand to God that he may punish me*, or *God do so to me and more also*, having been dropped. Here אִם = *assuredly not*; אִם לֹא = *assuredly*.

b. In the case of the first apodosis of two consecutive conditional sentences, this apodosis being easily supplied from the context.

c. In the case of the elliptical conjunction כִּי אִם = *yes, if*, the real apodosis having strictly to be supplied.ᵛ

d. In the expression of a *wish* which is not, or cannot be, realized.

REMARKS.

(a) For אִם in the sense of *although*, 1 Sam. 15:17; Jer. 5:2; 14:7.

(b) See Ex. 4:1; 8:22 and compare הִנֵּה, § 48. 8. c.

(c) See Judg. 9:15; 11:9; 1 Sam. 6:3.

(d) Cf. אִם אֹמְרִי (Job 9:27) *if my saying = if I say.*

(e) Cf. sentences introduced by כִּי *when*, § 47. 5. a.

(f) Cf. the distinction between אִם and כִּי in Ex. 21:2–5, where כִּי is used before a general ordinance, אִם, before the particular details.

(g) To be distinguished from this are other usages of כִּי אִם, viz., (1) *that if, because if, for if*, e. g., 1 Kgs. 20:6; Deut. 11:22, and (2) *but*, the אִם having lost its force, Ps. 1:1; Josh. 17:3.

(h) Here belong cases in which the protasis has been omitted, e. g., Ex. 9:15; 1 Sam. 13:13; 2 Kgs. 13:19.

(i) The voluntative Imperfect or Imperative may be substituted for the ordinary Imperfect, e. g., 1 Sam. 20:21; 21:10; 2 Kgs. 2:10.

(j) The Participle (according to § 20. 2. (h)) may also be substituted for the Imperfect, e. g., Gen. 4:7; Lev. 21:9.

(k) For cases in which the Imperfect in apodosis refers to the past in the frequentative sense, see Gen. 31:8; Ex. 40:37.

(l) While the Greek uses in the first form the subjunctive, in the second the optative, and thus distinguishes them, the distinction in Hebrew can be seen only from the context.

(m) When both members are parallel in thought, the particle is translated *if;* when contrasted, it may be rendered by *though.*

(n) Here, too, the Participle may be substituted for the Imperfect.

(o) Notice that this Perfect is continued by a Perfect with Wāw Consecutive, not by an Imperfect with Wāw Consecutive, e. g., Gen. 43:9; Job 11:13,14.

(p) Notice that this Perfect is continued by an Imperfect with Wāw Consecutive, e. g., Judg. 9:16–19.

(q) By the omission of the apodosis there arises a common expression for a *wish* that has not been realized, e. g., Josh.7:7; Isa. 48:18,19; 63:19.

(r) By the omission of the protasis and the use of כִּי עַתָּה arise such cases as 1 Sam. 13:13; Ex. 9:15, etc.

(s) Here the Greek likewise employs past tenses in both protasis and apodosis.

(t) Examine 2 Sam. 18:12; Ps. 81:14-17 and note the use of the Participle in the protasis and the Imperfect in the apodosis (as, *if I found him now, I would tell him*).

(u) Cf. § 23. 2. *d.*, under which many of the cases here cited may also be classified, e. g., *do this and live* may be *do this that you may live*, or *if you do this, you will live*.

(v) Here belong also אִם . . . אִם, *if . . . . if, whether . . . . or*, cf. ἐάν τε . . . ἐάν τε, *sive . . . sive.*

REFERENCES FOR STUDY.

Gen. 24:8; 32:9	3a.	2 Sam. 17:9	8c.
Gen. 32:29	9c.	2 Sam. 18:12	1c.
Gen. 33:13	1a.	2 Sam. 18:13	7a.
Gen. 42:15	9a.	1 Kgs. 1:52	3
Gen. 42:18	8b.	1 Kgs. 8:30	8a.
Gen. 42:38	8a.	2 Kgs. 3:14	1d.
Gen. 43:9	1b.	2 Kgs. 5:13	7a.
Gen. 43:10	2d.	2 Kgs. 7:4	5a.
Gen. 46:33	1e.	2 Kgs. 7:2,19	8c.
Ex. 4:14	8a.	Isa. 1:15,18	4
Ex. 7:9	8b.	Isa. 6:13	1a.
Ex. 7:9	1e.	Isa. 8:9,10	8b.
Ex. 19:5	3a.	Isa. 22:14	9a.
Num. 10:17,18	8a.	Jer. 2:22	4
Num. 14:28	9a.	Jer. 18:4,8	8a.
Num. 15:24; 35:22-24	6a.	Jer. 33:25,26	6
Num. 32:23	3b.	Jer. 49:9b	5b.
Deut. 4:29a	8a.	Ezek. 33:9	6
Deut. 6:20,21	3a.	Hos. 12:12	3b.
Deut. 32:26	7	Amos 3:7	9c
Deut. 32:27	1d.	Amos 5:4,6	8b.
Deut. 32:41	5	Ps. 7:4,5	6
Josh. 14:9	9a.	Ps. 7:4,5	1b.
Judg. 5:8	9a.	Ps. 23:4; 27:3; 50:12	4
Judg. 6:18	8a.	Ps. 63:7; 94:18	5
Judg. 9:16-20	9b.	Ps. 73:15	7
Judg. 13:23	1c.	Ps. 75:3	3
1 Sam. 3:17	9a.	Ps. 119:15	8b.
1 Sam. 17:34,35	8a.	Prov. 3:9,10; 4:8; 20:13,25	8b.
1 Sam. 20:6	3a.	Prov. 6:22,31	1a.
1 Sam. 25:34	1d.	Prov. 25:21	5
1 Sam. 25:34	7	Job 7:4; 21:6	5a.
1 Sam. 26:19	6	Job 9:15,16	7a.
2 Sam. 2:27	2d.	Ruth 3:18	9c.
2 Sam. 3:35	9a.		
2 Sam. 15:33	5a.		

INDEXES

INDEX OF TOPICS.

[The references are to sections, unless otherwise indicated.]

150 HEBREW SYNTAX.

INDEX OF TEXTS.

[The references are to sections, unless otherwise indicated.]

Num.26:55..............35. 1.
" 28:6..............8. 3. b.
" 30:6..............48. 6.
" 31:49..............5. 1.
" 31:49..............9. 3. a.
" 32:1...... 4. 1. a. R. (a)
" 32:7..............41. 4. d.
" 34:2..............6. 1. c.
" 35:14..............8. 2. a.
" 35:22b..............8. 2. d.
" 35:23..............41. 4. c.
" 35:28..............22. 2. b.
Deut.1:2 ....15. 3.
" 1:2..........15. 3. R. (d)
" 1:3........15. 8. c. R. (g)
" 1:12..............42. 6. c.
" 1:13..............15. 8. b.
" 1:15..............4. 2. b.
" 1:15..............9. 3. b.
" 1:23..............15. 3.
" 1:23..............15. 9. a.
" 1:27..............29. 2. c.
" 1:44..............4. 3. d.
" 1:44..............21. 3.
" 2:14..............4. 2. c.
" 2:14..............47. 5. e.
" 2:24.......... .... .36. 2.
" 2:25..........25. 1. c. R. (f)
" 2:30..............26. 1. a.
" 2:34..............34. 3.
" 3:6.......... ....28. 1.
" 3:18..............8. 3. e.
" 3:18..............10. 5.
" 3:21..............43. 2. b.
" 3:24......12. 2. e. R. (g)
" 3:26..............41. 1. b.
" 4:1..............27. 2. b.
" 4:5..............38. 1. b.
" 4:11..............45. 1. b.
" 4:27..............6. 1. e.
" 4:33..............24. 2. c.
" 4:42..............22. 4. a.
" 5:23..............10. 2. a.
" 5:23..........19. 4. R. (d)
" 6:20,21.......... 25. 2. d.
" 7:7..............37. 4. c.
" 7:12......25. 1. c. R. (f)
" 7:17..............48. 1. e.
" 8:3......29. 3. a. R. (a)
" 9:6..............9. 1. c.
" 9:14......23. 1. a. R. (j)
" 9:15..............15. 7. b.
" 9:16..............17. 4.
" 9:21..............28. 2. b.
" 9:25..............34. 7.
" 10:1..............8. 3. d.
" 10:9..............7. 6.
" 10:16..............25. 2. c.
" 11:1..............25. 2. c.
" 11:10..............25. 1. a.
" 11:12......34. 10. R. (k)
" 11:22......48. 1. f. R. (g)

Deut.12:6..........34. 1. R. (d)
" 12:23..............7. 6.
" 12:23..............29. 6.
" 12:23............ 37. 5. b.
" 14:12-18.....34. 1. R. (d)
" 14:21..............28. 4. b.
" 15:3..............23. 1. a.
" 15:9..............15. 8. c.
" 16:20..............39. 5. a.
" 17:13..............26. 2. b.
" 17:19. 20..... .. 41. 4. a.
" 18:16..........23. 1. R. (e)
" 18:21..............42. 6. c.
" 19:13..............8. 3. a.
" 19:13..............10. 1. a.
" 21:1..............45. 2. a,
" 21:14..........28. 3. R. (f)
" 22:2..............29. 2. c.
" 22:2..........29. 2. c. R. (i)
" 22:8..............37. 2. c.
" 22:19..........9. 3. b. R. (c)
" 22:26..........25. 1. c. R. (f)
" 26:5..............8. 3. b.
" 26:15..........23. 1. a. R. (h)
" 2:76..............2. 1. a.
" 28:27..............47. 4. a.
" 28:49..............13. 1.
" 28:49..............46. 1. c.
" 29:12..............29. 2. a.
" 30:19..............25. 2. c.
" 31:12..............36. 1.
" 32:1..............4. 3. e.
" 32:5..............8. 2. d.
" 32:6..............41. 5. a.
" 32:10..... .....16, 2. a.
" 32:10..............20. 1. a.
" 32:21...8. 2. d; 41. 5. a.
" 32:29..............48. 1. c.
" 32:29..............48. 7. a.
" 32:31......44. 1. d. R. (e)
" 32:35........20. R. (a)
" 32:41..............48. 5.
" 33:6........6. 1. e. R (d)
" 33:7 ......23. 1. a. R. (i)
Josh.1:2........11. 2. a. R. (g)
" 1:2..............39. 3.
" 2:5......28. 2. b. R. (g)
" 2:22......13. 4. b. R. (e)
" 2:22..............15. 2. a.
" 3:1..............47. 5. d.
" 3:7..............47. 4. b.
" 3:15......8. 3. f. R. (d)
" 3:17......28. 2. b. R. (g)
" 5:15..............7. 7.
" 6:11......28. 2. b. R. (g)
" 7:2..............9. 2. d.
" 7:3..............26. 2. b.
" 7:7......48. 7. R. (g)
" 7:7..............48. 9. d.
" 7:21......4. 1. b. R.(b)
" 8:33........4. 1. b. R.(b)
" 8:33......9. 3. a. R. (a)

Josh.9:8......22. 3. d. R. (c)
" 10:24..............4. 3. b.
" 10:24..............13. 4. b.
" 13:33..............8. 3. c.
" 14:11.....29. 2. c. R. (h)
" 15:3-11...25. 2. a. R. (b)
" 15:19..............11. 2. a.
" 16:2,3,6,7,8 ....
     ......25. 2. a. R. (b)
" 17:3......44. 1. a. R. (d)
" 17:3......48. 1. f. R. (g)
" 17:9......25. 2. a. R. (b)
" 17:18......44. 1. a. R. (d)
" 18:12-21...25. 2. a. R. (b)
" 21:39..............15. 5.
" 22:3........ ....12. 1. e.
" 22:18..............45. 2. e.
" 23:14..............10. 2.
" 24:10..........28. 3. R. (d)
Judg.1:7..............45. 2. c.
" 3:15..............5. 1. b.
" 3:16..............14. 1. b.
" 5:4..........30. 2. R. (b)
" 5:23..............28. 3. c.
" 6:3..............25. 4. b.
" 6:5..........44. 1. R. (a)
" 6:16-19...48. 6. R. (p)
" 6:25..............44. 1. c.
" 6:27..............47. 2. c.
" 7:4........12. 1. b. R, (a)
" 7:14 ....41. 5. c.
" 7:17......25. 2. d. R. (d)
" 7:19..............28. 4. a.
" 7:19..............39. 5. b.
" 8:5.......... ....3. 3.
" 8:11......9. 3. a. R. (a)
" 8:11..............33. R. c.
" 8:11..............44. 3.
" 8:19..............19. 4.
" 8:19..............48. 7.
" 9:1......8. 3. f. R. (d)
" 9:2..............29. 2. b.
" 9:15......48. 1. b. R. (c)
" 9:55..............40. 4. b.
" 10:9..............37. 3. b.
" 11:1..............8. 3. d.
" 11:9......48. 1. b. R. (c)
" 11:13......19. 4. R. (d)
" 11:20..............47. 2, a.
" 11:23......42. 1. R. (a)
" 13:2..............5. 3.
" 13:3. ....25. 2. b.
" 13:17..............42. 5. a.
" 14:15......42. 4. a. R. (d)
" 14:18..............10. 4. a.
" 16:5..............10. 3.
" 16:22..............1. 4.
" 17:5..............7. 3.
" 17:10..........38. 2. c.
" 18:3..............45. 3. b.
" 18:5..............27. 2. c.
" 18:17...........

2 Sam. 16:17............42. 1.	
" 17:3......6. 1. e. R. (d)	
" 17:5...........39. 4. b.	
" 17:14....29. 3. a. R. (a)	
" 17:22.....8. 4. c. R. (e)	
" 18:3.'..........47. 1. a.	
" 18:7...........40. 2. a.	
" 18:11....29. 4. R. (d)	
" 18:12....48. 7. R. (t)	
" 18:14..........45. 2. e.	
" 18:18....29. 3. a. R. (a)	
" 18:18....34. 1. R. (b)	
" 18:19..........30. 5.	
" 18:23........23. 1. b.	
" 18:29.....42. 1. R. (a)	
" 19:1...........11. 1. a.	
" 19:2..........24. 1. b.	
" 19:5..........32. 3.	
" 19:18.....9. 5. R. (f)	
" 19:20..........29. 2. b.	
" 19:20....29. 2. b. R. (f)	
" 19:21.........9. 5. d.	
" 19:23.....42. 1. R. (a)	
" 19:23.....42. 2. R. (b)	
" 19:25..........46. 2. c.	
" 20:10..........40. 6.	
" 20:19....9. 2. c. R. (f).	
" 21:4..........47. 1. d.	
" 21:9...........33. 2.	
" 21:17.........44. 2. b.	
" 22:34........12. 1. f.	
" 23:5............42. 1.	
" 23:10.....20. R. (a)	
" 23:15.........43. 3. c.	
" 23:15....... 42. 5. a.	
" 23:19....42. 3. R. (c)	
" 24:9.....2. 2. b. R. (e)	
" 24:24......39. 5. b.	

1 Kgs. 1:2...........23. 1. b.
" 1:24....42. 2. R. (b)
" 1:35............18. 1.
" 1:52...........48. 3.
" 2:2.....25. 2. d. R. (d)
" 2:21....40. 1. R. (a)
" 2:30....41. 1. c. R. (c)
" 2:31..........8. 3. b.
" 3:2..........27. 3. a.
" 3:4...........15. 6.
" 3:7..........29.1. d.
" 3:18....11. 2. d. R. (k)
" 4:14....33. 1. b. R. (d)
" 5:1........27. 2. a.
" 5:20,23.......4. 3. e.
" 6:16....34. 3. R. (e)
" 6:18.........41. 2. c.
" 7:8b.........20. R. (a)
" 7:13....24. 2. 9. R. (b)
" 8:5..........22. 2. a.
" 8:13....... 33. 3.
" 8:27....44. 1. a. R. (d)
" 8:33............25. 5.
" 8:47.........46. 1. d.

1 Kgs. 9:26,27............1. 4.
" 10:21...........41. 6.
" 10:22.........15. 9. b.
" 10:22....20. 2. R. (h)
" 11:22....41. 1. c. R. (c)
" 12:15....29. 3. a. R. (a)
" 12:16.........42. 5. b.
" 13:8..........22. 4. b.
" 13:12.........42. 5. c.
" 13:31.........25. 2. d.
" 14:11....... 38. 3. a.
" 14:24....9. 3. a. R. (a)
" 15:2...........17. 1.
" 15:23.........33. 8. a.
" 15:23...........34. 8.
" 15:31.........9. 5. e.
" 16:11........47. 5. c.
" 18:4..........15. 6.
" 18:11,12...25. 2. d. R.(d)
" 18:26.......4. 3. e.
" 18:32..........31. 6.
" 18:39............7. 6.
" 19:4.........29. 4. c.
" 19:4.........47. 2. a.
" 19:5....27. 2. c. R. (k)
" 19:21........33. 8. c.
" 20:6.....25. 1. c. R. (f)
" 20:6.....48. 1. f. R. (g)
" 20:13............5. 3.
" 20:21.........4. 3. c.
" 20:35.....9. 5. R. (f)
" 20:36....25. 2. d. R. (d)
" 20:36........48. 8. c.
" 21:6......,....20. R. (a)
" 21:15....44. 1. a. R. (d)
" 22:1.......... 8. 2. d.
" 22:1.........45. 2. e.
" 22:10 ....05. 4.
" 22:15.......42. 4. a.
" 22:20......'.11. 1. g.
" 22:28.......48. 2. a.

2 Kgs. 1:2 ....42. 4. b.
" 1:3............41. 6.
" 2:10....48. 3. R. (i)
" 2:24...........15. 5.
" 3:16 ....3. 1. c.
" 3:16.........6. 3. c.
" 3:26 ....40. 2. b.
" 4:13.......29. 3. c.
" 4:24....19. 3. R. (b)
" 4:43.........28. 5. b.
" 4:43....43. 2. d. R. (d)
" 5:11.........39. 5. b.
" 5:12....25. 1. c. R. (f)
" 5:13.........38. 3. b.
" 5:23.. ....3. 3.
" 5:23...........3. 5. b.
" 7:9.....25. 2. d. R. (d)
" 8:13...........31. 1.
" 10:1..........15. 4.
" 10:5.........46. 3. a.
" 10:6.........10. 4. b.

2 Kgs. 11:13..... ...44. 4. d.
" 13:19....48. 2. d. R. (h)
" 13:20........20. R. (a)
" 14:8..........33. 8. b.
" 14:10...25. 1. c R. (f)
" 15:16.....4. 1. b. R. (b)
" 16:14....9. 3. a. R. (a)
" 16:17. ....6. 1. a.
" 18:17.......8. 3. a.
" 20:4........ ....30. 4.
" 22:3..........15. 8. b.
" 23:17....9. 3. a. R. (a)
" 25:4....3. 5. c. R. (h)
" 25:9...........8. 3. a.

1 Chr. 5:9............6. 1. c.
" 7:2,9...........3. 4.
" 11:9....28. 3. d. R. (h)
" 13:4.........47. 3. d.
" 19:5.........40. 2. a.
" 21:18......47. 3. c.
" 28:18....6. 1. R. (a)

2 Chr. 1:6...........15. 6.
" 2:12...........18. 1.
" 3:4..........15. 4.
" 3:16..........15. 6.
" 13:9........15. 2. c.
" 16:14....44. 1. R. (b)
" 20:6.........41. 4. b.
" 29:3........15. 8. a.
" 31:10...28. 2. a. R. (e)
" 34:8..........15. 8. b.

Ezra 1:11...............1. 3.
" 3:10.........26. 1. b.
" 8:35..........15. 3.

Neh. 1:4......27. 2. a. R. (g)
" 1:7.........28. 3. R. (a)
" 2:2..........28. 2. b.
" 9.10,15....27. 2. a. R. (g)
" 9:33.. ....10. 3.
" 11:13........9. 5. b.

Est. 9:1...........14. 1. b.

Job 1:1...........11. 1. c.
" 1:1...........12. 1. b.
" 1:1........37. 5. c.
" 1:1....38. 2. c. R. (f)
" 1:1.........46. 4. c.
" 1:3.........10. 4. b.
" 1:14........2. 2. a.
" 1:15........39. 4. a.
" 1:16.........29. 3. a.
" 2:10.... 5. 3. R. (e)
" 2:20....15. 1. R. (a)
" 3:3..........13. 3. a.
" 3:3..........20. 1. a.
" 3:4....10. 3. R. (e)
" 3:13.......37. 3. a.
" 3:17....21. 3. R. (b)
" 5:7.........44. 1. b.
" 6:17.....20. R. (a)
" 8:12........41. 5. d.
" 9:2...........42. 5. b.
" 9:4............9. 1. c.

Ezek. 45:11......6. 1. e. R. (d)
"   45:16 ....5. 1. a.
Hos. 1:6.......41. 1. c. R. (d)
"   3:2.........15. 3. R. (d)
"   4:2.......43. 2. d. R. (d)
"   4:3 ....25. 1. b.
"   5:11..............36. 2.
"   8:11 .....39. 5. a. R. (e)
"   9:4...............8. 2. c.
"   10:6.........40. 1. R. (a)
"   10:12.....25. 1. c. R. (f)
"   12:1..............3. 2. c.
"   12:6......44. 1. d. R. (e)
"   13:8 (cf. 2 Kgs. 2:24)
............2. 1. b.
Joel 1:6..............41. 5. b.
"   1:14..............44. 4. e.
"   1:15............43. 1. b.
"   1:20.............40. 4. a.
"   2:3ff......20. 1. a. R. (c)
"   2:23 ..... 44. 1. d. R. (e)
"   4:9................2. 2. c.
"   4:18.........30. 2. R. (b)
"   4:20......44. 1. d. R. (e)
Amos 1:11............29. 5. b.
"   2:16...............33. 4.
"   4:2.......37. 2. a. R. (b)
"   4:7 ....37. 3. b.
"   4:13......27. 1. b. R. (e)

Amos 5:1............46. R. (h)
"   5:3........... ....33. 3.
"   6:1 ....43. 1. b.
"   6:12 ....37. 2. b.
"   6:13.....8. 2. d. R. (f)
"   7:7.....45. 3. b. R. (d)
"   9:5......44. 1. d. R. (e)
"   9:8........28. 3. R. (f)
"   9:11...........40. 7. d.
Jon. 1:11 ....26. 2. a.
"   1:3,5 ....1. 4.
"   3:3 .... 9. 5. a.
"   3:5 ....9. 4. b.
"   3:5 ....10. 4. b.
"   4:10.............8. 3. e.
"   4:10............10. 5.
"   4:10,11......42. 1. R. (a)
Mic. 1:10.........28. 3. R. (f)
"   2:4...........28. 3. R. (d)
"   2:6 ....40. 2. b.
"   2:12........4. 1. b. R. (b)
"   3:6. .. ..37. 3. b.
"   3:12.............4. 3. e.
"   5:2...............19. 3.
"   5:4...............8. 3. f.
"   6:5,16... 29. 3. a. R. (a)
"   7:4.......10. 4. a. R. (g)
"   7:10..............40. 3.
Nah. 1:3.........28. 3. R. (f)

Nah. 2:5.......20. 1. a. R. (c)
"   2:9.......37. 5. b. R. (e)
Hab. 2:17............8. 1. b.
"   3:8...........6. 1. R. (a)
"   3:10......20. 1. a. R. (b)
"   3:16........ ... 47. 4. b.
Hag. 1:1..............9. 5. a.
"   2:5 ....43. 2. b.
"   2:11.............31. 4.
Zech. 1:3.............25. 2. c.
"   1:9.............42. 5. b.
"   4:4,13...........42. 5. b.
"   4:5 ....37. 5. b.
"   4:10.......9. 3. a. R. (a)
"   7:1...............15. 8. c.
"   7:5......... ...11. 2. a.
"   8:2..............32. 3.
"   8:6................42. 1.
"   8:17.......34. 10. R. (k)
"   8:19 ....4. 3. d.
"   9:5.......23. 1. R. (f)
"   10:7.......23. 1. R. (f)
"   12:10............34. 10.
"   12:12-14..39. 5. a. R. (e)
"   13:6 ....37. 2. b.
"   14:4............8. 3. a.
"   14:4...............33. 7.
Mal. 1:2............24. 2. c.
"   1:11 ....37. 3. a.

INDEX OF TEXTS

Under "REFERENCES FOR STUDY."

INDEX OF HEBREW WORDS.

ELEMENTS OF HEBREW.

INTRODUCTORY HEBREW METHOD.

The testimony of teachers and pupils who have made practical use of these text-books is uniformly and enthusiastically in praise of both the books themselves and of the system embodied in them. ☞ *In the acquisition of the Hebrew language, more rapid and satisfactory progress can be made by means of these books than by the use of any others in existence.*

The publishers invite attention to the following testimony:

FROM PROFESSORS OF HEBREW.

"I like them very much. No better books, introductory to Hebrew exist." —Prof. T. K. CHEYNE, *Oxford University*, Oxford, England.

"The 'Elements' is a book above praise. I shall be glad to recommend it to my pupils; it would save them a world of trouble."—Prof. ARTHUR WRIGHT, *Queen's College*, Cambridge, Eng.

"* * An expression of the latest Hebrew scholarship, and the work of a practical teacher, who knows the wants of beginners."—Prof. R. V. FOSTER, *Cumberland University*, Lebanon, Tenn.

"I have used Professor Harper's 'Method' and 'Elements' two years in the class-room with most gratifying results. I regard them the best text-books for beginners in Hebrew."—Prof. EDWARD L. CURTIS, *McCormick Theological Seminary*, Chicago.

"I have used Dr. Harper's text-books in the class-room during the last year with the most gratifying results. They are stimulating to teacher and to pupil. I know of no better books for elementary drill, both for thoroughness and rapidity of progress."—Prof. R. F. WEIDNER, *Augustana Theological Seminary*, Rock Island, Ill.

"Dr. W. R. Harper's 'Elements of Hebrew' and 'Method' have been used in Garrett Biblical Institute during the last year, and have given very great satisfaction. They will continue in use as the elementary text-books for Hebrew study in this institution."—Prof. M. S. TERRY, *Garrett Biblical Institute*, Evanston, Ill.

"I have used Professor Harper's books for the beginning of the study of Hebrew during the past three years. The system is decidedly the best I have been able to find, for it tides the beginner over the initial difficulties of the language more quickly than the ordinary method."—Prof. F. B. DENIO, *Bangor Theological Seminary*, Bangor, Me.

"Success is the best argument. What the Hebrew Summer Schools under Dr. Harper have succeeded in doing, in giving the average minister and student a real grasp of Hebrew, that exactly the 'Method' and 'Elements' effect in the class-room. They are invaluable. What other books give a treatment so full and scientific, and yet so clearly put, of Hebrew nouns, *e. g.* and of the vowel-system? It is Davidson and Bickell and Gesenius combined. The debt instructors owe the Principal of the Institute of Hebrew has not yet been fully recognized."—Prof. W. W. LOVEJOY, *Ref'd Episcopal Divinity School,* Philadelphia, Pa.

AN ARAMAIC METHOD.

By CHARLES RUFUS BROWN,

Associate Prof. of Hebrew in Newton Theological Institution.

PART I. TEXT, NOTES AND VOCABULARY.

A Text-book for the study of the Aramaic, by a method at once comparative and inductive. Commended by eminent scholars and teachers. CONTENTS: I—Genesis 1-10, The Hebrew Text and Targum of Onkelos on parallel pages. II—Note of References to the Biblical Aramaic. III—Targum Pseudo-Jonathan, Genesis, ch. 8. IV—Targum of Jonathan Ben Uzziel, Joshua, ch. 20, Isaiah ch. 6. V—Targum on the Psalms, Psalm xxiv., Psalm cl. VI—Targum on the Megilloth, Ruth, ch. 2. VII—Notes on the Text: Onkelos, Genesis 1-10. Biblical Aramaic. Other Targums. VIII—Vocabulary.

12mo. Cloth. Pp. 132. Price, $1.75, net.

PART II. GRAMMAR.

The second part of this work includes brief statements of the principles of Aramaic Orthography, Etymology and Syntax. The method pursued is comparative and inductive. As in Part I, a knowledge of Hebrew is presupposed, and the agreements or disagreements of Aramaic therewith are carefully noted. Instead of bringing the principles for all the dialects under one head, the grammar of Onkelos is carefully distinguished from that of the Biblical Aramaic, and, to some extent, from that of the more corrupt Targums, and all dialectical variations from Onkelos are printed in special type. For the convenience of those using Harper's *Elements of Hebrew*, the *arrangement* has been adapted, as far as possible, from that work.

12mo. Cloth. Pp. 96. Price, $1.00, net.

"The result of my examination is altogether favorable. We shall use it in our Seminary."—Prof. WILLIS J. BEECHER, D.D., *Auburn Theological Seminary*.

"It is well adapted to the purpose which the author had in view."—Prof. HENRY P. SMITH, D. D., *Lane Theological Seminary*, Cincinnati.

"I have decided to use it in my classes."—Prof. BASIL MANLY, D. D., *So. Bapt. Theological Seminary*, Louisville.

"A real and valuable contribution to the study of the so-called Chaldee."—Prof S. BURNHAM, D. D., in "*Hebraica.*"

"The 'Method' is a manual of exceptional merit, and richly deserves recognition and success. It is just the kind of a book we need for our Seminaries, our Summer Schools and for private study."—Prof. GEO. H. SCHODDE. Ph.D., in "*Hebraica.*"

"Excellently adapted for purposes of instruction. A text-book of this character is very useful."—*The Independent*, New York.

"I have used Professor Harper's 'Elements' and 'Method' with the Junior Classes of this Seminary during the past year. The practical test has only confirmed the favorable opinion with which the books were introduced. I have no doubt that, for their purpose, they are the best works now before the public."— Prof. W. G. BALLANTINE, *Oberlin Theological Seminary*, Oberlin, O.

"I take pleasure in commending the Hebrew text-books of Professor W. R. Harper. They are in my judgment practical, convenient and adequate to introduce one to a good working acquaintance with the Hebrew language. We are using them in this Seminary in the Junior Class, and propose to continue to do so."—Prof. BASIL MANLY, *Southern Baptist Theological Seminary*, Louisville. Ky.

"* * I have found them both to stand the test of the class-room. The 'Elements' treats all principles thoroughly and exhaustively. The 'Method' is unique and in all respects *sui generis*. It seems to me to leave nothing un-done in helping a student to a knowledge of the Hebrew. It is a vast improvement on the old methods. The typography of both books cannot be excelled."— Prof CHAS. H. COREY, *Richmond Theological Seminary*, Richmond, Va.

"I have used Dr. Harper's Hebrew 'Elements' and 'Method' for one year. The results in the class-room have been not only exceedingly gratifying, but more satisfactory both as to amount and thoroughness than in preceding years. I not only expect to continue the use of the 'Elements' and 'Method,' but hope for them that which they richly deserve—a constantly increasing demand and usefulness."—Prof J. G. LANSING, *Theological Seminary*, New Brunswick, N.J.

"* * They are clearly written, so that no one can misunderstand what the author means to say. They are beautifully printed, so as to be in themselves attractive as mere works of art. The 'Method' is full, easy and progressive; and, above all, is liked and enjoyed by the students; while the matter of the 'Elements' is well chosen both as to quantity and quality, and is paragraphed and arranged in such matchless order as to make it most ready of acquisition and convenient for reference."—Prof. R. D. WILSON, *Western Theological Seminary*, Allegheny, Pa.

"* * Actual trial of these exponents of the inductive method has convinced me that they are the best text-books of elementary Hebrew that have yet appeared. The author has not only adopted the surest method of mastering the phenomena of the language, but he has also done for beginners what Bickell and others had done for more advanced students: he has led them back of the mere surface facts to the controlling principles, and encouraged that kind of analytical study which makes Hebrew a permanent acquisition. These two books are simply indispensable in my class room."—Prof. W. W. MOORE, *Union Theological Seminary*, Hampden Sidney, Va.

"It affords me pleasure to say, after a year's trial of Dr. Harper's Hebrew text-books in the class-room, that they have given entire satisfaction. Of the fifteen years during which I have taught Hebrew, this has been in all respects the most pleasant and satisfactory, and I cannot but attribute the fact to the use of Harper's method of teaching the language. As a consequence of its introduction, the students have exhibited unwonted enthusiasm, and found great delight in the pursuit of what is commonly regarded as a very dreary study."—Prof. F. A. GAST, *Theol. Sem'y of the Reformed Church*, Lancaster, Pa.

"I have used Professor Harper's books with my classes for the past three years, and am convinced that, for thoroughness and perspicuity of statement, for simplicity of analysis, and for economy of time, both in and out of the class-room, they afford just the aid which a teacher desires from the use of text-books. By systematic arrangement and appropriate reiteration they facilitate an accurate and rapid acquaintance with the Hebrew language, while, in the hands of an independent teacher, they may be so used as constantly to stimulate the pupil's curiosity and power of discovery, and thus greatly to promote his interest, in the introductory stages of his study."—Prof. CHAS. RUFUS BROWN, *Newton Theol. Institution*, Newton Centre, Mass.

FROM THE PRESS.

"* * A peculiar merit of the 'Elements' is that, although elementary, the book is not superficial but philosophical."—*The Congregationalist*, Boston.

"The whole grammar aims to lead the student not only into a practical knowledge of the language, but also into a rational explanation of its phenomena."—*New York Independent*.

"* * Remarkably full and precise, and appears well designed to train the learner in a sound philological method, and to lead him on gradually until he acquires a firm grasp of the principles of the language."—Prof. S. R. DRIVER, in *Contemporary Review*.

"* * So logically and self-consistently arranged that the student who goes faithfully through the lessons will, by a very natural process, come into possession of all the fundamental facts and principles of the Hebrew language. We are of opinion that for the beginner in the study of Hebrew no better text-books can be had."—*Northwestern Christian Advocate*.

"* * In this way the labor of acquiring the language becomes comparatively light and is always pleasant. * * Any one of moderate capacity can acquire from Dr. Harper's books a good working knowledge of Hebrew without a teacher. * * The arrangement throughout is clear, and the statement of principles concise and accurate. * * Will contribute much to the advancement of Hebrew learning."—*Reformed Quarterly Review*.

"The plan of the book ('Method') is admirable. In arrangement it is natural, simple and scientific. It comes nearer to being a satisfactory text-book for teaching Hebrew to beginners than probably any other that has ever been published. * * Every teacher must welcome this book ('Elements') as the best published aid to his teaching. There is certainly no other grammar of Hebrew so well adapted to the work of the class room as is this."—Prof. BERNARD C. TAYLOR, in *Baptist Quarterly Review*.

"* * The 'Method' puts the learner at once face to face with the language in concrete and connected form, and teaches him to derive its facts and principles from actual observation. * * The 'Notes,' 'Observations,' 'Grammar-Lessons,' etc., are distributed with great judgment and clear understanding, born of experience, of what students need. * * His plea for historical explanations of linguistic facts, as not only not foreign to an elementary treatment, but essential to its intelligent pursuit, is thoroughly sound, and the convenience, as well as accuracy of this course is amply illustrated in the 'Elements.'"
—Prof. FRANCIS BROWN, in *Presbyterian Review*.

"* * Two works which seem destined to supersede all the other introductory manuals now in use in our theological seminaries. * * A rigidly scientific and consecutive presentation of the elements of Hebrew grammar. * * A unique contrivance of lessons, exercises, vocabularies and explanations, designed to introduce the learner to the grammar and to the Bible. * * The combination of an unprecedented amount of help to the beginner with the scientific rigor of a Bickell. Everything is made as lucid as skillful explanation can make it, but nothing is passed over superficially. * Works which show upon every page the evidence of conscientious use of the latest authorities upon the Hebrew language, directed by a natural genius for teaching."—*Bibliotheca Sacra*.

"Your most valuable *Assyrian Manual.* * * Will undoubtedly find a ready sale in all English-speaking countries. I wish your book every success." —T. G. PINCHES, *Dep't of Egyptian and Assyrian Antiquities, British Museum,* London.

" An extremely useful and practical book, just as complete as is needed for beginners, and sufficiently clear, however succinct it be. * * You have rendered a great service to the study of Assyrian."—Prof. C. P. TIELE, *University of Leyden.*

"Your *Assyrian Manual* supplies a felt need, and will be most thankfully greeted on all sides. * * Your outline of grammar is carefully wrought out and gives all that is important in clear, synoptical form. The glossary satisfies in its form all reasonable demands."—Prof. EBERHARD SCHRADER, *University of Berlin.*

" Not a few will welcome this admirable manual, which has long been sought in vain from a cuneiform expert. * * It is at once modest and masterly. We will not say that it is unapproached as an introduction to Assyrian. Were its price one half of what it is, it would be unapproachable."—Prof. J. P. TAYLOR, Andover, in *Andover Review.*

"The best Assyrian text-book for beginners (it is indeed the *first* really practical *introductory* book). For advanced classes the book of Prof. Delitzsch will still be needed, even in this country ; but for elementary instruction, it will doubtless be displaced here, and Dr. Lyon's book might very well be brought out abroad in German and French."—Prof. C. R. BROWN, *Newton Theological Institution,* in *Hebraica.*

" It is altogether the most convenient and intelligible introduction that I have ever seen to the Assyrian language. * * I have no doubt it will not only smooth the path of those who attempt the study ; but allure many to undertake it who might otherwise be deterred."—Prof. BASIL MANLY, Louisville, in the *Religious Herald.*

"Prof. Lyon's *Manual* supplies a want very keenly felt heretofore by many students in Assyriology. * * A very useful volume in every respect, and exactness in philological research is noticeable upon every page of it."—*Sunday School Times.*

" We rejoice in it as a most skillful piece of work. * * We hope that our more cultivated and enterprising young ministers, as well as some in other professions, may be encouraged to undertake some elementary acquaintance, at least, with the language and literature toward the acquisition of which the book affords such well managed help."—*The Standard,* Chicago.

" The preface contains instructions for the use of the book by those who have no teacher. To such persons, and to many others, this manual, the first of the kind that has appeared in Assyrian, will be of very great service. * * Prof. Lyon has performed his task with conscientiousness and skill."—*The Nation.*

" In this *Manual,* the author has given us, in clear and precise manner, the most complete and correct grammar of the Assyrian yet published, * * The author has done his work well. Every page shows signs of critical and scholarly work. He has also shown good judgment in his selection and arrangement of the material, and in its adaptation to the wants of beginners in this language. * * The notes are very full and critical, explaining most of the difficult grammatical forms met with in the transliterations. * The book is singularly free from typographical errors and can be recommended as the best— and in fact the only practical—guide to beginners in the study of Assyrian." —ROBERT F. HARPER, Ph.D., in *New Englander.*

Date Due

2-14			
2/3			